IMMIGRANT

IMMIGRANT

A JOURNEY TO THE AMERICAN DREAM

SAL DIMARIA

Copyright © 2020 by Sal DiMaria.

Library of Congress Control Number: 2020909153
ISBN: Hardcover   978-1-9845-7970-6
                Softcover   978-1-9845-7969-0
                eBook   978-1-9845-7968-3

All rights reserved. No part of this book may be reproduced or transmitted in any form or by any means, electronic or mechanical, including photocopying, recording, or by any information storage and retrieval system, without permission in writing from the copyright owner.

Any people depicted in stock imagery provided by Getty Images are models, and such images are being used for illustrative purposes only.
Certain stock imagery © Getty Images.

Print information available on the last page.

Rev. date: 05/18/2020

To order additional copies of this book, contact:
Xlibris
1-888-795-4274
www.Xlibris.com
Orders@Xlibris.com
811301

CONTENTS

PART 1
Growing Up in Sicily

Chapter 1	Introduction	1
Chapter 2	Grandpa	4
Chapter 3	Vita Goes to Sicily	11
	At Nino's House	16
Chapter 4	Delia	23
	Lack of Hygiene	28
Chapter 5	Growing Up as an Orphan	36
Chapter 6	My New Mother	43
Chapter 7	In the Streets of Delia	49
	Totò the Little Thief	55
	Playing with Live Ammunition	58
Chapter 8	Totò in School	62
	Smoking Cigarettes	65
	My Old Home	70
Chapter 9	Then and Now	75
	Giulia Remembers	76
	Totò in Middle School	84
Chapter 10	Boarding School	88
	From Rascal to Model Student	93

Chapter 11 Before Leaving for America	97
At the American Consulate	100
Saying Goodbye to Delia	104

PART 2

Finally America

Chapter 12 Sailing to America	109
In Reading	118
Factory Work	121
Chapter 13 Moving on Up	124
Fun and Games	127
Carmen De Angelo	133
Chapter 14 In the Army	139
Boot Camp	141
Fort Sam Huston	150
Chapter 15 Fort Bragg	155
My First Car	160
D, the Doc	165
Chapter 16 In College	168
Last Days in the Army	171
Honorably Discharged	173

PART 3

College and Academia

Chapter 17 A Family Gathering	183
At North Carolina State University	186
Summer Job	197
Chapter 18 Junior Year Abroad	200
Driving to Greece	204
Amelja	207

Chapter 19 Pasquale's Death 211
                PhD Program, UW-Madison 212
                Marriage and Honeymoon 215

Chapter 20 At the University of Alberta 219
                At the University of Minnesota 224
                At the FBI? 226

Chapter 21 At the University of Tennessee 229
                My Parents Come to Visit 236
                Urbino 238

Chapter 22 Nino 241
                Return to Sicily 243

Epilogue 247

When I retired in 2017, I found myself with a lot of free time and little to do. I had difficulty adjusting to a life of *leisure* after over forty years in academia. I missed my students and my research. In a word, I was bored. My wife, tired of watching me piddling and diddling around the house, suggested I work on some of my papers. "Why don't you work on your diary? You always said, 'When I retire, I want to work on my memoir.'" She was right. I did plan to organize my scattered notes into my autobiography. I wanted my children and grandchildren to know where I came from and what I had to do to fulfill my lifelong dream. The project filled my time as I started reading and rearranging loose sheets and notes scribbled in old notebooks. Soon I was recalling memorable moments of my past and working them into a flowing narrative. Though I changed some people's names in order to respect their privacy, what follows is the truth-based story of my life. It is the story of a poor Sicilian immigrant who dared to dream. In the Sicily of my days, to dream of a better life was nothing but a seductive illusion, a pie in the sky. And that's why my entire family came to *lamerica*, as we used to say back home. We left nothing behind because we had nothing. But the land and the memories never left me. Whenever I went back, as soon as I landed in the airport, the sound of my old dialect and the strong aroma of espresso made me feel at home, among my people.

    I set out to write this book as a testament to my children and grandchildren with the intent of showing them that life favors those who dare to dream and never quit their dream. But more importantly,

I wanted them to know that my life story is not a mere memorialization of my achievements, but the celebration of America as the land of opportunity. It is the story of all immigrants who leave poverty and hopelessness behind and come to America in search of a better life. Whatever else America might be, it is still the land of plenty. It was for me when almost sixty years ago I left poverty-ridden Sicily and came to America, hoping to make it big. Not knowing a word of English, I took whatever job I could find while going to night school. Eventually, I earned the GED, a certificate equivalent to a high school diploma. Soon after that, I was drafted in the US Army for two long years. In the army, my English improved considerably. While serving at Fort Bragg, I took college courses offered at the base by the NCSU Extension Program. When I was discharged, I enrolled at the University of North Carolina-Chapel Hill and soon joined the UNC Junior-Year Program in France. Upon graduation from UNC, I entered the PhD program at the University of Wisconsin. It was in Madison that I met Lynn. Love at first sight, we got married within the year and soon started a family. I began my academic career at the University of Tennessee, where I taught Italian for more than thirty-five years. While at UT, I authored several books and dozens of scholarly articles. Now, old and retired, I enjoy my grandchildren and watch my own children—all three college graduates—prosper in their chosen professions. In all, I believe I can claim without reservations that this poor immigrant from Sicily lived the American dream.

Salvatore DiMaria
Knoxville, Tennessee

PART 1

Growing Up in Sicily

CHAPTER 1

Introduction

My grandchildren, just like many kids their ages, were curious about where and how I grew up. They were especially intrigued by their mother's uncommon name. "Vita, what kind of name is that?" They would ask jokingly. Sometimes, they would tease her by distorting the pronunciation of her name, just like most Americans do. They would call her Vita, with a long *i*—as in the word f$\underline{\text{i}}$ve—instead of the short *i*. Vita was proud of her Italian heritage and never missed a chance to show it. She was proud of her family, especially her immigrant father. The kids enjoyed hearing her stories about me, their *nonno*, as they called me, and constantly asked questions about my life in Italy and the reason I came to America. In a way, their interest reminded Vita of the curiosity she and her two siblings had when they were growing up. All three of them, Pat, Vita, and Jenna grew up in a household of professionals. I had a PhD in Romance languages, and my wife Lynn had a master's degree in elementary education. I was from Italy, and she was born and raised in Wisconsin. We met when I was a graduate student teaching Italian at the University of Wisconsin, and Lynn happened to take one of my courses. It was love at first sight. I was smitten with her happy face and beautiful smile; she was fascinated with my Italian accent, tailored clothes, and cosmopolitan flair. That was plenty for a girl who had never been outside the farmlands of Wisconsin. We were married within a year and started a family soon after.

Lynn grew up in a large working class family. She and her five siblings spent a lot of time outside, playing in the snow in the winter and going fishing or swimming in the summer. On occasion, they set up lemonade stands at the end of the street: 10¢ for lemonades and 15¢ for cupcakes. Most summers, she went to stay for couple of weeks with her grandparents, about a two-hour drive northeast of Madison. By the age of fourteen, she was babysitting for several of her neighbors, making good money and saving most of it. She was a good student and her grades were good enough to enroll at the University of Wisconsin. As much as our kids loved their mother and liked to hear about her typical American childhood, it was my life story that truly stirred their curiosity. They thought my background was exotic and rather mysterious: Where did he come from? What about those *strange* foods he eats? Why does he speak in a weird way? Why couldn't they understand him when he spoke to some of his friends or relatives?

They loved listening to me talk about my boyhood mostly because it was like hearing tales from a timeless past in imaginary lands. I described people and places from my poverty-ridden village in Sicily so vividly that they could actually see them in their mind's eye. Often, especially in winter evenings, they would jump on my bed and plead with me to close my book and tell them about my youth. It was during those evenings that they truly got to know me, their dad. From my stories emerged a man who dared to dream and came to America to live his dream. They learned that I believed that success comes to those with the determination to seek and seize opportunities. For me, the opportunity came when I, with my entire family, came to America. Coming from a world of poverty and despair, I rose to a respectable and rewarding place in academia. They thought of me as the perfect example of the little engine that could, I agreed and would add, "only in America, the land of dreams." Their admiration for me and my accomplishments never faltered, and their own kids never failed to remind them of it, albeit with a little humor. Vita's children, in particular, would often tease her about her *amazing* father. "Oh, my father is a great man! . . .

My dad did this . . . My dad said that . . ." they would say, mimicking her high-pitched voice.

But their ribbing, she knew, was a clear sign that they were growing genuinely interested in their nonno. Whether at the dinner table or on boring car rides, they would ask her to tell them more about the grandpa they barely knew. Though they had heard some of the stories before, they followed her retelling them with interest, expressing astonishment and disbelief. At times, they even wondered whether her filial affection colored her recollection. "Are you kidding me? . . . Are you serious? . . . You expect me to believe that?" Those were their typical reactions whenever they thought she was exaggerating.

Ironically, their suspicions did not prevent them from asking for more stories and more details. Their mother's ancestral pride was beginning to rub off on them. They were undoubtedly intrigued by this peculiar little man, their nonno. How old was he when he came to America? Did he speak English? Why did he come? However, much Vita knew about my life, she was not always able to answer all their questions. But she knew where the answers might be found. She knew that in a footlocker up in the attic, there used to be folders with my papers, including my personal diary. It was a mixed bag of recent and distant memories, some going as far back as my childhood days. In more than one occasion, I had said I planned to turn the scattered collection into a cohesive manuscript.

One day, while visiting with Lynn and me at our house in Knoxville, she asked me if I intended to work on my memoir, as I had said I would. I told her I had been working on it since I retired and was hoping to finish it in a few months. All three of my children were ecstatic when on Christmas Eve I presented them each with a copy of my autobiography: the best possible gift ever, they said. They were visibly moved, and judging by the way they were thumbing through the pages, it was clear they couldn't wait to begin reading it.

CHAPTER 2

Grandpa

Vita once told me that her two children had scant memories of their nonno. They remembered me as a little man who spoke with a foreign accent and liked to eat smelly pecorino cheese, figs, prickly pears, and other weird foods. Her daughter, Stella, recalled how I used to whistle and sing all the time. She even learned some words to the song "Santa Lucia." She also remembered how I would prompt her to try some of my *strange-looking* foods like fennel or pomegranates. She loved to sit and eat pistachios with me. How I would pry open the shell when she couldn't. How I thought her and her little brother Harrison to say *Buon giorno* when they got up in the morning. Undoubtedly, some of the kids' memories were a mixture of what they actually remembered from their frequent visits to our house and the stories Vita told them. She used to amuse them with accounts of some of my peculiar preferences, such as my insistence on eating whole cloves of garlic and using only Sicilian extra-virgin olive oil. She told them that I refused to eat hotdogs and never developed a taste for butter. "He finished a typical meal," she recalled for them, "by sipping the rest of his red wine and cracking nuts in the shell. His dinner was never complete without his espresso."

As my grandchildren grew older, they wanted to know more about their grandpa, especially how I grew up and how I became a professor.

Sometimes, their interest had to do with school assignments dealing with tracing a family tree or with foreign cultures in general. They were particularly fascinated with pictures of their nonno growing up in Sicily. They were shocked by the poverty those images revealed: rundown houses that looked more like shacks, unpaved muddy streets, shoeless children in rags, and women holding babies in their arms while carrying water jars on their heads. For them, the backdrop was not much different from that of Afghanistan or some other third-world country they saw on TV. They couldn't believe that their grandfather grew up in such an impoverished environment. Often, when Vita couldn't satisfy their questions, she would call to ask for my help while apologizing for her children's disbelief. I told her that for kids living in the comforts of our times, it was not easy to imagine the kind of abject poverty I grew up in. After all, I reminded her, she and her siblings, too, had doubted some of my childhood stories.

What puzzled my kids, especially the older two—Pat and Vita— was the contrast between their *peculiar* father and their *normal* mother. Lynn told them stories depicting a life very similar to their own: lemonade stands, picnics, Christmas trees, Mickey Mouse, trick or treat, and so on. My tales, instead, portrayed a world they could hardly imagine existed: danger, filth, and deprivation. One of the very first things they found strange about me was my accent. They thought there was something unusual about a man who, though showing a good command of English, spoke with a heavy foreign accent. I explained that most immigrants never lost their native accent, even if they mastered the language. Many others never learned to speak English, period. My parents belonged to this last group. They knew few basic words, which they spoke with an Italianate pronunciation, such as *waita mminutte* (wait a minute), *nisah* (nice), *bossuh* (boss or bus), *shuh* (sure), *jobba* (job), *bettirrummulu* (bathroom). I recalled for my children the time when my father would call them to him by waving his hand and saying, "Vieni cca . . . vieni cca" (come here. . . come here). Once in a while, my mother would offer them a piece of chocolate and asked, "You *allikah*?" (do you like it?). Their illiteracy was one of the reasons they never became American citizens. Even today, citizenship applicants must pass a test in basic language and cultural literacy, a test my parents couldn't possibly pass.

As for me, I developed my language skills working alongside Americans in the factories, and during the two years I spent in the US Army. In both places, I learned spoken English, especially street talk and four-letter words. I polished my speech later in college, first as a student and then as a teacher. Regarding my foreign accent, I told my kids, I didn't think I would ever lose it. Very few immigrants lost their accent, except those who came at an early age. My younger siblings, for instance, speak English like native speakers. In my case, I was in my late teens when I came to America, totally unfamiliar with both its language and its culture.

I used to tell my children about the culture shock that hit the entire family when we first arrived in New York. After a six-day voyage on a passenger ship, seeing nothing but skies and water, we beheld the Big Apple as it emerged in the distance. It was a true fairyland wonder. Watching from the ship's bridge, we were awestruck by all the high-rise buildings and the myriad of multi-hued lights illuminating the city's evening skies. It was a dazzling and intimidating spectacle for people who, like us, had never seen buildings taller than three stories high or night skies so brightly lit. We were as excited as we were apprehensive about entering a world that was full of wonder, promises, and uncertainties. We were anxious about the many obstacles that lay ahead, in particular, finding work and learning the language. But we were glad to be in the land of opportunity. For us, the old world offered nothing but a bleak future of enduring hardship and no hope of improving our lives. There, the sons of peasants grew up to be peasants, just as the sons of barbers followed in their fathers' footsteps. In Sicily, to dream of a better life was nothing but a seductive illusion, a pipe dream. And that's why we came to *lamerica*, as we used to say back home. We left nothing behind because we had nothing. But the land and the memories never left us. I used to tell my children that I never stopped being a Sicilian. Whenever I went back—I went back many times—the strong aroma of espresso and the sound of my dialect took me back to the world of my memories.

For my children, it was hard to believe their father had grown up in a dirt-poor family from a third-world country. Having seen my passport and other documents lying around the house, they knew I was born in 1942 and raised in Delia, a small Sicilian town. What the papers didn't tell was the degree of misery that plagued most of the town's six thousand souls who lived with no electricity or inside plumbing. Without running water, it was difficult for people to clean, do the washing, or practice basic personal hygiene. The resulting squalor accounted for many serious diseases and often death. People seldom went to the doctor and had no idea what a dentist was or did. For many, their doctor and dentist was the family barber. They usually called on him whenever they needed a tooth extraction or a medical bloodletting.

Once, when my father was running a high fever, my mother sent me to fetch Gianni, our barber. I was told to ask him to bring his leeches for a bloodletting treatment. I ran as fast as I could, but when I got to his house, his wife told me he was not feeling well. Still out of breath, I pleaded for my sick, very sick father. Apparently, my emotional appeal so moved the woman that she, turning away from the door, shouted to her husband to put down his bottle and go help Mr. DiMaria. After some back-and-forth yelling between the two, Gianni came out of the house huffing and puffing and muttering something about "the old hag." As if by mutual agreement, he put up with his wife's nagging as long as she put up with his drinking. People knew he enjoyed his wine but trusted in his *medical* expertise. Carrying his little, medical bag, Gianni— a fat little man in his early fifties with rosy cheeks and a large potbelly—kept pace with me, and soon we were at the house.

My mother was anxiously waiting at the door. When we walked in, Gianni's eyes went straight for the tall glass of wine my mother had set on the table just for him. But business before pleasure. To bring down the fever, Gianni attached a leech on my father's bare back. Almost instantly, the worm began to suck blood, and within minutes, it grew to the size of a small tomato. He pulled off the bloated creature, placed it in an empty glass. He then repeated the operation with another hungry leech. When he was done, he went for the wine he knew was meant for him. After my mother thanked him and gave him a small bag of almonds as a token of our appreciation, he left happy as a lark. Did bloodletting work? I don't know, but people believed it did, so much so they even used on their horses. In my father's case, the fever eventually broke, and by the following day, he was on his feet. I don't know whether he got well because of Gianni's leeches or simply because the fever ran its course.

My kids were sickened by such a primitive procedure and wondered about the potential health risks. A patient could develop a serious infection, they feared. While agreeing with them, I pointed out that the practice was not seen as harmful or painful as that of a barber's dangerous and excruciating approach to dentistry. I recounted an episode involving our next-door neighbor, a farmer in his late forties. The poor man, I told my kids, had put up with a toothache for over a week. When the pain became so unbearable, he couldn't take it any longer. It was time to send for Luigi, their family barber. Luigi was known more for his dental expertise than his shaving or hair cutting skills. I went with my friend Angelo, the neighbor's younger son, to fetch him. The man wasn't at his barbershop, so we went to look for him at his home. The old spinster who came to the door told us that her brother was taking his afternoon nap. But when she understood the urgency of our appeal, she went to wake him up and assured us he would be ready to go in a few minutes. Luigi, a confirmed bachelor who lived with his older sister, was in his early forties though he looked like an old man. He was of average height, gaunt, and bone-thin with a droopy mustache and a hooked nose. A set of thick eyebrows arched over his sunken brown eyes. He walked slowly and didn't say a word during the five minutes it took us to get to Angelo's house.

Knowing that in all likelihood he had to pull a tooth, Luigi brought along an old pair of pliers and a string about five feet long. Before starting the operation, he asked the man's wife to bring two glasses of wine and place them on the table. He began the procedure by trying to grab the tooth with his pliers but had difficulty reaching in the back of the man's mouth; the instrument was too big. After several vain attempts that caused the patient excruciating pain, he decided to use the string. He tied the infected molar to one end of the string and secured the other end to the doorknob. He then slammed the door shut and the tooth came out, followed by a scream of pain and a thin flow of blood. At that point, he handed the patient one of the two glasses of wine to rinse his mouth and soothe the pain. He then gulped down the other glass and asked for another.

When I first told this story, my children were appalled by the crude practices. The thought of the primitive anesthetic, the poor man's awful pain, and the blood streaming out of his mouth made them sick. Although they reacted with sincere disgust about some of the stories, they were often outright skeptical, which they expressed through questions such as "Did it really . . . ? Did you actually . . . ? How could it be. . . ?" Interestingly, their skepticism, though ever present, did not curb their curiosity about my childhood. They were always eager to hear one more story.

An episode they heard several times and questioned its plausibility every time they heard it had to do with my father's vain threat to shoot me. Once, when I was a bout eleven years old, my dad caught me high on a tree stealing almonds from a neighbor's farm. He made me come down, spanked me, and told me leave the loot at the foot of the tree, where the owner would be sure to find it. Then, he sat me behind him on his horse and fearing I might run away, tied my legs to the saddle. Riding double, we went for a few minutes until I managed to loosen the rope, jumped off the horse, and ran as fast as I could. He ran after me but was soon out of breath. So trying to scare me, he pointed his gun at me and threatened to shoot unless I stopped. I didn't stop, sure of being out of shotgun's range.

For my kids the story was a little over the top. They could not imagine a father trying to shoot his child, neither could they picture an eleven-year-old boy so knowledgeable about firearms, including the firing range of a particular gun. They also doubted my claim that my family was so poor that we had only one bed for the boys to sleep in. For them, who had their own rooms and their own beds, it was inconceivable that four teenagers could actually fit in one bed. But we did; three of us laid down vertically, head to foot, and the youngest slept horizontally at our feet.

Another story they weren't sure what to make of had to do with my undernourishment. I once became so weak that I couldn't even walk. I was in first or second grade, I told them when one day I felt so tired I couldn't walk the three blocks from my home to the school cafeteria. I felt my legs buckling, and unable to continue walking, I sat on the sidewalk and began to cry. A family friend happened to come by and asked me what was wrong. When I told him my legs were hurting, he picked me up and carried me home. My parents, when they saw me with my legs dangling lamely from the man's arms, immediately feared the worse. Did their little boy contract polio? They had reason to be anxious because the disease had paralyzed many local children my age. The doctor, who came to the house that afternoon, allayed their fears; their child was suffering from malnutrition.

My children were astonished to hear about my childhood poverty. But it was hard to tell whether they actually believed everything I told them. At times, after hearing one of my youthful exploits, they would give each other a puzzled look as if to ask, "You guys believe this? Did he really live like that?" I understood their suspicions. Born and raised in a prosperous middle-class family, I guessed they had all the reasons in the world to doubt some of my recollections. But one thing was clear: they always wanted to hear more. I took this eagerness as a sign they were beginning to believe my stories and understand the world of my childhood. But I knew that the ultimate proof would be for them to see with their own eyes where I grew up and meet some of the people and see some of places I often mentioned in my stories.

CHAPTER 3

Vita Goes to Sicily

Vita's skepticism about my *embroidered* recollections ended when I took her to Sicily, just before she started college. At that time, I was directing a six-week study-abroad program in Italy for students from my university. She didn't know any of the kids in the program as most of them were already in the second year of college. Nonetheless, she fit right in because many had never been out of the country just like her. It was an eye-popping and unforgettable experience. Besides studying and getting to know local Italians, she and her friends got to visit famous cities, like Venice, Florence, and Rome. They were in awe of the country's rich cultural history displayed in its artworks, buildings, and ancient ruins. How could they forget the first time they saw the coliseum or the Leaning Tower of Pisa! Neither could they forget their impression of awesome Venice with its many bridges and canals. Some of them took rides on the gondolas and posed for pictures in front or next to famous buildings, such as the beautiful San Marco's Basilica and the famed Rialto Bridge. She had some of those pictures framed and are now hanging on the wall in her study.

But for her, the best part of the trip was the time she and I went to Sicily. After the program ended and the students returned to the States, the two of us boarded a flight for Palermo. She would soon see the houses and walk the streets where my *incredible* stories had taken place. She would also meet some of my friends, relatives, and neighbors who could bear witness to some of my escapades. This was the right place to test her skepticism. Here, folks could corroborate or deflate my tales. She wondered whether they still remembered me. "Sure, they remembered me," I told her. Since I started taking students to Italy, I have returned almost every summer.

"But you came back more than twenty years after you left. Why did it take you so long?" Vita asked me one day while taking a walk in the streets of Delia.

My reason, silly as it might seem to some, was that I swore to my friends I would not go back until I made a name for myself. For all those years, I feared that coming back without having achieved some sort of success I would look like a failure. I waited until I could show that in *lamerica* I was living the dream, just as I swore I would. Call it pride, stupid pride, but then in my culture, pride was a highly valued currency—people admired a man of his word more than they valued a man of wealth. After I became a university professor, I returned every summer for a couple of weeks, and everybody in town referred to me as *lu professuri*, the professor. I loved coming back. It felt as if I had never left. My buddies and I got together, taking walks, playing cards, reminiscing about the old days, and having dinners that lasted well into the night. Sadly, there weren't that many of us left; some had died and others had moved somewhere in Italy or emigrated to various parts of the world. Of those who left, a few came back to visit almost every summer just like me; others returned to retire and live in the same homes they were born and raised. Their retirement checks went a long way in a small town where life was comfortable among friends and relatives.

Vita and I stayed in Delia for almost two weeks and totally enjoyed it. In the beginning, she feared it would be a long and boring visit, especially because she didn't know the people and barely understood the language. But as it turned out, it was exciting and time went by very fast. Every day she met different people, and some days she and I went sightseeing in nearby towns. We didn't have a car and didn't need one.

From the moment we arrived until we left, there was always a friend or relative eagerly waiting to drive us places. When we landed in Palermo, my best friend Nino was already waiting for us. As we came out of the airport's security area, there was Nino waving wildly and hollering, "Totòooh . . . Totòooh." Nino was in his early sixties, short, fat with a round head, and strands of long black hair pulled straight back. He had a happy face with a thin mustache and a set of brown and smiling eyes that immediately made you feel comfortable. When we spotted each other, we ran and embraced in a bear hug. Then, Nino gently hugged Vita and exclaimed, "Welcome to Sicilia, Vita!"

"Nice meeting you, sir" she said timidly, wondering how he knew her name.

"Don't call me sir, just Nino," he said, dismissing all formalities. "I recognized you right away from the pictures your papà showed me of the entire family," he said, mixing English and Italian, mostly Italian.

He had a way of making people feel at ease, and within a few minutes, Vita felt at home. He tried to make conversation, asking about her studies and her impressions of Italy. But his broken, middle-school English and her rudimentary Italian made it difficult for them to carry on a conversation. Naturally, I was there to translate when necessary. Nino assured her that once we got to his house, language would not be an issue because his twin daughters spoke perfect English. With pride in his voice, he told her that both girls had studied English and spent time in England.

We finally made our way out of the airport and to the parking lot, put the suitcases in the trunk, and Nino began to navigate our way out of Palermo. It was hot. The afternoon traffic was frantic in the big city, and Vita was nervous. She wondered how drivers managed to avoid accidents on a street too narrow for a two-way traffic. There was no visible yellow line dividing the two-lane road. People drove in the oncoming lane just to pass slow-moving vehicles. Adults and teenagers on scooters rode on either side of moving cars, often coming dangerously close. Noticing Vita's nervousness, I assured her that there was nothing to fear; Nino was used to driving in this kind of city traffic. In fact, he drove just like the rest of them—honking the horn, passing slow-moving cars, and shouting obscenities at unruly motorists. The deafening sound of blaring horns and the muggy air were unbearable. Sitting in the back seat, Vita asked me why Nino didn't raise the windows and turn on the air condition. It would definitely cut down on the noise and the noxious exhaust fumes. I explained that he was reluctant to turn on the air condition because, like many other Italians, he was afraid of catching a cold. But when I told Nino that Vita's asthma was starting to act up, Nino did not hesitate to roll up the windows and turn on the air.

We were soon out of the city. All the while, Nino and I were engaged in lively conversation. As we talked, it intrigued Vita that Nino referred to me as Totò, which she first noticed at the airport. I told her that Totò is a nickname for Salvatore, just as Bobby is a nickname for Robert or Bill for William. Nino and I continued speaking in our native dialect and never stopped talking. Of course, Vita couldn't understand a word we were saying. But she found it entertaining, watching the two of us talk, using our hands and raising our voices. At times, she later told me she had the impression we were about to punch each other when all of a sudden we would let out a loud, hearty laugh. We argued and laughed throughout the drive home.

Vita didn't mind being left out of the conversation. She was actually relieved not having to stress over Nino's halting English. Sitting quietly in the back seat, she enjoyed looking at the countryside on either side of the road. The terrain was mostly hilly. Some slopes were rocky and treeless, outlining a desolate landscape. Others were dotted with thick patches of vegetation and small farmhouses. Once in a while, she saw shepherds keeping watch over their flock grazing on boulder-strewn slopes. She could hear the barks of the dogs rounding up stray sheep and the soothing sound of sheep bells, now rushed, now slow and distant. The mellow echo of bells jangling far away in the shimmering heat of summer reminded her of the idyllic scenes often described by poets. Ghostly and timeless, the sound was the echo of a bygone era.

"It's so quiet and peaceful. It seems so far removed in time and yet so present," Vita thought aloud.

I explained that sheepherding, once a common activity in the island's hinterland, was now a dying tradition. Few young men want to live in the hills among the animals like their parents and grandparents before them. Nowadays, as soon as they are of age, they go look for work in the big cities up north or abroad, mostly in England or Germany.

As we drove on, Vita saw men on tractors plowing fields, women watering vegetable gardens, and water sprinklers spraying fruit orchards with a gentle mist. The sight stood in stark contrast with sheep and shepherds roaming the barren landscape. It was strange to see the old and the new side-by-side and yet unmindful of each other. All that green foliage in a mostly arid region baffled her. Sicily had hardly any measurable rainfall during the summer months. She finally interrupted the spirited conversation between Nino and me and asked, "Dad, didn't you say that when you were a kid, most of the Sicilian countryside looked like a wasteland? I remember you telling us that it never rained in the summer, and the soil was drought-parched."

"As you can see for yourself," I answered, "Sicily is still hot and arid in the summer. Actually, I think now it rains less than it did fifty years ago."

Nino, who understood the gist of the question, jumped in and explained that in the last decade farmers began to dig water wells to irrigate their fields. The practice had turned the once arid landscape into large areas of lush vineyards, fruit orchards, and vegetable gardens. In a sense, it revolutionized the local agriculture from a lackluster wheat and beans industry to a profitable variety of food products more in keeping with market demands. Now, there were huge tractor-trailers full of fresh fruit and vegetables headed to markets as far as Milan and even Berlin. No sooner was he done explaining, we turned back to our chatter, and Vita went back to looking out the window.

We had been driving for little over an hour when we reached Mussomeli, Nino's hometown. He did not drive through town; instead, he took a dirt road that took us straight to his country house. It was here where the family stayed to escape the oppressive heat of Sicily's hot summers. Originally, Nino explained, the house was a barn that served to store the harvest and shelter the family's farm animals. The place was big enough that during harvest time; some of the farmhands slept there, in the stables with the cows and the mules. He was in his early teens when his father gave up farming and turned the structure into a rustic summer residence. Though his sisters came and went as they pleased, he was the sole owner of the property. Tradition entitled him to the estate because he was the family's only male heir, and therefore the only one who could carry on the family name. Vita saw this custom as archaic and as blatant gender discrimination. And it was. But she was glad to hear that the practice was no longer as common as it used to be.

At Nino's House

Waiting for us at the house were Nino's wife and children, his octogenarian mother who lived with them, and two of his three sisters. They were all excited to receive their guests and eager to make us feel at home. Much of their attention was on Vita, *lamericana*, whom they met for the first time. They took turns kissing and hugging her and saying things such as "Piacere" (nice meeting you*)*, "Devi essere stanca" (you must be tired), "Ti piace l'Italia?" (how do you like Italy?), and similar other phrases. The twins, a year or so younger than Vita, were the last to step up and greet her. She was impressed by their appearance. They wore knee-high black skirts, white polka dot shirts, and black sandals. Their tall and slender figures with long black hair hanging down their shoulders did not fit the stereotype of the short Sicilian woman Vita had seen in the movies. The contrast of their deep dark eyes and the pale skin of their faces gave them a strikingly beautiful look. As always, they were happy to see me, Uncle Sal.

"You girls, speak English with Vita," hollered Nino, eager to show off his daughters' foreign language skills. But the girls, their father's pride aside, were fully aware of their beginner English and visibly flustered to have to talk to a native speaker. As it was to be expected, their conversation did not go beyond first-encounter pleasantries, such as "How are you? What do you study at the university? How long have you been in Italy?" Everyone attributed the embarrassing silence that followed the sputtering conversation to the girls' shyness.

Though language was a major hurdle and I had to translate here and there, the hosts' gestures and body language were enough to convince Vita that they were truly happy to have her as their guest. But what really made her feel at home was my behavior. I acted as if I was a member of the family. On our arrival, I didn't ask where Vita and I were going to sleep. I simply took the suitcases to the room I normally slept in whenever I visited. I didn't ask if I could do something, such as rearranging the furniture in the bedroom or taking a shower. I just did it. I didn't have to explain how I preferred my coffee; the women of the house knew how I liked it—*stretto e senza zucchero* (black and strong). If I asked that my spaghetti be prepared in a certain way, they were more than happy to oblige. Clearly, I was at home and that made Vita feel at home.

On our second night there, Nino had company. A dozen or so of his friends—all males in their forties—came over for what turned out to be an elaborate dinner. They were all college graduates and knew each other. Vita couldn't tell if the banquet was intended to honor the Americans or a monthly gathering hosted on a rotating basis. She and I were properly introduced to the arriving guests though I knew some of them from previous visits. To relieve the tension typical in these situations, some of them took pains to follow their greetings to Vita with an English word or expression, such as "Jack Daniels . . . Elvis Presley . . . Clinton good president . . . allikah America . . ."

Eventually we took our seat at a long table out on the terrace. Vita sat between Nino and me. It was a cheerful and friendly bunch. The wine that kept on coming throughout the evening contributed to the cacophony of good-natured banter, jokes, and singing. The men were especially gracious to Vita though the language barrier kept their interaction to mere smiles and familiar gestures. At one point, perhaps to make her feel more part of the group, they asked her to sing an American song. She hesitated, but I encouraged her, and she sang "Summer Time." They all listened politely and at the end gave her a loud and prolonged "Braaava! Braaava!" At first, she wondered if the applause was genuine or a mere polite gesture. But my look assured her they were truly pleased with her singing.

For his part, Nino kept on telling Vita how much his family and his friends liked her. "Everyone thinks you're wonderful," he told her at one point during the meal. At least, that was what she thought he said. Between the noise and his broken English, she could barely make out much of what he was saying. At times, she asked me to translate, but for the most part, she simply smiled, feigning polite agreement. As the wine was beginning to have its relaxing effect, some of the guests made it a point of saying the few English words they thought they knew, mostly words they had heard in some American movies or seen in advertisements. A dentist, who thought he knew English because he had studied it in college, tried to make conversation. From what she could make out, his questions sounded something like "How many years you have? What do you call you? Me and your papà friends." Others, placing a cannoli or a piece of cake on her plate, would say, "You allikah?" (Do you like it), "Gut?" (good), "Eatta! . . . Eatta!" (Do you like it? Good? . . . Eat! . . . Eat!). Clearly, they were not showing off their beginner English or the local cuisine; they were simply trying to make her feel at home. And she did!

Soon and with an extra glass of wine, Vita felt totally relaxed. But she couldn't overcome the strange feeling of being the only female at the table. The women of the house stayed mostly in the kitchen and came out only to bring out the food and clear the dishes. Of course, they knew all the visitors and interacted with them, exchanging pleasantries and accepting compliments for the *great* meal they had slaved the whole day to prepare. Vita found it odd they didn't stick around and socialize more. Were they too busy cooking and serving or were they supposed to stay in the kitchen where they belong? But if it was a men/women thing, why was she sitting at the table?

Feeling awkward about being the only female at the table, she went in the house and invited Angela, one of the twins, to come and sit at the table next to her. After some hesitation, the girl followed her to the table and pulled a chair next to Uncle Sal. She had hardly put a piece of food in her mouth when her mother came out and told her to go inside where she was needed. Maria's brusque tone startled Vita who, turning to me, asked, "What was that all about? Why was Maria so gruff with her daughter? The only thing Angela did was to sit down next to me."

"It's just that. Angela was not supposed to come out and sit at the table with a bunch of men," I told her, further explaining that it was not customary for women to join in such a gathering.

"Why?" she asked, wondering what was the harm if women mingled with male guests, especially in their own homes.

"For one thing," I tried to explain, "a woman's presence would inhibit the jovial atmosphere, which, after a few glasses of wine, could easily deteriorate into profane allusions and dirty jokes. Also, her exposure to foul language and sexual innuendos could taint her reputation."

"Am I risking my reputation by sitting here and socializing with these guys? Is my honor compromised?" she asked sarcastically. She was clearly contemptuous of a mindset she considered chauvinistic and outright primitive.

I pointed out that her situation was different. It was OK for her to sit at the table since she didn't understand enough Italian to dampen the men's carefree mood or blush at their jokes. Also as an outsider, she was not bound by local customs, at least for the short time she was going to be around. My explanation did little to tamp down her disgust at the blatant sexism she was witnessing.

"Chauvinism is chauvinism, wherever it is practiced and accepted," she told me with irritation.

For a while, I feared she might make a scene, but happily she managed to hold back her contempt, choosing to grin and bear it. In the meantime, it was already one o'clock in the morning and the feasting was beginning to die down. Some of the guests started to get up, a clear sign they were ready to leave. They finally said their goodbyes, told Vita how delighted they were to have met her, and some even teased her about her *promising* singing career. She was surprised to see that though a lot of wine was consumed during the evening, no one appeared to be visibly inebriated. Her observation caught me off guard; I had never given much thought about excessive drinking. I don't believe I ever saw a friend of mine intoxicated. We mostly drank at dinner and in moderation. "This society," I told Vita, "frowns on public drunkenness, especially if it involves educated, *respectable* people."

The following day, Vita got up late. Nino and I were already gone, and the women were in the kitchen working on the noon *pranzo*, the day's main meal. After greeting Vita with the usual, "Good morning! Did you sleep well? Was your bed comfortable?" They made her breakfast. While she was eating, she and the twins did their best to keep up the semblance of making conversation in English. Maria was visibly proud to hear her daughters speak English though she didn't understand a word. In her limited Italian, Vita made it a point of talking to Nino's mother, complimenting her on her nice family. The poor woman looked at her with an appreciative facial expression while, at the same time, asking the twins "*cchi dici*?" (What is she saying?). Within a few minutes, the language barrier led to an awkward silence, with everybody in the room looking around aimlessly and hoping for something to happen. On the pretense of finding out what was on the agenda for the day, Vita asked if they knew where I was. She was told that Nino and I had gone to town to visit an elderly relative. We actually did more than that. We went to buy some fruit and stopped by the house to pick up a few bottles of vintage wine. Nino kept a well-stocked wine cellar in town. We were back by lunchtime. Soon after we returned, everybody sat down to eat with Grandma at the head of the table, her usual place.

We didn't start eating right away because we had to wait for Nino, the man of the family. He had gone to his bedroom to change and would join us in a few minutes. He finally showed up, shirtless and sporting a pair of baggy, knee-high shorts. On his head, he wore a hair net that kept straight back the few strands of hair he had left. His large breasts hung shamelessly over his hairy chest, and his beer belly drooped low over his flowered shorts. He looked like a colorful toad on its back. The sight was so ridiculous that Vita, forgetting her manners for a moment, burst out laughing. He was clearly taken aback by her reaction. Nobody at the table, except his mother perhaps, would have dared laugh at him. Then, turning to me and nodding toward Vita, he asked, "Cchi c'è, pirchì ridi?" (what's matter, why is she laughing?).

Pointing to his appearance, I chuckled, "Did you look at yourself?" It was hard to tell whether his big ego was hurt, but he took it gracefully, especially when everybody at the table started giggling, including his mother. After lunch, some of us sat outside under the shade of a large medlar tree, talking about cultural differences between America and Italy; others went to take their regular afternoon nap. Later in the evening, we all went to town to watch a spectacular display of fireworks in honor of the town's patron saint.

The next day, Vita and I left for Delia, my hometown. We thanked the family for their warm hospitality and invited them to come and visit us in America someday. After the usual hugs and kisses, we set out for the hour-long drive with Nino at the wheel. The ride was not much different than the drive from the airport earlier in the week—the same landscape for Vita, the same chatter between Nino and me. The town itself was not that far, about twenty-four miles. But the winding and narrow roads were so riddled with potholes and loose gravel that we couldn't drive faster than thirty miles an hour on a good stretch. When a truck or a bus came from the opposite direction, Nino had to slow down or move aside to let the big vehicle through. In some places, old landslides caused us to get off the main road and proceed on dirt-packed trails for a mile or so. At one point, we had to stop to let a flock of sheep cross the road. When all the animals were finally across, the shepherd, leaning on his staff and shouldering a shotgun, approached the car. Pointing to a corncob pipe in his hand, he politely asked for a light while peeping inside the car to see if he recognized the passengers. Nino quickly produced a match, struck it, and his hand trembling, held it up to the man's pipe. The man thanked him profusely, wished us a safe journey, and proceeded to catch up with his flock.

As we drove on, I wondered aloud at how things had hardly changed since I left. The roads, for instance, were as bad as they were fifty years ago. Vita didn't understand how people put up with this type of neglect.

"Seems as though nobody cares. This would not be tolerated in the States. People would complain to their elected officials until things got done," she said.

"Sadly, this is Italy," I agreed.

Nino, who was apparently listening and understood the thrust of what we were saying, broke in, "Uh-huh! We are not in America," he said in dialect and asked me to translate for Vita.

"I can see that you got used to the American way of thinking and find it easy to criticize our way of life." Nino went on. "You went away and had the opportunity to change. Unfortunately, people do not change that easily around here. We are so used to bad roads, corruption, and criminality that we simply grow jaded. I understand why an outsider might wonder why people don't demand better roads and for that matter, better living conditions. Don't forget, Totò, you too once thought all this was normal."

Although agreeing that things needed to improve, Nino couldn't bring himself to share my belief in the ability of the individual to affect change. While we continued arguing over the causes underlining the country's problems, Vita couldn't erase from her mind the encounter with the shepherd. She kept asking herself why Nino's hand was shaking when he lit up that man's pipe. She had to ask.

"In this culture," I answered, "shepherds have always been a fiercely independent lot barely affected by urban values. They tend to live by their primeval sense of justice, righting a wrong in secrecy and with little regard for the law. In these hills, they are the law, their own law. It is not unusual for someone to disappear without a trace."

Vita understood Nino's nervousness.

CHAPTER 4

Delia

As we came up over a hill, I turned to Vita and pointing to a cluster of houses on a distant hilltop, exclaimed, "There is Delia, my hometown."

With its three church steeples, Delia did not appear different from some of the communities we had seen along the way. We entered the town and soon arrived at Aunt Lucia's house. I had already explained to both Nino and Vita that Aunt Lucia was my father's younger sister and that her house was the same house where she and my father were born. Due to recent construction, the place was no longer visible from the main street and its entrance was from a side alley. As the alley was too narrow for a vehicle to get through, Nino stopped the car on the main street. We had barely got out of the car when a crowd of relatives and curious neighbors surrounded us. After the introductions and the conventional hugs and kisses, Uncle Filippo, Aunt Lucia's husband, carried the suitcases inside, telling us to follow him, "Avanti! Avanti! Andiamo dentro" (Let's go! Let's go! Let's go inside). The table was already set for a huge *pranzo*, a sign that they had been preparing for our arrival since early morning.

The welcome was somewhat similar to the reception we got at Nino's house with one exception— nobody spoke a word of English. Vita had to marshal all her language skills to try to keep up with the small talk that dominated the moment. It was a struggle. At times, she just smiled or blurted a hesitant, "Sì . . . Sì . . . Bene . . . Bene" (Yes . . .Yes . . . Fine . . . Fine). But when it got to be too much, she turned to me for help. I told her to be patient for a while longer. Those who came to see and welcome *lamericani* would soon leave, and things would calm down a little. A few minutes later, Aunt Lucia announced in a loud voice that the food on the table was getting cold and that it was time to sit down and eat. The well-wishers took the hint and began to file out, promising to come back later. Nino, too, left. He regretted having to leave, but he had promised his family to be home for a late lunch. He thanked Aunt Lucia, gave Vita a hug, and insisted that she visit him again and *make friends* with his daughters. She promised she would. Then, he and I walked to the car and talked about our plans for the coming days. After the usual hugs and kisses, he drove away.

The three-course meal was delicious and lasted a long time. For almost two hours Vita had to fend off Aunt Lucia's insistence that she eat more of this and more of that. She ignored Vita's repeated but polite, "No, grazie! . . . No basta!" (No, thanks . . . No more, please!). She just kept on putting food on her plate, urging her to try it, "Mangia! Mangia! Delizioso!" (Eat! Eat! Delicious!). Vita watched her manners throughout the meal, smiling and saying, "Sì! Sì! . . . No! No! . . .. Grazie!" But she felt the stress of all the attention she was getting. The sweltering heat—they had no air condition—and the noise of people talking over one another added to the strain. Nobody, except her, seemed to mind the TV with its volume set at full blast. She breathed a sigh of relief when the meal was over and the men filed outside for a smoke and the usual small talk. Against Aunt Lucia's objections, Vita joined the women in clearing the table and doing the dishes. When the kitchen was finally cleaned and the commotion had died down, the hosts began to give hints that they were ready to retire for the customary siesta or *pisolino*. Aunt Lucia told me our beds were already made and that we could go take a nap if we wanted. A catnap would have been the thing to do, mostly to escape the afternoon heat and to take a break after a long day with so many people. But Vita, at last free from the crowd and the noise, felt that it would be more relaxing if we went for a stroll around town. She wanted to have her own space for a while, just the two of us. Also, she could hardly wait to see the house where I was born.

"Not in this heat? People will think we're crazy," I tried to discourage her. But she insisted, saying that she didn't mind the heat and couldn't care less about what people thought.

"What the hell, let's go? They think Americans are weird anyway," I said, changing his mind.

As we expected, not many people were out on the streets. Here and there, a woman was sweeping the sidewalk in front of her house; another was watering her flowerpots on the windowsill, yet another was hanging her laundry on the line. A man, fresh from a short nap and still in his summer T-shirt or *canottiera*, was standing on his balcony smoking a cigarette.

Today's homes

Vita was excited to see the houses and walk the streets that my stories had etched in her childhood memories. Most houses looked very modest with only a ground floor and a single entrance door, just as I used to describe them. Some were old structures in disrepair and seemingly abandoned; others were new with wraparound balconies and up to three stories high. One would swear rich people lived in them. Vita found it strange to see these big fancy homes rising next to humble ones. Sadly, there were quite a few left unfinished with boarded-up windows and rusty rebars sticking out from roofs and columns. "What a waste!" Vita said. But what she found truly puzzling was the display of so much wealth in an otherwise poor town. Delia had changed beyond recognition since I left for America, I told her. Then, only the well-to-do resided in two-story buildings, usually with balconies. Others lived in old homes consisting of a simple ground floor. The truly poor lived in squalid shacks. But we never saw boarded-up houses, and seldom did we see new ones being built. Occasionally, young couples inherited family homes or moved in with their parents, at least temporarily. The less fortunate rented a place, hoping to get back on their feet someday and have a house of their own. For many, the dream never came true.

"How could a town change so much in such a short time? What happened?" Vita was curious to know.

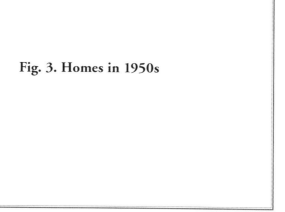

Homes in 1950s

Homes in 1950s The simple answer, I explained, was emigration and the money that returning immigrants brought back with them, mostly from Germany. With regard to the unfinished constructions, one of the first things some returnees did was to put all their hard-earned savings into building the big house they never had. But not everybody had the means to finish what he or she started. As construction dragged on and expenses mounted, many realized they didn't have enough money to complete the project. Some emigrated again, hoping to come back with enough savings to finish the job. Others simply decided to live in the part of the house already finished, leaving the rest to stand as an eyesore among beautiful homes. Whether finished or unfinished, most of the new homes were too big for the owners' needs and far beyond their means to maintain it. A fair number of households consisted of aging couples living alone as their children had already left home. Most young adults went to look for work in other parts of the country or aboard; others went away or simply got married and moved out of the house. Yet they built! It would have made more sense to let their savings grow by investing in some sort of business instead of wasting it in mansions they didn't need or could afford. At worst, they could invest in the stock market, purchase government bonds, or just open interest-bearing bank accounts.

I conceded that my criticism of the way people made use of their hard-earned money reflected my embrace of the American business mentality, as Nino often reminded me. Only someone who had lived abroad and assimilated a business culture could engage in such judgmental views. Unfortunately, this part of the country never developed a strong entrepreneurial spirit. Risk-taking was anathema to most Southern Italians whose distrust of business adventures was deeply rooted in their culture. I could think of several reasons for this cautious mentality. First and foremost, people never had enough money to live comfortably, much less to invest. For centuries, Sicily and most of Southern Italy had been a very poor region under the yoke of a feudal system that oppressed and exploited its people, consigning them to lasting ignorance and misery. Those with money eschewed unsecured investments, preferring instead to buy land or built big houses, both the symbols of wealth and social status. By and large, people continued to honor a tradition that was largely short on substance and big on appearance.

"In Sicily in particular, what has always mattered is not who or what you are, but what you appear to be," I told Vita while leisurely strolling through the town's narrow streets. "In the eyes of the community, a pretentious residence stands as a sign of its owner's prosperity. Sadly, many of these homeowners, by the time they are done building their dream house, have little left to show except the false image of wealth. Indulgence in appearance is not always harmless. Sometimes it leads to unpleasant or even tragic consequences." I recall the often-told story of a supposedly prosperous shopkeeper who borrowed a lot of money to pay for his daughter's lavish wedding. The bridal gown alone cost him more than he earned in a month. He also chose an exclusive wedding venue and hired an expensive catering service. For entertainment, he engaged a five-member band to play during the four-course meal and the dancing that followed. The costly event was the talk of the town, and he reveled in the people's praise of the sumptuous ceremony. Two months later, they found him hanging from a tree behind his house. The note he left behind read: "I was broke and too ashamed to face my family, my friends, and my creditors. Please forgive me."

Lack of Hygiene

Vita and I were enjoying our walk so much that we lost track of time. By all indications, siesta time was over, and the town was coming to life again. Children were playing in the streets. Women were beating the dust off their rugs or bedding, hung on the railing of their balconies. Men were out for a stroll or simply standing in front of their houses. Some looked at us with squinting eyes, wondering who we were, or who was the young lady with the *professuri*. Many greeted me with a typical hand gesture accompanied by "Buona sera, Professu" (Good afternoon, Professor). Some men I knew stopped to say hello and exchange pleasantries. After the customary introductions, they made it a point of greeting Vita, shook hands, and went about their business. Vita was puzzled to see so many people with beautiful smiles, showcasing mouths full of perfectly healthy teeth. She had always assumed that dental hygiene had never been a common practice among these folks. Wasn't that what some of my stories were about? Didn't I often say that when I was growing up, the town had no dentists and that most people didn't even know what a dentist was, much less see one?

No doubt, I had said that. But times have changed. Now there were plenty of dentists and doctors familiar with the latest medical advances. People trusted them and didn't hesitate to go see them on a regular basis. One may hear locals complain about slow medical services, but in the end, they were satisfied with the care they get. It was a far cry from the dismal care we used to get in my days. The town had come a long way since the 1950s when I was growing up. Back then, there were only two doctors and no dentists. Folks were reluctant to see a doctor and had no concept of dental hygiene. In my eighteen years in this town, I never knew or heard of anyone who went to the big city to see a dentist. None of the people I knew had ever seen a toothbrush. I saw my first toothbrush at the boarding school, where all students were required to use one. No one else in my family had ever seen a toothbrush until we came to America.

Lack of dental care was part of the reason people had bad teeth or hardly any left. Young people lost their teeth to unattended cavities or gum disease; adults viewed tooth decay as the natural process of aging. The thinking went: you get old, you lose muscle mass, you lose your sight and hearing, you lose your teeth. When a toothache became unbearable, they called the family barber who with a string and a pair of pliers, extracted the infected tooth. "Didn't these people understand that a pair of unsterilized pliers or a dirty string in one's bleeding mouth could lead to serious infections?" they wondered. I assured them that the educated and the well to do understood the risk of infection and did not hesitate to go to the big city to see a real dentist. The problem was with the ignorant poor, that is, most of the town's people, my family included. The notion of hygiene was by and large alien to our way of life. Two basic reasons, besides poverty, accounted for our awful sanitary conditions: widespread ignorance and more importantly, lack of running water. Without water, we could not wash clothes or ourselves as often as we needed to. Neither could we have a working sewage system. Farmers in particular emptied their chamber pots in their stables, mixing it with animal manure. Every other day or so, they would take the manure to a heap they kept on the outskirts of town. In the fall, they would use the composted dung to fertilize their fields. The filth we all lived in! Should it surprise that many children, the most susceptible to serious infections, died at a tender age?

Since children spent most of their time playing outside in the open, they were less susceptible to contagion. But in the winter months, as people spent a lot of time in crowded and enclosed spaces, germs and viruses spread rapidly, at times with serious consequences. Common colds often developed into croup or whooping cough, resulting in death among babies. Then there were the more common and less serious infections such as the constant runny nose, the occasional earache, and the unavoidable pink eye. It was not unusual for kids to wake up in the morning with their eyelashes so encrusted they could barely open their eyes. At times, the encrustations were so hardened that mothers had to loosen them up by dabbing at them with a cloth dipped in warm water.

In the summer, the most common germ carriers were houseflies and mosquitoes. Flies, in particular, were everywhere and people learned to live with them on their food, clothes, and skin. If you left a piece of bread on the table, within seconds it would be totally covered with flies. You swatted them away and went back to eating your bread. Imagine the health risk! Relief came in the late forties when the Americans promoted the use of DDT. The chemical was first used in large quantities by the American military during WWII to combat spreading diseases, such as typhus and malaria. For the poor communities plagued by housefly infestations, it was a godsent remedy. It was particularly effective during the summer months when the flies were most numerous and very active. Unfortunately, the insecticide was not readily available. It wasn't sold in stores and could be gotten only through family connections or by bribing the right official. But there was always the black market. Once I went with my father to a man's house to pick a gallon of the milk-like substance, the man reminded my father to dilute it one part to three parts water before using it. My mother would often send us children out of the house so that she could spray the chemical and close the door on her way out. An hour or so later, the floor would be entirely covered with dead flies sometimes close to a quarter inch deep. She would then sweep the dead insects out into the street. And this she did almost every other summer afternoon.

One may rightly argue that by using DDT we jumped from the frying pan into the fire; the pesticide didn't just kill flies, it also harmed humans. But at that time, we didn't know that it was a cancer-causing chemical. Only of late have people learned that it was a serious health hazard. But what other choice did we have back then? There is no question the immediate benefit outweighed the health risk associated with its use. There and then, we were relieved to see a drastic reduction of the nuisance, which undoubtedly led to a notable decline in infectious diseases.

Sad to say, there were other sources of disease that threatened people's health. One such source was the repeated use of the same syringe on different patients. Doctors and some self-proclaimed neighborhood *nurses* sterilized needles by wiping them clean with a rag; others dipped them in isopropyl alcohol. My mother was one of those nurses who used the same syringe over and over though she made sure to wipe it with a cotton ball doused in alcohol or *spiritu*, as she called it. Somehow, she learned how to give injections and before we knew it, she was thought of as the neighborhood's nurse. Women would come by the house and ask her in confidence to stop by their place to give a shot to someone in their family. They were discreet about their requests because people were sure to spread all sorts of alarming speculations about the *disease*. Although fulfilling the many requests was quite an imposition on my mother, she never said no and never charged for her services. People were expected to help each other, especially when it didn't cost them anything. What about their time? Wasn't their time worth something? One may ask. The simple answer is that the notion that "time is money" was alien to the local culture. In such a backwater environment as ours, the pace of life was slow, and time was something everybody had plenty of. There were no time cards to punch and no appointments to keep.

Time telling was generally approximate. Seldom did people make appointments. If you wanted to see the doctor. For instance, you simply went to his clinic. There you sat and waited for your turn on a first-come-first-serve basis. People didn't really mind not knowing how long it would take to see the doctor. They just sat there gossiping and socializing with other patients who, like them, were waiting for their turn. A lawyer might tell a client to come by his office. As in the doctor's clinic, here too, people sat in the waiting room and waited and waited. In some instances, after waiting for hours in vain, they would be told to come back the next day. At the post office or at the city hall, they might be told that the official or clerk they were looking for had gone for coffee and would be back *soon*. And they waited. Most people didn't have watches and very few households had alarm clocks. My grandmother had an alarm clock. It was a huge decorative piece sitting majestically on the only table in her one-room house. Ironically, she didn't know her numbers and couldn't tell time. She had to ask others, usually her grandchildren, to tell her what time it was. Every time she asked me, she usually gave me a five-cent coin or *5 lire*. Sometimes, I would stick around, hoping she would ask me for the time. A lot of older folks told time by listening to the church bells, which rang on the hour and every fifteen minutes. The number of loud tolls signified the hour, the mini ones the quarter-hour. So if you heard the loud ring three times and the mini ring once, it was three fifteen. Some relied on the trajectory of the sun or the arrival of the intercity bus, which came by three times a day generally on schedule.

With all this time on their hands, my children asked, "Why didn't they make more of an effort to improve their unhealthy living conditions?" Again, it was not a question of time or indifference. People were simply unaware that some of their habits or practices were unsanitary and caused diseases. They just didn't know any better. Ignorance was definitely a serious obstacle to improved health care. To treat common injuries, such as skin infections, cuts, or burns, they relied on old remedies. Once my older brother developed a huge boil on this back. Neighbors urged my mother to dress the wound using fig leaves. The leaf's heat would draw out the pus and dry up the wound, they said. When I was twelve, I fell off my bike and got a deep cut on my leg. Again, the neighbors came to the rescue. They suggested stuffing the cut with coffee grounds to absorb and stop the bleeding. My mother followed their advice and swaddled my leg in gauze. In both cases, the wounds eventually healed, leaving permanent scars. Hard to say whether the healing resulted from the home remedies or from long months of recovery.

Whatever the effectiveness of these old wives' tales, the fact is there weren't many other choices. If ignorance were not enough, there was the question of money. Folks were too poor to pay for needed drugs though drugs were not that expensive. Even those who could afford them were unwittingly taking risks whenever they needed to have a prescription filled. Those days, not all medications came prepackaged in bottles or boxes. Often, pharmacists had to prepare them by mixing the right ingredients in the right proportions. The town's pharmacist, a man in his sixties, was not always dependable even when he was sober. In addition, he was barely familiar with the latest standards of the profession. In some cases, if he were not around, his wife or his daughter— neither a pharmacist—would take it upon themselves to fill a prescription. God only knows how many people got sicker or even died after taking the wrong medication. Also, people rarely went to the doctor. They sought medical assistance only when they could no longer ignore whatever afflicted them. This reluctance had nothing to do with lack of time; they had all the time in the world. Neither did it have to do with their inability to pay because healthcare was free under Italy's national health insurance. For most people, the main reason was fear— fear to learn that they might have a deadly or contagious illness, such as typhoid or tuberculosis. As the notion of privacy was totally unheard of, they worried that the whole town would find out and brand the entire family as *diseased* or *segnata*, as they said back then. To be so branded was tantamount to a social death sentence; the community would shun them, marriage prospects would vanish, and work opportunities would dwindle.

There was a family in our neighborhood whose older daughter had contracted tuberculosis. Soon, the entire family was considered dangerously contagious and to be avoided at any cost. They were branded, and the disease was their scarlet letter. To be sure, folks talked to them in the streets, always from a safe distance, but would never go inside their house. Not surprisingly, the other two sisters never got married, and their only brother could not find work. Nobody would hire or work with someone who might be carrying and spreading a deadly disease. So the family managed to scratch a living off a piece of land they owned on the outskirts of town, where they went to live.

I don't know if the fear of been shunned justified people's reluctance to seek professional help. Social isolation could kill as easily as a fatal disease. But it was not just the fear of being *segnata*; it was also the general lack of confidence in the town's doctors. The two local physicians were so professionally limited that they were often of little help. They relied by and large on the knowledge they acquired in medical school early in the twentieth century or on the battlefield in WWI. Seldom, if ever, did they read about the latest medical breakthroughs. Heaven knows how many people were misdiagnosed and died as a result. My birth mother was one of those victims. She was afflicted by fatigue and low-grade fever for several months after giving birth. The doctors, failing to recognize she had developed a postpartum infection, treated her with the usual antiquated and quackish remedies. Untreated, the infection spread into her bloodstream and killed her. She died at the age of thirty-eight, leaving behind four children ranging in age from a newborn to a six-year-old. The baby girl died a few months after her first birthday.

One day during our visit to Delia, something I don't recall exactly what, made me think of the child's death. When I tried to tell Vita about it, she reminded me I had already told her the story.

"I'll never forget the time and the way you told us how your baby sister died. When you began to think about the reasons that might account for her death, your words faded into sullen silence," she recalled. "You became reflective, just as you did whenever you drifted back to your unpleasant, boyhood memories. I remember asking myself, Why does he become so withdrawn and introspective? Is he trying to fight back dreadful recollections or simply searching for the actual causes that led to the baby's passing?"

Thinking back, there was no obvious cause of death and no one asked why the infant died. Some relatives suspected malnutrition as the cause of her death. They thought the wet nurse routinely gave her whatever little milk she had left after feeding her own baby. Whatever the reason, she was one of several toddlers that died every month in Delia. Those days, so many babies died within the first years of their lives that it was difficult to tell what really killed them. Hardly a week went by without hearing the joyful tolling of church bells; it was the sound announcing the death of a child. Announcing one's passing was one of the bells' many functions. The number of strokes, tone, and frequency distinguished each death. Slow and mournful tolls announced the death of an adult: six for a woman, seven for a man. For the death of a child, the bells rang a joyous peal or *gloria* as we called it. The common belief for the merry tolling was that the blessed innocents went straight to heaven. A joyful event for the believers! Death, premature death, in particular, was commonly accepted with devotional resignation. "God wanted them and called them to Him," the saying went.

Comforting as this belief might be, it's hard to reconcile how a religion could glorify the death of an infant. People might have found solace in the thought that their beloved went to heaven and was rejoicing in the grace of God. But the relatives left behind had to go on living with the painful memory and in some cases, with the nagging doubt whether they could have done more. Perhaps that's what really bothered me the most—the suspicion that the family didn't do enough to save the child. Could she have died of malnutrition? was the question that nagged consistently at my mind. But if that were the case, how was it possible that nobody noticed she was wasting away? Couldn't they look for another wet nurse? Maybe they thought of that! But who? Where? In a small town like Delia, it would not have been easy to find another woman with enough milk to breastfeed an additional baby even if they paid good money.

CHAPTER 5

Growing Up as an Orphan

Good money is just a matter of speaking, for the family had barely enough to make ends meet, especially after the payment for the care and the funeral expenses for both my mother and later my baby sister. Also, cash was a scarce commodity when I was growing up. There was very little currency in circulation. Most people didn't use money; they simply exchanged services for goods and goods for services. My father, for example, paid the family barber with wheat or *grano*. Every year, at harvest time, the barber's two boys would come by the house with their wheel barrel to collect the amount of wheat agreed upon as payment. Wheat, locally known as *frummientu*, was a common trading item. It was also the main staple of our diet. Following the summer harvest, most people kept whatever *grano* they thought the family needed for the coming year and sold the rest. Every month or so, they would take a certain amount of it to the flourmill. With the flour they made bread, pasta, pizza, and other flour-based foods. Often they bartered small amounts of the cereal for minor household needs, including kitchen utensils. Sometimes they traded other foodstuff for processed foods, such as salt or sugar. They exchanged chickens, almonds, and beans for spices and cured meats, such as pepper or *mortadella*, a type of cheap luncheon meat. For small purchases, say below a dollar, they usually traded eggs or paid in cash. I recall being told that my baby sister's wet nurse preferred to be paid with wheat. She also insisted on having her pick of my dead mother's things. She even kept the baby's clothes.

There were times when I asked myself why the nurse was given such a free rein over our things. I didn't expect my father to oppose her overreach; he was a total wreck to even think about baby clothes and other keepsakes. But what about the relatives? Didn't they care enough to want some of the baby's things, for memory's sake if for nothing else? I guess what I was really asking was why did they let her die? Wasn't there something they could've, should've done? In the absence of a specific answer, I began to resign myself to the most obvious cause, namely the grim conditions that awaited all four of us orphans. Innocent and without a mother, we entered a world void of loving care and full of misery. The relatives tried to help out of sheer compassion or sense of duty. But they were not in a position to help, neither were their scanty efforts enough to ease our misery. They were poor and lived in tiny houses with their large families. Whenever I entertained these thoughts, I couldn't help wonder why I was brooding over the relatives' seemingly token support? Was I trying to fault them for their indifference or simply understand their situation and forgive them?

Undoubtedly, I was conflicted. On the one hand, I expected the relatives to help; on the other hand, I knew they couldn't. But I never doubted my grandparents' compassion. They truly cared. From both sides of the family, they were more than willing to help though they were sickly. Soon after my mother's death, they took turns caring for us. For over six months, we stayed with them. First, we went to live with our grandparents on my father's side, and then we moved in with the other grandparents. Fortunately, they lived near our house and across the street from each other. But the arrangement was hardly a suitable one. They lived on meager pensions and in small houses without plumbing or electricity. Just like most poor people's homes, theirs consisted of a front room and a stable in the back. They lived in the front room; in the stable they kept the donkey, the chickens, the rabbits, and whatever farm tools they still had. As if the tiny spaces and the lack of utilities were not a huge problem, both grandmothers were in poor health.

One of them got around with the aid of a cane, and the other, though crippled with arthritis, had to take care of her bedridden husband.

We were virtually left to fend for ourselves, spending most of the day out in the streets, often hungry and always dirty. The filthy environment we lived in gave us constant runny noses, frequent pink eye, earaches, huge pus-filled boils, and other minor illnesses. The upshot of this exposure was that it helped us develop a strong immune system. But whether it was because of a tough immune system or simply pure luck, we survived while many rich kids got sick more frequently and often seriously. Sadly, the average person was not aware that unsanitary habits caused and spread diseases. It was not unusual for people to hack up wads of yellow phlegm, splatter it on the ground and smear it under their feet. This happened even in the waiting room at the doctor's office. Whenever the doctor happened to see that muck on the floor, he would yell at everybody in the room and lecture them on the risk of infections. And then, he would throw his hands up in disgust and go back in his office, slamming the door in resigned frustration. For him, it was a daily occurrence.

Schools tried to teach children basic sanitary procedures aimed at curtailing the spread of infections. But whatever the kids learned at school couldn't possibly practice at home. Most of them lived in grimy dwellings that lacked running water, the ABC of good hygiene. Whatever water people had to have for their basic needs, such as cooking and drinking, they got from a public fountain in their neighborhood. Usually, housewives would make one or two daily trips, carrying the water in a two-gallon clay jar or *cuartara*, which they typically carried on their heads. Placing a jar on their heads was a careful balancing act requiring skill, concentration, and careful movement. It wasn't difficult for an experienced woman to put an empty crock on her heard and walk to the fountain. But once the jar was filled, it was too heavy for one person to lift; other women at the fountain had to help. When they got home, either a family member or a neighbor helped them to take it down.

The task was nerve-racking, physically demanding, and time-consuming. Besides having to walk carefully to prevent the jar from falling, women had to drag along their restive children who were constantly trying to pull away from them. Also, once at the fountain, the kids wanted to run around and play instead of standing in line waiting with their mothers for their turn to fill their jars. Depending on the hour of the day, the ordeal could take as long as a half-hour, especially in the morning when most women went to get water. Sometimes, patience gave way to frustration and even altercations. Scuffles happened mostly when someone tried to cut in line with tried, made-up excuses such as "I left my baby alone in the crib" or "I have a boiling pot on the stove." But these incidents were rare and inconsequential. Most women were eager to get home and start their daily chores.

Helpful as it was, the routine trip to the fountain did not provide enough water for bathing or doing the wash on a regular basis. Due in part to the chronic water shortage and the need to heat it up, people bathed no more than two or three times in the winter months. They also wore the same clothes for weeks on end. Did they smell! But then, everybody else smelled. The noxious scent was noticeably strong in enclosed spaces such as cafés where people reeked of stale smoke and dirty clothes, especially socks and underwear.

Body odor was not a big issue during the summer. Older boys, in particular, would go wash and swim in the small river on the outskirts of town. Also, women could do the laundry more often as they didn't have to heat the water. Some even went down the river to do the wash. And of course, there were plenty of sunny days to dry up the clothes on the line. In addition, there was less wash to do because people wore fewer and lighter clothes. Most teenage boys spent the summer wearing shorts, no socks, no shoes, and no shirts. Adults, many in *canottiera*, passed a lot of time out in the open, sitting in the shade and trying to sweat as little as possible. Late in the afternoon, when a gentle breeze made the day's heat more bearable, men mingled in outside cafés—always in the shade—playing cards, smoking, and bantering with each other. Women in small groups of four or five gather in front of a neighbor's home and sat around gossiping or reciting afternoon or evening prayers. With no house chores left to do, they relaxed and enjoyed each other's company. They didn't have to worry about their children playing somewhere in the neighborhood. Those days, the streets were safe, especially in small towns where there was no crime, no drugs, and no traffic to speak of.

Winter was not as easy going for women, especially when it came to doing the laundry. First, they had to haul enough water from the public fountains. Then, they had to heat it up. This was particularly difficult since it could be heated only a pot at a time on the family's small primitive wood stove. By the time the last pot started boiling, the first ones were already getting cold. Also, since the wash was done by hand, women had to keep on pouring hot water into the washtub to prevent their hands from getting numb and chapped. It was quite a challenge to wash big items such a bedsheets. Most importantly, the laundry had to be done on sunny days so that it could dry on the line. This was long before the age of weather forecasting, and women didn't know what the day would bring: rain or sunshine? All the while, they had to tend to the daily domestic drudgery, such as cooking, caring for their babies, and watching a houseful of bouncy youngsters. A woman's day was long and truly exhausting.

Undoubtedly, it was this life of hard toil that led my grandmothers to throw in the towel and declare the boys were too much for them. They told my father they were too old and too feeble to continue taking care of his kids. He needed to find an alternative. But what? Where? How? Who could help? He was at his wits' end. My grandmother, moved by her son's desperate pleas, agreed reluctantly to help for a while longer. Needless to say, she found the task overwhelming, especially during the winter. She constantly had to remind us kids to be quiet and stop running around the house. But her threats couldn't possibly keep three lively youngsters cooped up for long in the one-room house. Before we knew it, we were at it again, playing rough and making noise. At times, she made us go outside and play in the streets. But the cold and the frequent rains made it hard for us to stay out for long. In addition, little Pasquale started wetting the bed where all three of us slept. That became a huge problem, especially because it was quite an undertaking to wash and dry the sheets. As a result, we often slept on damp sheets and smelly mattresses. Pasqualino was yelled at and punished for being too *lazy* to get up and pee in the chamber pot like everybody else. No one thought that bedwetting might be related to the severe emotional distress we were experiencing. Today, most people would understand we were unconsciously living the profound loss of our mother but were too young to verbalize our grief. We were three lost children in the world that our mother's death had suddenly turned upside down.

Clearly, the situation was getting more and more untenable if not desperate for my father. There he was with a little baby girl in the care of a wet nurse and three boys at his mother's house. As for him, he had to tend the farm, which he worked as a sharecropper. Every day he went out at dawn and didn't return until dusk. How did he deal with all of this? I was too young to know how he felt. But it is not difficult to imagine how distressfully aware he was of his predicament. Years ago, my aunt put the situation in perspective for me. There was no question in her mind that my father needed a woman to do the cooking, the washing, the cleaning, and taking care of us kids. The problem was that no self-respecting woman would agree to come and work in a widower's house. To be in the home of an unmarried man would compromise her reputation and that of her entire family. The other option would have been to simply pay a woman to care for us boys in her own home. But that, too, was not a workable solution. Those who might be willing to take the job lived in cramped spaces with their typically large families. They had no room for three more kids.

There we were alone in our misery with little to look forward to except cold, hunger, and the token compassion of our neighbors. I say token not because they didn't care but because they were in no condition to help. They could only offer words of sympathy. We would hear women say to us with heartfelt pity, "Poor little orphans! My heart goes out to you! Only if your mother were here!" But in the end, we were left to fend for ourselves against a cruel fate without fully understanding why. My father once told me that some winter evenings, he would run into us on our way to meet him as he was coming back from the fields. He said that more than once he cried on seeing us hungry with runny noses and shivering in the winter cold.

Not long ago, my younger daughter, Jenna, reminded me that when I first talked about this episode, tears welled up in my eyes.

"Then, wiping your eyes with the back of your hand and regaining your composure," she recalled, "you said, 'It was heartbreaking for me to hear my father say that he cried. Those days, men of his temper did not cry.' I will never forget, those words, the tone, and the distant look in your teary eyes. I had the impression you were actually reliving that far away moment. I also remember asking if you were one of *those men*. In my entire life, I have never seen you cry. You looked away, and after a short pause, I heard you murmur to yourself, 'I do cry, alone, like my father.'"

CHAPTER 6

My New Mother

Rescue finally came as my father decided to remarry. Eight months after my mother's death, he married a charitable and loving woman. She took care of us as if we were her own. When my children first heard the story, they wondered why he didn't take this step sooner instead of letting his kids wallow in wretched conditions for so long. At that time, we were too young to dwell on such questions; we were simply glad to start living a normal life in a normal household with a *mother*, food on the table, and the sense of stability that came with it. But as I grew older, I could see why my father didn't remarry earlier than he did. There were two major reasons, both steeped in our culture. First, it was difficult to find a marriageable woman ready and willing to marry a forty-five-year-old widower with four young children—the baby girl was still alive. Society frowned on a woman who would jump into such an arrangement. So it had to be someone past her prime who for some reason hadn't married, a spinster. But even an old maid ran the risk of been made to feel like an outcast. Also, whoever married my father had to consider the possibility that the children might resent her as an unworthy substitute for their dead mother. In addition, she would undoubtedly be under the scrutinizing eyes of her new neighbors. They would be watching her every move toward the orphans, ready to label her a *wicked stepmother.*

The other reason that prevented my father from getting married earlier was also rooted firmly in our customs. Those days, local traditions expected people to mourn the death of a relative for a certain length of time, depending on how close the relationship was. A mother, for example, would mourn the death of a child for as many as ten years. During the grieving period, she would wear black, the most common symbol of mourning. Within that time, other deaths would occur in the family, causing her and others like her to wear black for the rest of her life. Naturally, grieving people were expected to abstain from participating in festivities or showing signs of cheerfulness in public. One of the most widely held beliefs was that a widower should not remarry—widows seldom remarried—during the mourning period, that is, within the first year of his wife's passing. Going against this tradition would surely meet with widespread public censure. The town would view the transgression as a blatant desecration of the deceased's memory and a serious insult to the grieving family.

While my father was expected to honor these traditions, we continued to live virtually in the streets, waiting for him to come home in the evening from the fields. Lucky for us, a close family friend made it his business to get involved. He took it upon himself to approach a thirty-year-old neighbor of his and ask her if she would marry my father. At first, Filippa, that was her name, refused because she was planning to serve God by entering the convent and becoming a nun. But after several heart-to-heart talks with her confessor, she relented. The padre assured her there was no better way to serve God than taking care of the four wretched, little orphans. The Lord would bless her sacrifice. But what really changed her mind was when the priest, reaching down into her deeply buried memories, reminded her that she, too, had been a young orphan. She was barely eleven years old when her father died, living a widow with five mouths to feed.

Filippa's consent to the marriage met with opposition from family members, especially her older brother, Paolo. He argued that her marriage to a man thirteen years her elder, and worse, a widower with four children would disparage the family name. The fall out would jeopardize his and their siblings' prospects of a good marriage. He also warned that she would be committing herself to a life of hardship, having to care for four young children. But in the face of her determination to go through with her decision, he relented and the wedding took place as scheduled. But in no way was he going to let her forget what she getting into. On the wedding day, while Filippa was receiving her guests, I—just over three years old— decided to relieve myself on the steps leading to the reception room. Filippa's mother immediately went to clean the mush, but Paolo stopped her, insisting that it was Filippa's *new* job. She had better get used to the life of drudgery she had chosen for herself. And so it was that Filippa, still in her wedding gown, was initiated to the toilsome life that awaited her.

My father, too, had to deal with social criticism and family opposition. Some folks criticized him for disregarding a tradition long enshrined in the local culture. For them, he should have waited the usual year of mourning before thinking about getting married. His *rush* to replace his dead wife was a brazen insult to her memory. But most people were more charitable. They understood the precariousness of his situation and were willing to overlook the transgression. They knew he had no other option and that the children had suffered enough. Not surprisingly, opposition came from my mother's side of the family. My grandparents, aunts, and uncles expressed their disapproval by not going to the wedding. No one expected them to attend; they were the aggrieved party. Their situation was a complicated one. Publicly, they were supposed to show outrage over a wedding that was taking place barely seven months after the passing of their beloved one; privately, they were glad the children were now living a normal life in a normally functioning household. What's more, they were no longer expected to shoulder the burden of caring for the little orphans.

The ceremony was a very low-key affair out of respect for the groom's recently deceased wife. The guests were treated to a *bomboniere* (a small bag of sugar-coated almonds), a handful of roasted chickpeas, and plenty of red wine. There was no music or dancing. The day after the wedding, Filippa, now my stepmother, moved in with us and made it her priority to clean the place from top to bottom. One of the first things she did, always according to my aunt, was to boil all our clothes, including the bedsheets. Some of the clothes were so infested with lice that she simply threw them away, together with the ones too tattered to mend. My father welcomed the stability the marriage brought to his life, with him going to work in the fields and his new wife taking care of the household. For us kids, the marriage meant the deliverance from filth and hunger and the comforting feeling of being loved and cared for. Our new *mother* immediately accepted us as her own children, and we embraced her as our only mother. The neighbors, ever suspicious of stepmothers, soon came to view her as a genuinely caring woman and a model wife.

One of her primary tasks was to replace the clothes she had thrown away. That presented a serious problem since my father didn't have much money. His meager savings had been spent on the wedding. But she didn't feel discouraged; she was a resourceful woman. By selling eggs, some chickens, a few pounds of wheat, and other spare household goods, she was able to put aside enough money to start buying clothes for us kids. She usually bought used clothes at the open market or bazaar that took place once in while in the town square. Every now and then, a vendor came to town with a truck full of used American clothes and some kitchen utensils. The merchandise was generally clean, hardly used, and dirt-cheap. Some said that the goods were generously donated by kind Americans to help Europeans recover from the ravages of WWII. Others suggested, rather cynically, that the American government was primarily concerned with winning over the hearts and minds of the masses in order to fend off the *red* menace of Communism. Be that as it may, for the poor folks of Delia the *donations* were a godsend.

The vendor would spread his goods out on the sidewalk: pots and pans, boxes of shorts, shirts, skirts, shoes, jackets, and winter coats. Just like other women with little money to spare, my mother would look for items she thought the family needed and could afford. Some of the clothes she bought didn't look like anything we normally wore. I was fascinated with those white-tipped saddle shoes with thin rubber soles.

I had never seen shoes so pretty and so lightweight. We kids loved them because unlike our typical shoes, they were light on our feet, and we could run really fast. Our regular shoes were handmade ankle boots and consisted of rough cowhide, thick leather soles, and metal heel plates. People asked their shoemakers to make them to last. And they lasted! Sadly, our parents didn't realize that as our feet grew, the heavy and indestructible shoes tended to stunt foot growth in many of us. With the feather-light, low-quarter American shoes, we felt liberated. Another item of clothing I really liked was the soft cloth and the bright colors of some of the shirts my mother bought at the *mercato americano* as people called the occasional bazaar.

Although I still have vivid memories of my early childhood, there were times when I doubted my own recollections. I often wondered whether I actually remembered or simply heard some of the things I was writing about in my diary. Did I remember, hear, or imagine certain details about my mother's death or my father's wedding with Filippa? My memories could very well be mere recollections of what the relatives or neighbors might have told me. After all, I was barely three years old when my mother died and not yet four when my father remarried. How could I know, for instance, that Pasquale used to wet the bed? Did I really remember that on my father's wedding day I pooped on the steps, and Filippa, still on her wedding gown, had to clean it up? Where did I learn about Filippa boiling our lice-infested clothes? After serious and frequent reflections, I concluded that some of my *recollections* were actually from stories my aunt Lucia used to tell me. But I do recall that my new mother, a year or so after she married my father, would sit us down on a chair out in the street and comb our hair with a gray fine-tooth comb to remove lice and their eggs. I particularly remember how she would crush the little creatures by placing them between her thumbnails and squash them with repeated twisting motions. I also recall that in an effort to prevent the spread of the itchy bugs, each spring my father would tell our barber to shave our heads and keep them shaved until late fall.

Totò's family

CHAPTER 7

In the Streets of Delia

Strolling through the streets of Delia, Vita and I stopped and talked to a lot of people, each with a story to tell about my childhood. It got so late that we didn't get to visit the house I was born in. We needed to go back to Aunt Lucia's house; they were undoubtedly waiting for us to start dinner. So we hurried home and wouldn't we know the food was already on the table? We could tell my aunt had been fretting over our tardiness; we had been gone for more than four hours. The first thing Uncle Filippo said when we arrived was "Unni astatu?" (roughly, where have you been?). Aunt Lucia, noticing that the wine was loosening her husband's tongue, told him to shut up, "zittiti." Filippo was not really upset. His reproachful tone was his way of expressing the family's wish to see us spend more time at his house. He was proud of his American relatives and wanted everyone in town to know that they came to see him and his family.

Eventually we all sat at the table and after Filippo murmured a routine blessing, began to eat. There were eight of us at the table, and the noise quickly rose to a festive pandemonium. But there was no actual conversation. Everybody was talking at the same time, TV blaring out ads, babies crying, and a six-year-old banging his spoon on the plates. Vita had already gotten used to the "mangia! mangia!"

urgings, and made sure to say *sì! sì!* Whenever someone asked her if she liked the meal, "You allaikah? You allaikah?" All that hubbub of laughter and shouting aside, there was no mistaking the hosts' genuine pleasure in entertaining their guests.

After dinner, the women cleared the table while the men went outside to smoke and had the usual chitchat. As a guest and an American to boot, Vita was not allowed in the kitchen to help the women with the dishes. This time, Aunt Lucia insisted and encouraged her to join the men outside and relax. She resented being kept out of the women's *club*, but she had argued the issue before and wasn't about to argue it again. So she came out and sat between Filippo and me, just in case she needed help with translation. While the guys were reminiscing about the olden days and bantering with one another, Filippo began to talk about flying and airplanes. Perhaps he wanted to involve Vita in the conversation by bringing up a topic she was familiar with. Or he just wanted to show off his flying experience and appear worldly. Whatever the reason and with everybody's attention, he went on to boast about his familiarity with jumbo jets, stressing that they were "grande . . . grande" (big . . . very big), bigger than three buses put together. At first, Vita thought she misunderstood his childish notion of airplanes, but my winking and my condescending smile assured her that she had gotten it right; the guy had no idea what he was talking about. But what led to hilarious laughter was Uncle Pietro's taunting questions. Knowing that his braggart brother had never been near an airport, much less on an airplane, he dared him to explain.

"How do you know? Have you ever been on an airplane?"

"No! Never," answered Filippo with determination, as if to say, "So what?"

"Then, how do you know what an airplane looks like?" Pietro insisted, determined not to let his brother off the hook so easily.

"I just know," Filippo replied, refusing to admit his barefaced ignorance.

Vita didn't understand why Filippo had to pretend knowledge of things he knew nothing about, especially in front of us who had been on airplanes many times. She was puzzled by his pretentiousness and wondered if it was a common tendency among the locals to claim knowledge of things they knew nothing about. I explained that many Italians found it embarrassing to come across as ignorant. They have this urge to appear knowledgeable about everything. They often make up stories or give wrong information rather than simply say, "I don't know." I gave her an example. Once in Rome, I was talking to some of my students about this annoying cultural trait and proceeded to demonstrate it to them. While walking in the EUR neighborhood, we met a local gentleman and asked him if he knew what the acronym EUR stood for. Without hesitation, the man answered, Ente Unione Romana. A young woman also gave us an improvised answer. Finally, we met an elderly lady who gave the correct answer, Esposizione Universale Roma. She added that the area was the site of the world's fair Mussolini planned to open in 1942. The exhibition never took place because of WWII.

Vita agreed that the EUR anecdote reflected the attitude of people who didn't want to come across as uneducated nitwits. But in Filippo's case, no one put him on the spot. No one asked him to comment on things he knew nothing about. Also, she added, his refusal to admit his ignorance made him resistant to new ideas. How can he learn anything if he thinks he *knows* everything? She was right. The sense of irony informing Filippo's arrogant ignorance, I told her, was a deplorable cultural trait. I illustrated this point by telling her a story I heard from a friend. One summer afternoon, some friends and I were sitting at a sidewalk café having a drink and reminiscing about the old days. As usual, Giovanni, a wealthy landowner and the most jovial of the group, was entertaining us with humorous stories he claimed really happened. One of his stories had to do with Neil Armstrong's historic landing on the moon.

"A few days after the Americans landed on the moon in 1969," Giovanni began, "I was coming out of the bank when one of my farmhands approached me."

"Sir," he said, "may I ask you a question?'

"Of course, you may, Fabrizio. What is it?"

"People are saying the Americans went to the moon, last week. Doesn't it strike you as another CIA propaganda scam?"

"No, it's true," I assured him. "There are pictures of the astronaut walking on the moon and planting the American flag."

"How can it be? The moment he landed up there, he would have fallen straight down to Earth," he argued with the conviction of one who is not open to discussion.

"No, Fabrizio, you see, the moon is—"

"You don't expect me to believe all that garbage, do you?" he interrupted. "I wasn't born yesterday, you know?" he said as he walked away proud of his suspicion and unaware of his foolish wisdom.

We all laughed at the poor man's presumptuousness, but I couldn't help wonder how many of the people I knew shared the farmer's suspicion. I was about to give Vita other examples, but it was getting late, the chatter was dying down, and people were beginning to take their leave. Finally, it was time to go to bed. But first, there followed a seeming heated discussion between my aunt and me that appeared to trouble Vita. She understood some common words, like "dormire . . . letto. . . notte . . .no! no! sì! sì . . . domani" (to sleep . . . bed. . . night . . . tomorrow), but she wasn't sure what it was all about. I summed it up for her. Aunt Lucia insisted we sleep in the master bedroom and wouldn't take no for an answer. It was her way of showing how honored she was to have us as her guests. Vita couldn't understand why I tried to turn down the offer. I knew she would've accepted it right away because among other reasons, she was exhausted. The bed was comfortable and she slept like a log.

Vita woke up late the next day, oblivious to the early morning clatter of pots and pans coming from the kitchen. She didn't even hear the bullhorns of street vendors ballyhooing their fresh produce or whatever goods they were selling. Rested and ready to start the new day, she got up and joined the living. Everybody was glad she was up and greeted her with a festive "Buon giorno." I was already on my second cup of espresso and talking to Gino Paradiso, an old buddy of mine, who had stopped by to say hi. Our laughter and constant backslapping made it obvious we were old friends from way back. Gino was about my age, a bit taller and with a slender built. He had a happy angular face with a slightly hooked nose and a graying handlebar mustache. His thinning salt and pepper hair was pushed straight back and held in place by a generous layer of hair gel. As Vita approached, he took his cigarette out of his mouth, placed it in the ashtray, stood up, and introduced himself.

"I am Gino. Me and your papà old friends."

He went on to tell Vita that he "talked good English" because he had worked in Canada for a number of years. When he retired, he chose to come and live back home like many other immigrants. In a small town like Delia, his Canadian pension went a long way toward enjoying a comfortable life. He made a point of ingratiating himself with her by telling her that he and I were childhood friends. We lived across the street from each other and were schoolmates. We were always together, playing in the street and getting into mischief. Sometimes we skipped school, and other times we roamed the countryside looking for foodstuff to steal and sell or eat. In the summer, we often went swimming, which angered a lot of farmers and sometimes got us in trouble with the police.

Water trough

Vita wondered what he meant by *swimming*. As far as she knew, in the area there was no lake or a big enough river to swim in. The sea was a good twenty miles from Delia. "And why did swimming anger people? Was he making stuff up?" she asked me.

"Actually, no! He was telling the truth," I told her. We did go swimming, so to speak, but only in one of the town's water troughs. The trough, which I showed her during our visit, was about five feet wide, two feet deep, and around forty feet long. In hot summer days, we would take our clothes off and jump in the seemingly clear water. But as we swam and splashed around, we stirred a lot of mud from the trough's bottom. This enraged many farmers whose animals, though thirsty, refused to drink from the murky trough. They were forced to wait around until the mud settled and the water was clear enough for the animals to drink. Their repeated complaints caused the local police to crack down on the young offenders.

"What did they do to you kids? Did they arrest you?" she asked.

"First they had to catch us," I said with a self-satisfied smirk.

And how could they? I thought to myself. The sheriff deputy couldn't possibly outrun us kids. He was too old and too fat. So he would sneak up on us and try to seize our clothes, which we normally hid behind a bolder near the trough. The rare time he managed to get to our clothes, our parents had to go to city hall and pay a fine in order to get them back.

"Did that keep you boys away from the trough?"

"Not really!" I answered.

We didn't fear our parents or the old policeman as much as we feared the farmers. So when they were at the trough with their animals, we would go on to do other things. Our favorite pastime was wandering around the countryside looking to steal goods, such as almonds, olives or other foodstuffs we could sell at a local store.

Totò the Little Thief

Most shopkeepers were hesitant to buy our stuff. Suspecting it was stolen, they asked all sorts of questions to make sure it was ok with our mothers. Of course, we lied our little hearts out, but we weren't always convincing. Sometimes, we were told to take our *wares* somewhere else. We generally avoided going to these shopkeepers, preferring to go to Mr. Giuliano's who never asked questions but paid us a fraction of the loot's actual value. He knew the goods were stolen, and we would accept anything he gave us. Clearly, he was an unscrupulous man, untroubled by the fact he was encouraging and abetting juvenile delinquency. We could get caught stealing and get in serious trouble. If this didn't concern the merchant, it definitely didn't bother us, ever careful not to get caught. We made sure the owner was not around before attempting to steal from his property. Sometimes, a farmer would set up a trap to catch us.

But we were streetwise and good at spotting an ambush. Also, when it came to running away from a pursuing farmer, he was no match for us; we were fast, especially when running with our *American* shoes. At my mention of the shoes, Gino nodded in proud agreement and went on to boast about our ability to outsmart and outrun anybody trying to catch us. But I cut him short, reminding him that we got caught once in a while even with our *americani* shoes. I also recalled that sometimes we even got a sound spanking.

"OK, we got caught, but once in a moon," Gino admitted grudgingly.

I recalled we were never seriously beaten. Typically, the farmers did not lay a hand on us before asking who we were, "Di cu si figliu?" (Who is your father?). At first, I didn't quite understand why they wanted to know who our parents were. But I soon understood why; they didn't want to run the risk of roughing up the son of some local notable. In fact, it didn't take me long to notice that the moment Gino said he was the son of the shoemaker Vincenzo Leone, they did not hesitate to slap him around. I figured I would get the same treatment if I said I was the son of Giuseppe DiMaria the peasant. So I told them I was the grandson of Mr. Calogero, "lu zi Calò." It worked. When they heard that name, they didn't lay a hand on me. They wouldn't dare. Instead, they waived a menacing finger and vowed to tell *zi Calò*. My grandfather was highly respected in our hometown, not because he was a mafioso—he was not—but because in his younger days he had stood up to the mafia and at times to the local authorities.

The conversation was interrupted when Gino's cell phone rang. It was his wife. She wanted him home right away because a water pipe had burst in the kitchen, and he needed to go get the plumber. Gino had hardly put the phone back in his pocket that he was out of the door, promising to come back and continue the conversation another day.

Vita, still eager to hear about my childhood escapades, wasn't going to wait for Gino to come back, so she prodded me to talk about those wild days of my youth. She was particularly interested in knowing where I got my spending money during the winter when there was nothing to steal in the countryside. Whenever I had a chance, I told her I stole eggs from our chicken coop and sold them at one of the town's grocery stores. She was shocked to hear that I stole food form the family. But I justified my action by pointing out that we seldom ate our eggs. Most of the time, my mother sold them or bartered them for spices or other foodstuffs.

"Didn't your mother notice the eggs were missing?" She asked.

"Most of the time she did, but there wasn't much she could do other than getting to the coop before I did. But then, if I couldn't get eggs, I found something else to sell."

"Like what? It's not like the family had valuables lying around for you to run off with?"

"You're right! We didn't have much. But I could always sneak out a bagful of wheat, which I could sell without any problem."

"But I thought you guys sold the wheat and kept only what the family needed to make pasta and bread for the rest of the year?"

She was right. I had said that. But we usually kept a little extra for bartering and trading. Also, my father didn't sell the surplus right away. Sometimes, he waited for a favorable market price. For the week or two it took to see if prices would go up, we lived with a huge pile of grain in the middle of the house. The pile was so big that no one would have noticed if I took a bagful or two. Obviously, I couldn't do it with my mother around and my siblings running in and out of the house. I had to wait for the time when everybody was away, which was rare.

I remember a particular episode when I devised an elaborate scheme to steal about five pounds of wheat. The summer 1953, we were waiting for Uncle Charlie and his wife, Aunt Enza, to arrive from America. Most of us didn't know what they looked like since they had emigrated more than thirty years earlier. But we knew that they, like all Americans, were rich and would be bringing many gifts. Everybody was excited, including the neighbors who hoped *lamericani* would remember them from the old days. For a week, there had been several false alarms about their arrival, "arrivaruuu . . . arrivaruuu" (they have arrived . . . they have arrived) people in the neighborhood would call out to each other. But to the disappointment of those who ran to welcome the distinguished visitors, no one had arrived.

One day, I schemed to get my mother out of the house by telling her that the Americans had just arrived and that she should go to Grandma's house to greet them. In the excitement, she immediately left for my grandmother's house, barely a block away from our house. I only had a few minutes to work with. Unable to find a bag, I quickly filled two knee-high, heavy-duty socks with wheat. As I was about to go out of the house with my booty, my mother came back convinced I was up to no good. I immediately buried the socks in the mound of wheat and playfully admitted to the ruse. That same afternoon, she started to scoop up a few pounds of the cereal to take to the flour mill when all of a sudden she saw what appeared to be human feet sticking out of the pile. Scared out of her wits, she screamed bloody murder. It took her a few seconds to realize that the *feet* were actually socks full of wheat. She quickly put two and two together and rightly blamed me for the wicked attempt to steal the *frummientu*, the family bread and butter.

"Need I ask how she dealt with you?" Vita asked, feeling amused and somewhat dismayed about my adolescent trickery.

She slapped me around a bit and, as usual, scolded me for robbing the family of its meager resources. But I had grown so impervious to guilt or spanking that nothing bothered me anymore. I did what I wanted to do, even stealing from my own family. I was not afraid of anyone or anything.

Playing with Live Ammunition

I couldn't think of anything I was afraid to do. I even played with live ammunition, totally heedless of the danger. Once, I did something that could've maimed or killed me.

"My God, what did you do?" she asked, wondering what an eleven-year-old could have done that was so dangerous.

Running around the countryside with my buddies, I explained it was not unusual for us to find unexploded ordnance left behind from WWII. Our favorite spot was a small creek, where we found all sorts of things, including rusty handguns and live ammunition. We sold the guns to a local blacksmith who forged them into something useful. As for the ammunition, mostly rifle and machine gun cartridges, we blew them up, after taking the necessary precautions. We would place it on top of a pile of hay, light up the fire, and run for cover behind a large tree or simply lie flat on the ground. By the time the fire heated up the ammo and caused it to explode, we were safely far enough to enjoy the fireworks. We loved hearing the loud explosions and watching the red-hot pieces of metal flying above our heads. We were not scared. We were too young to realize how deadly those flying fragments could be. But once, we came so close to being injured that we understood how dangerous was the game we were paying.

One hot summer day, we were down in the creek looking for stuff. One of the boys called everybody's attention to what appeared to be an unexploded bomb the size of a small melon. We were all excited at the prospect of blowing it up, just like we had done with live bullets many times before. But this time, it was different. For one thing, we knew it was going to be a huge explosion with a lot of shrapnel flying around. So we decided to build the fire on a small hill so that we could run and take cover down in a swallow ditch less than a hundred feet away. There we waited, watching the flames rise and slowly die down. But nothing happened. *Maybe we needed a bigger fire to heat up the rusty bomb*, we thought. So we decided to get up and gather more hay to place on top of the smoldering pile. We had barely gotten up when the bomb went off with a bright flash and a deafening boom. We froze panic-stricken and hit the ground. The bloodcurdling whistling of shrapnel flying just above our heads was terrifying. When we finally stood up, we were numbed and speechless. *We could have been killed,* we thought.

The townspeople thought so too when they heard what we did. They had not forgotten the deaths of four teenagers who four years earlier had died trying to defuse a large bomb they found in the creek. The boys thought the device was too old and badly rusted to be active and hovering over it, began to take it apart, using a hammer and a screwdriver. Only one of the five boys survived the explosion; the other four died instantly or days later at home. The accident was mourned as the most tragic accident ever to visit Delia. But even the fresh memory of this terrible loss didn't stop us from keep on looking for rusty guns and unexploded ordnance.

"So you sold rusty guns, took from your family, and stole from farmers. All for what? What did you do with all that money?" Vita asked, wondering what a little boy could possibly do with the money in a town where there was little to do.

Actually, we didn't get that much money, I told her. The storekeepers paid us peanuts just enough for us to buy gelato, rent a bicycle, or go to movies.

"The movies?" Vita was surprised to hear that a town where many people didn't even have inside plumbing offered the luxury of a movie theater. But it did. The town's first theater opened in the early fifties and ran movies three evenings a week. The projectionist was the local plumber, who had learned from his brother-in-law how to operate a movie projector. Due perhaps to his lack of understanding of how easily the heat from the projector's lamp could cause the celluloid reel to catch fire, there were frequent fires and long interruptions. Waiting impatiently for the film to resume, people in the audience hurled all sorts of insults at the poor man who was desperately trying to restart the picture. These disruptions, though a running nuisance, didn't keep people from going to the movies, the town's only venue for fanciful entertainment. Boys—girls didn't go to the movies—never missed the opportunity to go see films about swashbucklers, American Westerns, and bandits and robbers. Admission for us kids was relatively cheap. The drawback was that we had to sit in the first two rows, very close to the screen. At times, we had the scary sensation that we were about to be trampled over by the galloping horses on the screen. Fearing that the animals would leap out of the screen, some kids would start screaming and slide under the seat in front of them for cover. Besides these fearful moments, we enjoyed the show and never passed up a chance to go to the movies.

My friends and I were regular moviegoers. When we couldn't come up with enough money for the admission ticket, we tried to sneak in through a side door. We had a friend whose father worked at the theater. When his dad was busy doing something away from the side entrance, he would open the door and let us in. At other times, we took advantage of a practice that allowed adult patrons to bring a child along, free of charge. Kids usually stood in front of the theater's main entrance waiting for a relative to take them along with him. This did not happen often, as adults, unlike us kids, preferred dramas and love stories. They particularly enjoyed kissing scenes, the most explicit sex acts ever shown on the local big screen. Though rare these *risqué* moments often caused a cheerful brouhaha in the hall with some men applauding, others whistling, and a handful yelling something like "Go . . . go. . . go." Ironically, many believed that kissing scenes were not real. They thought that an invisible glass separated the kissing actors, which would prevent their lips from touching. For most folks, it was inconceivable that a man and a woman would kiss without provoking an immediate and passionate sexual experience of some sort.

This rather naïve idea was rooted in the belief that men and women should be kept apart for fear that their passions might flare up. *Putting them in the same room would be like pouring fuel on the fire,* it was thought. To be sure, not everybody shared these foolish notions. But the traditional view was so prevailing that schoolboys and girls were normally taught in separate classrooms and often in different buildings. Only after the fifth-grade boys and girls were taught in the same classroom due largely to lack of space. But even then, the boys had to sit on one side of the room and the girls on the other. The reason for the separation was partly born out of the deep-rooted fear that a girl's reputation might be compromised if she sat next to a boy though they were just children. Another reason for the separation was that girls, likely to become homemakers, had to go to domestic education classes that included cooking, sewing, cleaning, and other household activities. Reflecting on the gender distinction of my school days, I'm not at all surprised that a stubborn chauvinistic culture persists in today's Italian society. Italian women, especially in small southern communities, are still fighting for their relevance in society, be it at home, in the workplace, or the political arena.

CHAPTER 8

Totò in School

My children found it hard to imagine the awful times I grew up in. "How primitive!" they would say. They couldn't believe that ten-year-olds were allowed to roam the countryside, stealing and playing with live ammunition. "How was it possible," they asked, "for children to skip school so frequently without anyone putting a stop to it? Where were the parents? Were there no truancy officers?" They were appalled by the lack of adult supervision; kids were essentially left to their own devices in a world fraught with danger and disease. They got no argument from me; they had reason to be dismayed. But in more than one occasion, I pointed out that in the end our environment was safer than that of today's children. Sure, kids today are closely supervised and don't play with live ammunition, but they and their parents live in constant fear of drugs and street violence.

    The question of whether children are safer today than they were in the old days came up again one afternoon at Aunt Lucia's house while Gino was visiting. Ever eager to get in the conversation, Gino agreed that the country and the times in which we grew up were backward. True, no truancy officers, he said, directing his comments to Vita. If a kid was not in school, he went on, the teachers assumed he was sick at home or working in the fields. As for the role of school officials, they didn't think it was their responsibility to inquire about a pupil's absence. Then, he stopped and remembering an episode that had to do with me, conceded that there were some exceptions. Turning to me, he said, "More than once, our *professuri*, Mr. Luna, sent one of us to tell your parents that you were not in school. I remember the time when you missed school three days in a row and your papà brought you in, pulling you by the ear. When he got in the classroom, he started hitting you until our *professuri*, fearing he might hurt you, stopped him."

"I don't get it," interrupted Vita, confused. "Why did the teacher bother to notify his parents? You said that school officials didn't feel obligated to report truancy."

"Yeah, that's right," Gino answered, "but our teacher took a personal interest because he thought your papà was really smart. One time, he said to Mr. Giuseppe, your grandfather, 'Giuseppe, I wouldn't care about him skipping school if he were an average kid, but he is a very intelligent boy. It would be a waste for him to grow up to be a peasant like you. He has the smarts to go to college and become somebody, someday.'"

"I remember that day as if it were yesterday." I joined in. "I also recall my father's reaction. '*Professu*,' he said, 'beat him to a pulp if you have to, but make sure he learns. I don't want him to grow up to be an ignorant farmhand like me.'"

The teacher's belief in my potential resonated powerfully with the entire family, most of whom had barely finished third grade. From that time on, grandparents, uncles, and aunts never lost the opportunity to remind me that I would be the first on both sides of the family to get an education. I would be the *onore* of the family. They would no longer need to go to a priest or schoolteacher to have a letter read or written or a document filled out; they would have their own Totò to help them. Their pride and encouragement bolstered my self-confidence, and from then on I never doubted the course of my future in higher education. But if pride and encouragement abounded, the resources to send me to college were lacking. The family was too poor to afford to send me to school; they could only talk and dream about it.

While I was recalling the time when the family began to believe they had a bright star in their midst, Vita was thinking about the frequent and harsh beatings I received as a child. Phrases such as "beat him to a pulp," "slapping around," or "pulling by the ear" hit a sensitive nerve with her. *A child could be physically hurt and / or psychologically traumatized by that kind of treatment,* she thought. Barely able to contain her dismay, she turned to me and asked why did they have to resort to beating. Couldn't parents try less barbaric ways to discipline their children? Those days, I reminded her, most people believed that the only way to deal with unruly boys—girls were rarely a problem—was the whip. Just like their fathers and forefathers before them, they never thought misbehavior might be rooted in some underlying causes, such as ADHD or emotional traumas. Naturally, they grew unusually frustrated when their kids did not respond to corporal punishment. But they didn't know what else to do other than more beatings. I was one of those kids who were not deterred by a sound whipping. Let me tell a story.

Once, when I was nine years old, my father told me to go buy a bottle of wine. "The money," he said, "is in the basket on the counter."

I went to the counter, picked up the coins, and quietly slipped them under the waistband inside my shorts. Then, I turned to my father and with a straight face told him there was no money in the basket. Convinced that I was the only one in the family who would dare take the money, he demanded I hand it over. When I swore I didn't have it, he became furious and started slapping me. Sobbing and with tears running down my little face, I implored him to stop. He was hurting me. But he kept on hitting me while my mother was trying to hold him back. With my hands joined and raised in prayer, I knelt before him and continued to cry out my innocence. At one point, I saw a hint of doubt on his face as if he was beginning to wonder whether he had misplaced the money and was now hitting his child for no reason. But right as I was kneeling down, the coins fell out from under my short, making a jingling sound as they splashed and rolled onto the hard floor. The man lost it. He went wild and couldn't stop beating me. Finally, my mother managed to get in his way and stopped him. Then, with the tears on my cheeks barely dry, I went outside and started playing with the other kids as if nothing had happened. I was ready for mischief again. Still today, I can't figure out what caused me to get into trouble almost on a daily basis, heedless of the beating I was sure to get.

Smoking Cigarettes

Aunt Lucia, tired of listening to my story without understanding a word, chimed in, '*cchi dici?*' (roughly, what are you guys talking about?). After I told her that I had just recounted the coins incident, which she knew so well, she proceeded to add her own story. She too wanted to underscore how bad or *cattivo* little Totò really was. In a stew of Italian and local dialect, she proceeded to recount the episode of the cigarettes, her favorite story. Filippo immediately cut in, claiming it was his story to tell. But she wouldn't have it, insisting he didn't know how to tell a story. In addition, she reminded him, his memory was already showing signs of forgetfulness. He resented the insinuation and accused her of suffering from Alzheimer's. After a few minutes and back and forth, Filippo conceded and Lucia began her story. I translated for Vita.

"Totò," she recalled, "must have been no more than nine or ten years old when Filippo sent him to buy five cigarettes, four *Alfa* and one *Nazionale*. He gave the kid the exact change and urged him to make it fast because he had to go to work. *It shouldn't take more than ten minutes,* he thought. After waiting for about a half an hour, a frustrated Filippo, unsure of what to make of the boy's tardiness, went to work without his smoke. He was fuming, understandably. As hours passed and still there was no sign of Totò, the family grew concerned and began to look for him around town. It was getting dark and everybody was worried, including Filippo who never got his smoke. When Giuseppe, my brother, went to the stable to feed the horse for the night, he was surprised to find his child sound asleep on a pile of hay. He gently took him upstairs and put him to bed."

Vita was amazed at how proud Lucia was of her memory. Despite her age, the old woman was able to recall the story so lucidly and so excitedly as to give the impression she was actually seeing it in her mind's eye. I explained that for these older people, in particular, memory was one of the most cherished faculties. It allowed them to enter and bring to life the world of the past, their past. It was the soul of a culture that fed on its past and kept its dead alive, oftenelevating them as legendary protagonists. In Lucia's memory, for instance, my dead mother, Vita, continued to live as the fearless woman—the amazon—who, together with her husband Giuseppe, held a bunch of cattle rustlers at bay. Also, she literally saved Giuseppe's life by forcing him to quit his job when the local mafia decided to claim it for one its own. When the stubborn Giuseppe ignored the *mafiosi's* threats, Vita stood on his way and physically prevented him from going to work. She would not be made a window at her young age. Of course, living in the memory of the living came with variations as people's recollections were often creative or simply fading with age.

Lucia's memory, good as it might have been, was not what it used to be, judging by the omissions in her story. It didn't surprise me that her version of the cigarettes incident left out details she had emphasized in previous accounts. According to what she used to tell me, the day after my adventure with the cigarettes, I told my parents the whole story. On my way to the tobacco shop, I told them I kept debating whether to buy the cigarettes or spend the money on myself. I thought of buying a chocolate bar and maybe a big gelato and maybe something else. While mulling over my options, I arrived at the store and bought the cigarettes. On my way back, I pondered whether I should bring the cigarettes to Filippo or just smoke them myself. I chose the latter and ambled toward the outskirts of town to avoid been seen by family friends or relatives. I met a farmer returning from his field and a cigarette in hand asked him for a match. The man at first hesitated but then pulled out a cigarette lighter and lit my cigarette. Coughing my lungs out, I chain-smoked all five cigarettes, lighting the next cigarette from the one I was done smoking and about to throw away. By the last cigarette, I was feeling lightheaded and threw up a couple of times. After resting a few minutes by the roadside, I noticed that it was getting dark and began to think about the beating I knew I was going to get. So I went home and though fearing sure punishment quietly slipped into the family stable and fell asleep on a pile of hay.

Vita found the story amusing. But there were a couple of things she didn't quite get. What did Lucia mean by four *Alfa* and one *Nazionale*? Also, what kind of man would enable a child to smoke by lighting up his cigarette? Regarding the different types of cigarettes, I explained that those days a lot of folks could not afford a full pack so they bought them individually—three of these and four of those—or simply rolled their own. Also, not all cigarettes cost the same as the *Alfa* brand being the least expensive and the most unsavory. Folks tended to buy as many cheap cigarettes as they could afford. If they had enough money, they indulged in a few of higher quality, such as *Nazionale*. When I got older and started smoking, I always tried to get the best bang for my buck by buying several different brands. My favorite tobacco vendor was an old man who had difficulty with addition and subtraction. My buddies and I would ask for three or more types of cigarettes each at a different price. The poor man, a pencil stub in hand, had a hell of a time trying to figure out how much we owed. After adjusting his thick wire-rimmed glasses, he would lick one or twice the pencil he held in his left hand and sweat beads forming on his forehead, begin to add up the different prices, which he repeated aloud, "Six lire each for the four Alfa, plus eight lire each for the two Nazionale, plus eleven lire for the Espo . . ." By then he would get so frustrated that he would throw the pencil away and unwittingly give us more cigarettes than we paid for.

Going back to Vita's dismay at abetting cigarette smoking by children, I pointed out that most people disapproved of it. Many objected on the grounds that smoking was for grown-ups only. People were not aware that smoking was a health hazard. They knew the cough associated with smoking was not good, but they had no idea it was a cancer-causing habit. Smoking was rooted in a culture that glorified it as a sign of manliness. Kids could hardly wait to assert their manhood through smoking. For us, daring to smoke, first in secret and then in front of our parents, represented our boyish claim to manhood. We wanted to be like our fathers and especially, like the macho characters played by movie stars such as Clark Gable, Marcello Mastroianni, and other leading men of the big screen. Sadly, by the time we reached adulthood, we were hopelessly addicted to this dreadful vice. I, for one, started smoking when I was fourteen, and by the time I was twenty-two I was going through two packs a day.

Being a man's thing, smoking was taboo to women. I never saw a woman light up a cigarette, except in the movies. Some women thought it was a bad vice and left it at that; others were vocally against it. For one thing, they resented their husbands' waste of the family's meager resources. More importantly, they were apprehensive about the deep hacking cough that inevitably afflicted their cigarette-smoking men. But they had no idea that smoking caused cancer; they only knew that spewing out one's lungs had to be no good. Ironically, now that it has been proven to be a cancer-causing agent, many women have started smoking. Indoors and outdoors, men and women, young and old, continue to puff away their health. The habit is so deeply ingrained in the culture that a great many Italians continue to smoke even though cigarette prices have skyrocketed. Clearly, the government's effort to educate people about the link between cigarette smoke and lung cancer—started in the eighties—has barely made a dent in this deadly menace.

The national campaign against smoking has not been an easy fight to win. Once, while waiting for our flight out of Rome, Vita and I were standing near a man who pulled out a cigarette and began puffing away. As the smoke caused her asthma to act up, I approached a policeman standing nearby and called his attention to the man smoking, ironically, under a NO SMOKING sign. Following the *carabiniere's* warning, the man put out his cigarette and moved a little further away from the sign. Five minutes later, he was smoking again. When I asked him to stop because the smoke was irritating my daughter's asthma, he brazenly suggested we move somewhere else or just go back to America. At this point, we realized that it was a lost cause and moved away from the man who continued puffing on his cigarettes.

Reacting to my story, Gino, himself a smoker, thought I had no business telling the man to stop smoking or move somewhere else.

"Nowadays," he complained, "there is no *somewhere* else for smokers to go. There are NO SMOKING signs everywhere."

He went on to dismiss the health hazard of cigarette smoking as another example of CIA propaganda. But before he could go on with the usual conspiracy theories, a favorite pastime of many poorly informed Italians, I cut him off. He was being silly. I told him. "There is no conspiracy, just as there was no CIA conspiracy behind the assassination of President Kennedy or the American moon landing or the September 11 attacks. Scores of scientific studies have left no doubt that cigarette smoking is a primary cause of lung cancer. It's time for people everywhere to stop smoking though for some it might be too late already."

My serious tone left Gino speechless, and the conversation died down, fading into an embarrassing silence. Aunt Lucia, sensing the uneasiness of the moment, began to speak and proposed to tell another story about little Totò. But Filippo, maybe because he heard her tell it many times before or because he was still smarting over the cigarette story he didn't get to tell, reminded her that it was time to start making pranzo. Gino, who was sitting quietly and waiting for the right opportunity to leave, took advantage of the interruption. He couldn't join us, he apologized, because he had to pick up a few things at the grocery store before going home. He promised to stop by again the next day. Eventually hosts and guests sat down to eat, just the four of us. Pranzo was much like the dinner of the evening before, minus the chatter and the clatter, except of course for the blaring TV, which was on as usual. But this time, Vita did not hesitate to ask Aunt Lucia if she would mind turning it off. She did, perhaps unaware the thing was on to begin with, so used she was to the noise. Throughout the meal, we talked mostly in dialect, which spared Vita the strain of having to listen and participate in the conversation. Once in a while, Aunt Lucia would ask her, out of politeness, if she liked what we were eating. As always, Vita answered with her polite "sì! . . . sì!" When lunch was over, Lucia and Filippo retired for their habitual siesta while Vita and I decided to go for a walk through town, just as we did the day before. It turned out to be a memorable afternoon for her. She met some of my old friends and neighbors and heard all sorts of stories about the old days.

My Old Home

Vita suggested we go straight to the house where I was born. The previous day, we spent so much time looking at homes and talking to people in the streets that we never got to the old place. In retrospect, I wondered whether that was the real reason. Strangely, I had walked by the house many times before and never once tried to see the inside. Did I subconsciously fear revisiting unpleasant memories? Was the past within those walls still haunting me? I didn't know. What I knew was that at that time I was determined to show my daughter the home of my childhood. Though we stopped here and there to chat with old acquaintances, we managed to get there and actually go inside. It was the first time I made the effort to overcome my anxiety and walked into the very heart of my childhood memories. The place looked modern with marble front steps, a brand-new door, and large windows. It was hardly the house Vita had imagined from listening to my old stories. I stood in front of it and for a few seconds, looked at it in contemplative silence. Then like a man in a trance, I murmured in a stirring slow cadence, "I grew up here." Submerged memories began to pop up in my mind, and the echo of familiar voices sounded faintly in my mind's ear. I snapped out of my dreamlike moment when a young couple, fresh from their siesta, stepped out on their balcony—the husband smoking a cigarette, the wife watering her plants. They eyed suspiciously the two strangers below, wondering why we were looking at their house so intently.

Finally, I told them who I was and that I wanted to show my daughter the house I was born in. The couple said they were happy to show us around and would come down to let us in. "Just give us a few minutes," said the wife as she withdrew quickly inside undoubtedly to tidy up a bit. The house was small but no longer the rustic abode of old. Though it had been remodeled, Vita was able to reconstruct it in her mind, thanks to my description of what the place looked like in my days. She could see in her mind's eye how six children and two adults lived in such cramped quarters. I first pointed to the space where we used to keep a small table on which we ate, played cards, and did our schoolwork—when we did it. Then, I indicated the spot where my parents slept and the corner where my brothers and I had our bed. To the right of the entrance, there used to be a tiny cubicle that served as a kitchen.

"What about the bathroom? Where was the bathroom?" Vita asked, looking around for some space where the bathroom might have been.

We didn't have one. How could we? First of all, there was no running water in the house; second, we didn't have space. For our nightly needs, we kept a chamber pot in the kitchen. I went on to explain that the kitchen was the only enclosed area with enough privacy to go pee and that we used the pot only at night. During the day, the kids usually went outside and the adults used the stable on the ground floor. Though the place was updated to reflect modern living, I had no difficulty picturing it the way it was back when I left for America, some forty years earlier. It was a moving experience for me to revisit the house where I spent the first eighteen years of my life. Distant memories flooded my mind, some painful, others pleasant or made pleasant by the passing of time. I described the old place for Vita's benefit but mostly for myself, pointing to every little corner that reminded me of a particular story or incident.

After congratulating the owners on their beautiful home, we thanked them for their graciousness and left. Back on the street, I couldn't help commenting on the progress the town had made since my days. Now, people lived in larger spaces, enjoying the comforts of modern appliances and facilities: TVs, refrigerators, bathrooms, gas stoves, bright lights. Yes, bright lights! Though such a common feature as *lights* was hardly a novelty, it represented huge progress from the times when we used oil lamps in the homes and gas lamps to light up the streets. Back then, only the town's main streets were connected to the electrical grid. The rest of the town was illuminated by gas lamps mounted on street corners. Some areas were not illuminated at all.

One of my uncles was a lamplighter. His job was to go around town shortly before dusk and light the lamps using a wick attached to a pole about six feet long. Just before dawn, he would make his rounds snuffing the lamps with an aluminum hood attached to the same pole. Folks began to have electricity in their homes in the late forties. But the hook-up to the electrical network was so slow that some neighborhoods didn't get connected until the mid-fifties. Until then, many households continued to use oil lamps, including my family. The lamp's dim light cast shadows so dark that children were often frightened when they saw a ghost-like shadow behind them. They were especially terrified when they noticed that the shadow followed them everywhere, moving when they moved, running when they ran. Sometimes my brothers and I took pleasure in scaring our three-year-old sister by telling her that *the monster* was following her. She would scream in horror at the sight of that dark *figure* behind her and terror-stricken she would run into mother's arms. We called it fun, but in retrospect, it was nothing short of childish cruelty.

The *fun* didn't last long. The electrical grid reached our neighborhood, and we finally had electricity in the house. It was quite an improvement from the days of the oil lamp: no more kerosene smell, no more risk of knocking the lamp off our rickety table. But electricity was very expensive, and my mother, ever the penny pincher, insisted on using a very low-wattage light bulb for the entire room. The bulb shed barely enough light to avoid tripping on things. My kids once asked how my brothers and I managed to do our schoolwork without decent lighting. We didn't. Surely we could do our homework during the day, but that seldom happened. We simply didn't do much studying, period. How could we? The whole environment, from the cramped quarters to the constant noise of so many people coming and going, made it impossible to concentrate on our school assignments. During the day after school was over, we usually went home to drop off our books and went back out to play till dark. In the evening, we were too tired to even attempt to do our schoolwork, assuming we could see what we were doing under the dim light of a fifteen-watt bulb.

The best part of the day was going to the school cafeteria for lunch, which was free for poor kids like us. We looked forward to sitting with our buddies and eating things we didn't normally have at home. They usually served minestrone soup or spaghetti, bread, crackers, and a wedge of Swiss cheese. Some days, they even served chicken soup. Once a week, they gave us small chunks of white chocolate for dessert. It was a well-balanced meal, especially if we compared it with what we ate at home when school was not in session. Our typical lunch at home consisted of a piece of bread and some black olives or an onion. It was a treat the rare times our mother gave us five lire each to go buy some anchovies to eat with our piece of bread. The oily and salty fish made the stale bread go down much easier. I remember that rather than eating the anchovy and the bread together, I would often eat the little fish first and then try to eat the stale bread still in my hand. My older brother, instead, did the opposite. First, he ate the bread and then he teased me by just licking his anchovies still intact. More than once I managed to grab his last anchovy from his plate and ate it before he could react. Of course, my mother had to put up with the fighting that usually followed these incidents.

While finding these stories amusing, one of my kids, I don't remember who, couldn't help noticing the seeming contradiction between my lack of desire for book learning and my teacher's belief I was a bright kid. I didn't see the paradox. One can be smart without being a bookworm. I think my teacher considered me *bright* because I had a remarkable memory. Those days, schools placed special emphasis on memorization, and I was able to recite most assignments by heart. I didn't study for it; I merely listened to my brother Pasquale doing his homework. He and I were in the same grade because he had been held back a year. Since he was not doing well in school, the teacher suggested that the best way for him to learn was to read the assignments aloud. So every morning before going to school, he would read aloud over and over the day's homework. Casually hearing his reading, I managed to memorize the material long before he did. And so it was that I became the teacher's pet and sat in the first row while my brother was relegated to the last bench in the back of the classroom.

Seat assignments could have lifelong implications for many schoolchildren. Back then, it was common practice for teachers to arrange seating according to a pupil's perceived ability to learn: those with potential in the front, the others in the back. This allowed the instructors to focus on the good students and pay a little attention to those in the back. Teachers thought they would be *wasting* their time trying to teach kids unable or unwilling to learn. As far as they were concerned, those knuckleheads or *asini* (donkeys), as they called them, would never amount to anything. Most likely they would follow in the footsteps of their peasant parents. Sadly, a teacher's view of a pupil as *unteachable* carried a lot of weight in determining a boy's future. It was not unusual for parents to pull their *asini*-labeled children out of school and put them to work in the fields or the sulfur mines. It was a decision that inevitably destined the children to a life of ignorance and hardship. Fortunately, those days are long gone. Today's teachers practice a more progressive educational approach, and schoolchildren are all treated with kindness and given equal attention. Also, parents are more involved in their children's education and the label *asini* is no longer acceptable.

CHAPTER 9

Then and Now

Times had changed, indeed. But in some ways, the old was still casting its shadow on the present. Looking at the centuries-old houses lining the winding streets and the way some older people dressed gave me the feeling that in Delia the past was somehow present. Streets that in my days were wide enough to allow ox-drawn wagons to creak through unencumbered were now barely large enough for a car to get through. Widows and spinsters peeking through semi-closed doors or the lowered slats of their windows were like living ghosts of a bygone era. Hidden in the darkness of their homes, they watched passersby, wondering who they were and where they were going. They never failed to comment on people's appearance or disparage their modern ways. Most of the older women standing in front of their houses or walking in the streets were dressed in black from head to toe, barely showing their faces. To the outsider, the town was still living in the Middle Ages.

Men of all ages milled around the town's only park. Many sat outside cafés and social clubs nursing a beer and reminiscing with their friends. Others played cards while interested onlookers followed with keen interest in their every move, which card was played and why. At the end of each game, the bystanders would comment on the good or bad moves that determined the outcome of the game. Their remarks usually led to loud arguments, questioning the players' strategy and slamming the losers' skills. Some were so passionate that their shouts and gestures made one fear they were about to come to blows. But as usual, it was typical friendly banter, consisting of local gossip and humorous jabs.

A few feet away some older men sat silently, leaning forward on the walking canes they held between their legs. Their deep wrinkles and weathered skin spoke of years of hard work in the fields under the scorching sun of the Sicilian summers. Wearing the traditional *tascu*—a type of newsboy hat—they sat, looking vacantly in front of them. The spent look in their leathered faces gave the impression they were staring at the ghost of their past. They seemed fixed on memories that had given meaning to their existence. I stopped to talk to a couple of them I recognized, but their glazed eyes and the look of stupor on their faces told me they had no idea who I was. They seemed to come alive when I told them I was Giuseppe's boy from *lamerica*. They even remembered the old days when my grandfather *lu zi' Calò* was alive. The more Vita listened to these people, the more real became the ghost-like characters that populated the stories she heard as a child. In a way, I told her these old folks were a living reminder that my past was still living here. She understood why I kept on coming back to this place. The old town helped me unlock my childhood memories and bolster my sense of belonging. This was my home, they were my people, and I was one of them.

Giulia Remembers

As we strolled along, some folks waved to us, and others stopped to greet the *professuri* and said something nice to and about Vita. They didn't linger, perhaps sensing that my daughter and I were sharing a private moment and wanted to be left to ourselves. But one elderly lady did approach and talked to us at length. When we first noticed her, she was hanging clothes on the line in front of her house. As we got closer, she stopped what she was doing and looked at us, at first casually and then with growing interest. She was small, scrawny, and about five feet tall. Her wrinkled face accentuated her piercing brown eyes. She was dressed in black, with a long skirt down to her ankles and a headscarf tied under her chin. She must've been in her late sixties; at least she looked that old. The way she kept staring at us betrayed her curiosity. Who were these two strangers ambling along her street? As she was surveying us, we were pointing to this or that old house, some of which were dilapidated and seemingly abandoned. They were crumbling memorials of time past.

Abandoned houses

But as we stopped and I reminisced about the people who used to live in them, Vita started wondering why that woman continued to look at us so searchingly.

"Dad," she whispered, "have you noticed how intently that old lady is been looking at us?"

I did, but I didn't recognize her. Strange! I knew most every everybody in town. I didn't know who she was though I knew the people who lived in that house. Whoever she was, she was most likely wondering who Vita was and what she was doing here. Her foreign looks and mannerisms definitely made her stand out as an obvious outsider.

Still gawking, the old woman put down the clothes she was hanging and walked hesitantly toward us. Squinting her strained eyes, she stopped in front of me and after a few seconds of peering at me closely, finally said, "You look familiar. I don't know where, but I think I have seen you before. Who are you?"

"You tell me," I replied, humorously putting her on the spot. After allowing her to search her mind for a few seconds, I reproached her, "Giulia, are you so old that you don't remember me?" This tongue-in-cheek scolding clearly struck a chord in her mind, for she became visibly excited and all of a sudden shouted,

"Oh, my god! It's you, Totò!"

We embraced and kissed as it was the custom. Perhaps it was my voice that stirred her memory and brought her face-to-face with the little boy of decades past. Arms flailing and talking excitedly over one another, we inquired about each other's life, where we had been and what we had done. We talked about the old days, recalling and sharing childhood memories.

In the meantime, Vita, standing a few feet away from us, wondered what all the excitement was about.

"I'm confused," she finally said. "Just a few minutes ago you were practically strangers. Now you're carrying on like two old friends who haven't seen each other in years. Didn't you see her during your frequent visits? You have come to Delia almost every year."

"No! I haven't seen her since I left for America," I said. "She just told me that after she got married, she moved to the big city. Once in a while, she comes to visit her older sister, who still lives here in the old family home. It is pure coincidence that we both happen to be in town at the same time."

"But you had no trouble recognizing her."

Truth be told, I didn't. I simply assumed she had to be Giulia since she didn't look like her sister, whom I know well.

Our chat was excluding a fidgeting Giulia, who, having waited impatiently to say something, abruptly cut in and started talking to me. We spoke in dialect and too fast for Vita to understand. But I did my best to include her in the conversation by translating here and there. And so, between my translation and Giulia's gestures and changing facial expressions, Vita was able to gather that the old lady was especially pleased that little Totò had become a university professor. Giulia just could not get over how the mischievous boy she remembered had become the distinguished professor standing before her now. But she didn't dwell on that. She was more interested in talking about our families; she told me about her children and wanted to know about mine. She asked about Vita. When she learned that her name was Vita, her eyes lit up in happy approval and said, "Bravo, Totò, bene. . . bene!" And turning to Vita, she said, "Vita . . . lu nnomu di ta nanna" (your grandmother's name).

Vita was somewhat confused because, though she understood some words, she couldn't figure out what they meant. Noticing her perplexed look, I filled her in. Giulia was congratulating me for having followed the venerable tradition of naming the firstborn after one's parents.

"I honored my mother's memory by naming you after her. As you know," I continued, "my birth mother's name was Vita."

I had hardly finished translating when Giulia started talking again. We just couldn't stop chattering, accompanying our words with hand gestures. Our voices shifted from loud to soft, depending on whether we agreed on whatever we remembered. Though Vita couldn't understand much of what we were saying, our body language made it obvious that we were dredging up happy moments from our youth. I explained that Giulia had been a dear neighbor and that her mother had been very charitable toward my siblings and me after our mother died. I was still talking to Vita when Giulia took her by the arm and, looking intently into her eyes, told her that she had beautiful eyes and that she looked like her grandmother Vita, God rest her soul. Clearly, she was trying to establish the legitimacy of her long-term memory. And so, still holding her by the arm, she started to tell her a story.

She spoke so excitedly that she didn't stop to think that poor Vita did not understand much of what she was saying. But through her gestures, Vita was able to figure out she was talking about something I had done in my youth. As usual, I came to the rescue.

"When I was a kid," I began to paraphrase Giulia's tale, "I was the terror of the neighborhood. Frustrated with my mischievousness, some neighbors threatened to have me sent to a correctional institution. And they had all the reasons in the world to want me off the streets. I was a little devil, always causing trouble and getting into trouble. One day, I decided to go around the neighborhood and stuff fresh clay in the keyholes of peoples' doors. Those days, outside doors had large keyholes to fit the big iron keys commonly used in small towns and villages. Imagine the women's reaction when they came home and tried to unlock their doors. It didn't take them long to find out who had done it, and they swore to give me a serious thrashing should they catch me. My mother, aunt, grandmothers, and other relatives —they all lived in the same neighborhood—went door to door and began to break up the hardened clay, using knives, screw drivers, and whatever other means they could find."

Giulia finished her story with a look of satisfaction for her vivid memory, but she wasn't ready to leave it at that. She had many other stories to tell. I told her we really had to get going, maybe another time. She gave in but only after she made me tell Vita the story of the dead chickens as she put it. And so I did. One hot summer day, bored with sitting around doing nothing, I decided to make a bow and arrow. When finished, the *weapon* consisted of a smooth pliable olive branch curved by a taut string tied at both ends. For arrows, I used umbrella ribs from my father's umbrella. I sharpened the ribs into pointed arrows by repeatedly striking their ends on rough stones. That day, I chose to *hunt* chickens caged in makeshift coops people kept outside their front door. Within hours, I killed two chickens. When I got home, my mother was so upset she was crying. Two enraged women had come to the house complaining about what I had done and demanding compensation for their dead fowl. My mother apologized and promised to pay for the damage. As I expected, I got my usual spanking. But within minutes, I had forgotten all about the incident and went outside to play. When I finished telling the story, Giulia muttered something about my mother being at her wit's end trying to figure out what to do with me. Actually, no one knew what to do with me other than sending me away to some sort of reform school.

It didn't surprise Vita to hear that I had been such a little rascal. She had heard enough about my childhood adventures to know that. But she was shocked to hear I had come so close to being sent to a correctional institute. Where was Grandpa Giuseppe? Couldn't he lay down the law? Hadn't I told her more than once that back then people believed in beating their kids into shape?

It was true. I had said that. But all my father's efforts to straighten me out didn't work. Hardly a day went by that I wasn't up to no good. And almost every day, I felt his belt. Sometimes, to prevent me from mischief, he would chain me to the foot of our heavy iron bed and leave me there until he came home from the fields. The first time he tied me to the bed, my mother went around the neighborhood looking for keys that might unlock the chain. Neighbors offered all sorts of keys, none of which worked. Once he whipped me with a thick rope, which coiled around my chest and knocked the wind out of me for a few seconds. That was the time when he broke my mother's little finger as she tried to shield me from his lashing. The rope looped around her hand and broke her finger.

Although Giulia had promised to let us go after I told the story, she went on to relate several other incidents. It was clear she drew great pleasure from her role as a storyteller, the bard who had witnessed and was proudly memorializing Totò's exploits of long ago. For her, her enduring memories helped to define her life and lend relevance to her old age. As she talked, Vita listened to her intently trying to catch a word here and there. She was particularly interested in the meaning of her hand gestures and her constantly changing facial expressions. At times, looking straight at her, Giulia seemed to say, "He was a bad boy, but we all loved him. We saw him as the poor little orphan he was." But she was saying much more. Filippa, she was saying, was a wonderful woman who cared deeply about the little orphans. No one doubted she embraced her role as a loving and caring mother. She was careful not to punish too harshly her *newly adopted children*, fearing the neighbors would see her as a wicked stepmother. At times, this fear, coupled with her inability to handle this daring little devil, led her to ask Uncle Filippo to deal with him. That, too, didn't work; nothing seemed to work.

It was obvious that Giulia was happily aware that her stories were jogging my memory and allowing me to relive the precious moments of my childhood. She also sensed with great satisfaction that Vita had taken a keen interest in her stories. I could tell she was ready to tell other tales, but we really had to go. So after the usual goodbyes and promises to see each other again, Giulia went back to hanging the rest of her clothes on the line while Vita and I resumed our leisurely stroll around town. As we walked, she asked me why Uncle Filippo had to help *to handle me*. Why not my father? Where was Grandpa Giuseppe?

My father immigrated to Venezuela in the early fifties when I was in fourth grade. At that time, this South American country was the place to go for the thousands of poor Italian workers. Its booming economy offered them the chance to break the cycle of poverty that enslaved them and their forefathers before them. They hoped to earn enough money to get out from under years of recurring debts and perhaps buy a small farm or open a mom-and-pop shop. After WWII, thousands of Italian immigrants arrived in Venezuela where the government, awash with oil revenues, began to invest in the country's infrastructure, especially roads, schools, hospitals, and commercial shopping centers. Its need for a large workforce was such that it welcomed all sorts of skilled and unskilled foreign workers. My father was one of the countless immigrants lured by the prospect of jobs that paid much more than toiling in the fields or the sulfur mines. There was hardly a family in Delia that didn't have a friend or a relative who was or had been in Venezuela.

To pay for the cost of the ticket on a passenger ship, my father sold his horse and some of the summer harvest. He borrowed the rest from his brother-in-law Carlo, who was already in Venezuela. Within two months, he secured passage on the transatlantic *Irpinia* and off he went. With him, there were three other men from Delia; they all knew each other, and each shared the other's hopes and fears. Of the many Delia immigrants, some went into a prosperous business, arranged for their families to join them, and made Venezuela their new home. Occasionally, they returned to Delia but only for a short stay and *casually* flaunt their success. Others came back after saving enough money to build a house and buy a piece of farmland. My father stayed for four years, working as a laborer and at times as a security guard at a construction site managed by Uncle Carlo.

He always had a job and never shied away from hard or menial work. Sadly, he and other immigrants had to put up with the resentment of the many native Venezuelans who accused them of *stealing* their jobs. But their hostility was misplaced and unfortunate. Perhaps unbeknownst to them, they were living the paradox of being poor and illiterate in a country that was rich and striving to be modern. Among other things, they lacked basic trade skills and a strong work ethic. In most cases, they refused to do or were ill equipped to handle the work foreigners were willing and able to do. Immigrants did most of the jobs that required expertise, including masonry, plumbing, electrical wiring, and other skilled work.

All in all, the immigrants made good money, but it was a life of sacrifice. To save money, my father used to tell us kids he lived in a room with two other men from Delia. They cooked their own meals, usually pasta or rice, and ate lots of bananas, a cheap staple of the local diet. Every other month or so, he sent home whatever he managed to put aside. It was thanks to these remittances that my mother was able to pay tuition for me to attend middle school. Actually, my father sent more than enough for all his children to continue their studies. But only I appeared to have the potential to pursue higher education, at least according to my elementary school teacher, Mr. Luna. The others were not interested in staying in school beyond fifth grade, the mandatory minimum. They each chose to learn a trade: one became a cabinetmaker, the other a farmer, and the little one a mechanic.

Totò in Middle School

Education in Italy was and had been free of charge for over a half a century. But for us kids from Delia, it came at a price because the town was too small to have a state-funded middle school. In other words, there weren't enough students to justify the expense of maintaining a public school beyond fifth grade. To serve the needs of the few kids wishing to further their education, unemployed teachers obtained permission to open a small school, which was funded with student tuition though state-approved and fully accredited. Those who wanted to attend a free public school could do so by enrolling at a school in one of the larger towns about twenty-five minutes away. But this alternative was not convenient when considering the cost of the bus ticket and the time spent coming and going. Also, there was always the risk of being a couple of minutes late and missing the bus. In addition, the bus was not an option for girls. A young lady in an overcrowded bus, with all the inevitable shoving and pushing going on, could not avoid coming into physical contact with boys and risk tainting her good name.

Usually, girls who wanted to go on to high school or college went to the big city and either lived with a relative or at an all-girls boarding school, normally run by nuns. These were the two options Nino gave one of his daughters when she enrolled at the University of Palermo. When she expressed her intent to share an apartment with another girl, Nino refused to hear of it. He was troubled that she would even consider such a possibility. Didn't she know she would be the talk of Mussumeli? In the end, he told her that if she wanted to go to the university, she would have to live with the nuns, period. The need for such an arrangement followed from the established belief that women's behavior must always be above suspicion to avoid tarnishing the family name. When I suggested that times had changed and there was nothing wrong with the girl sharing an apartment, he got defensive and reminded me that Sicilians were still abiding by the same centuries-old customs. In his view, I had become too *americanu*.

"Totò," he said in frustration, "your life in America has clearly blurred your memory about our old ways. You know as well as I do that if I allowed my daughter to live without the strict supervision of a relative or the nuns, folks here would never stop gossiping about it, labeling her a loose woman and me a permissive father."

I couldn't really argue with him. He had no choice but to honor the local customs. I could only observe that women had a steep hill to climb. In this regard, little had changed since my middle school days. Back then, boys and girls, though barely in their teens and hardly aware of gender prejudice, were kept apart: the boys sat on one side of the classroom, the girls on the other. But even apart, the girls were a constant distraction for us boys trying to impress them. True to my character, I tried to be the center of their attention by acting up and frustrating the teacher, usually a woman. My disruptive behavior amused my classmates—especially the girls—and I took their laughter as a sign of approval. It wasn't. I have often tried to understand why I misbehaved at school. If the reason was to get attention, I could have gotten it by studying more and being a good student like some other kids. Why then did I not study, like the others? I don't know. But I do wonder whether my unwillingness to do my homework was due to my inability to sit still and concentrate or due to the home environment.

Since elementary school, little had changed around the house: no room to sit down and focus on my studies, poor lighting, and the constant noise of my siblings playing or fighting. In addition, I was too restless to actually be still for any length of time. I wanted to go out and play. The report card said it all. My mother would scold me for the bad grades I brought home and would remind me of the family's financial burden to send me to school. Even my grandmother kept on lecturing me about my father's *great* sacrifice away from home in a foreign land. She never missed the opportunity to make me feel guilty by reminding me that her son, at the old age of fifty, sailed across the ocean to provide for his children. But the repeated appeals to my sense of guilt had little effect on me; they went in one ear and out the other. I was a teenager and interested only in having fun.

No one was surprised when I had to go to summer school because I failed sixth-grade Latin. The following year, I failed every single subject and was therefore required to repeat seventh grade. When my kids first heard about it, they were flabbergasted. They couldn't believe that their father, the professor who had written several books and dozens of scholarly articles, had actually flunked seventh grade. "What happened to the *bright little Totò*?" they asked. What troubled them most was that of all the childhood stories I told them never once did I mention I had been held back a grade. For all those years, they were led to believe I had been an excellent student. Why the deception? Was I embarrassed? They wondered. No, I was not embarrassed and no, it was not a deception. I intentionally refrained from talking about it for fear that they might see it as a justification for neglecting their own studies. How could I insist my children do well in school, I explained, if they knew their father had been a bad student?

My strategy worked. All three kids studied extra hard because they didn't want to disappoint me. But while admitting my seventh-grade debacle, I reminded them that it was the only time I failed in school. The incident served as a wake-up call for both my family and the local authorities. They could no longer ignore that my misbehavior in school and in the streets had reached a critical point. Something had to be done to save me from myself. In a sense, the seventh-grade debacle turned out to be a providential setback in that it led to a definite turnaround in my dysfunctional life.

It was around this time that the city police got tired of the many complaints they received about me. They told my mother that if she didn't send me to a boarding school, they would take me to a detention center for juvenile delinquents. Either way, I had to be taken out of the environment that abetted my unruly behavior. That was enough to put the fear of God into my poor mother, who immediately turned to a local politician for help. Within a few weeks, the man was able to find a state-run boarding school for orphans, free of charge. The place, about seventy miles from Delia, was a reform school, the nearest thing to a juvenile correctional facility. It housed about sixty boys, ranging from twelve to sixteen-year-olds, several with a police record already. Some of the older kids, or *students* as we were called, were mature, young thugs. Organized into gangs of three or four, they bullied the younger kids and did not hesitate to disobey and even threaten the instructors.

I was definitely out of my comfort zone. Perhaps for the first time in my life, I lived at the mercy of others and in absolute terror. Such was my fear of the bullies that I wrote home and threatened to jump out of the window if they didn't come and get me right away. I stayed in that hellhole for more than a month before Uncle Filippo—my father was still in Venezuela—came to take me home.

The experience at the facility had a chilling effect on me but not enough to discourage me from misbehaving again. Back in my environment, I was back into my old bad habits: fighting, stealing, annoying neighbors, and pestering teachers when I didn't skip school. Another place had to be found to prevent the authorities from acting on their threat to take me away for good. It so happened that in Delia there lived an influential Dominican monk who agreed to start the paperwork to have me sent to a reputable boarding school run by Dominican friars. Within a month, I was admitted to the Collegio Domenicano in the town of Linguaglossa, near Catania. It was there that almost overnight I, the little *devil*, became a model teenager and an excellent student.

CHAPTER 10

Boarding School

When my kids first heard about the Dominican school, they thought it was a prep school. Naturally, they wondered how a poor family like mine could afford to send their child to a private institution. I made it clear that it was not an elite school but an inexpensive, semi-public institution partially subsidized by the state. In addition, the Dominican order, one of the oldest religious orders in the Catholic Church, provided some generous assistance for needy students. The cost to my family was minimal but a significant sacrifice, nonetheless. It should not be a surprise that both the state and the Dominicans helped to fund the school. It was in the state's interest to help wayward youngsters before they matured into actual criminals. As for the Dominicans, they hoped that students receiving financial aid would embrace the order and become padres. At the end of high school, students not interested in the priesthood left the *collegio* and continued their studies in public schools. Those who heard the calling to religious life entered the seminary or *convento* and began the novitiate. There they shaved the top of their heads in the shape of a small circle, called tonsure, put on the white robe and the black cape worn by the Dominicans, and started their theology studies. I never intended to become a priest and just like most of the other kids, left the school before having to enter the convento. By then,

I had turned my life around. I had become a well-behaved young man, one of the best students in the school and an outstanding soccer player.

The transformation from daredevil to *good boy* occurred almost overnight. I never forgot the moment and the circumstances that brought it about though I didn't know why it happened exactly. As far as I could tell, it was not a religious awakening or something in particular about the place. Perhaps it was the environment, that is, the monks, the kids, the discipline, all, or none of these factors. Even after so many years, I found it difficult to pinpoint the actual reason for my turn around. One day, while in Delia, I suggested to Vita we go see the place. Who knows? Revisiting the *collegio* and talking to some people there might provide a clue to my remarkable turnaround. The town of Linguaglossa, located at the foot of Mount Etna, was little more than two hours drive from Delia. Vita liked the suggestion and looked forward to visiting the school, but she wondered how we would get there. We didn't have a car, and someone would have to drive us there. She worried Uncle Filippo might volunteer.

"Is Uncle Filippo going to take us?" she asked, concerned about the man's unsafe driving and notoriously unreliable jalopy.

"No, don't worry. Nino can take us," I reassured her. "I'm sure he will want to come, as he, too, went to that school. In fact, that's where we first met." The next day, Nino arrived around ten o'clock in the morning. He was driving his wife's brand-new car. He, too, was looking forward to visiting the school he hadn't seen since he was a teenager. The drive was not much different than the one from Palermo to Nino's house, except for the new car with its new air conditioner and comfortable leather seats. He and I sat in the front and as usual talked excitedly with our arms flailing in the air and paying no attention to the potholes that carpeted the narrow road. Vita, sitting in the back, looked at a landscape, which was very similar to the one she had seen on the way to Delia: barren mountain slopes, hills dotted with huge boulders, and here and there, a lush vegetable garden or an olive grove. But as we approached the coast, the scenery changed dramatically. On our left rose Mount Etna with its smoking volcano; on our right shimmered the calm blue sea gently slapping the rocky shore.

On the mountainside, there were small farmhouses nestled in the middle of vineyards, thickets of chestnut trees, and fruit orchards neatly planted on the terraced slopes. On the other side, there was the majestic view of the coastline with rows of perennial flowers lining the highway and dozens of tiny lava-cooled clusters of huge rocks that looked like tiny *islands* rising from the sea. Kids were playing on the rocks; some were plunging into the water, others were scuba diving, and others yet, in small rowboats, were trying to reach the rocks or returning to shore. I told Vita that local folklore identified the *islands* with the boulders that the one-eyed cyclops Polyphemus threw from the heights of Mount Etna. She remembered the Greek myth from Homer's *Odyssey*, where Ulysses and his men escaped from the man-eating giant after they burned his eye and slipped out of the cave undetected. Blinded, in pain, and outraged, the monster began to hurl enormous rocks at the fleeing Greeks, thus the *islands*.

Eventually, Nino turned inland and after a few miles, we arrived at the school. No sooner had the big old building came into view than distant and intimate memories began to stream through my mind in rapid succession. It was here that I turned my life around; here I brushed my teeth for the first time, took a real shower for the first time, learned how to study, became an excellent soccer player, and learned to speak proper Italian. Strangely, the closer we got to the place the more we noticed its ghostly stillness.

"Why so quiet"? Vita asked, suspecting the place might be abandoned.

"This is the hour of the study," answered Nino in his best English. He went on to explain that around this time of the day the students were in the study hall, sitting quietly at their desks.

When we reached the main entrance, Nino rang the doorbell and within a few seconds, a clean-shaven, middle-aged monk about five feet eight inches tall greeted us. He introduced himself as Father Tommaso. Vita had never seen a Dominican padre before and was taken aback by the way he dressed. He wore a full-length, one-piece, snow-white tunic, and a white scapular over his shoulders. On top of that, he had a long black cloak with a hood resting on his shoulders. A foot-long rosary hung from his wide, leather belt.

"He looks like a penguin," she whispered in my ear.

"Yes, we do!" admitted the friar who heard the comment. Noticing that his perfect English startled Vita, he added that he was the son of Italian immigrants and was born and raised in Boston. When she tried to apologize for her remark, he graciously told her not to worry about it. He heard it many times before, especially when he went back home to visit his parents in Boston. In the meantime, Nino and I, talking at the same time as usual, explained who we were and asked if any of the old padres were still around. The monk said that only the aging Padre Domenico was still there and volunteered to go get him. But before going upstairs to fetch the old man, he invited us to come inside and make ourselves comfortable in the waiting area. About ten minutes later, a monk in his late eighties shuffled through the door.

"Padre Domenico," Nino and I called out, "remember us?"

Without hesitation, he said, "How could I forget! Nino and Totò. I remember the two you very well. You were my best soccer players. I still have a picture of the team with the trophy we won in 1956."

We each knelt, reached for the old padre's hand, and kissed it, just as we used to do in our days at the school. After the necessary introductions and small talk, Padre Domenico told Vita that I had been an excellent student. As her blank facial expression told him she did not speak the language, he asked me to translate.

"I would have made a great Dominican priest," I translated, "and regrets that I opted out of the ministry. But he is happy I had a successful career in academia and more than that, fathered such a beautiful daughter as you." Vita accepted the man's compliment and, in turn, congratulated him on his impressive memory.

"Eh! It's not what it used to be," he said. "With my short memory practically gone, I now live in the memory of things past."

After a few minutes of reminiscing about the old days, the monk invited us to follow him upstairs for a stroll down memory lane. Exactly what Nino and I had come for. Going through rooms and hallways, we recalled special moments and showed Vita where we studied, slept, prayed, ate, and went to class. In our exuberance, we kept on challenging each another about who remembered better a distinct incident or the name of a particular classmate. In contrast, Vita found the place rather dull though she was amused by our excitement in reliving our days of youth. When we walked by a large room, known as the auditorium, Padre Domenico pointed to an upright piano standing against the wall and turning to me, asked, "Ti ricordi?"

"How could I forget?" I answered. It was the same old piano I loved to practice on. Without hesitation, I sat down and tried to play a song we used to sing in church every Sunday, but the piano was dreadfully out of tune.

"I didn't know you learned how to play here. Did they actually give you boys piano lessons?" Vita asked, thinking it was a luxury the school could hardly afford.

"The school didn't offer music courses," I told her, "even though most monks could play the organ and could have given us music lessons." It was a local concert pianist Maestro Profumi, who volunteered to teach a small group of select students. Leaning on his cane, the old man came to the collegio once a week often bringing us sheet music—always classical—he bought in Catania. He was a baldheaded scrawny little man in his sixties with a pencil mustache and a grandfatherly smile that never left his face. He was one of the most amiable men I had ever known, never a word of disapproval and always reassuring. When I asked him to allow me in the group, he smiled at my ingenuity and politely told me it wasn't possible. Without a basic knowledge of music, I would be too far behind the rest of the class. I was disappointed but not discouraged. I got hold of a piano book for beginners and within two months I taught myself how to read music well enough to join the class. For the next two years, I went to the auditorium every other day and practiced on that old piano.

We had already made it back down to the first floor when Padre Domenico led us outside. The area in the back of the building had a big vegetable garden and meticulously kept flowerbeds. The multicolored flowers offered such a magnificent sight that we just lingered around enjoying the sweet fragrance and complementing the padre on the beautiful garden. But we had to move out of the way because the students were beginning to file out of the building headed for the playground. Some boys, in soccer attire, set out for the soccer field and quickly lined up for a game. Pointing to the field, I asked the old friar if he remembered whacking me on the head for having lied about a fight I had on that field. Of course, I didn't expect him to recall something as common as slapping a kid; the monks did that all the time back then. I simply wanted to bring up the incident that led to my *transformation*.

From Rascal to Model Student

"What fight?" Vita asked. "You actually continued to misbehave here, too? I thought the school changed you?"

"It did and it all started with a scuffle, here on this field," I said. One day, during my first week at the school, some students were playing soccer, just as they were about to do now. At one point, I ran onto the field and began chasing and kicking the ball around. One of the players, an older boy twice my size, confronted me and told me to "*please*, get off the field because they were playing a tournament game." I took his polite *please* as a sign of weakness and roughly pushed him aside, telling him to get out of my way. I had as much right to play as he did. The boy reacted by shoving me with such a force that I staggered backward, lost my balance, and fell to the ground. I quickly wobbled to my feet and started throwing punches. But his long arms kept him far enough that my punches were falling ridiculously short. Padre Domenico saw the whole thing and blew his whistle, a signal for all activities on the playground to stop. He called the two of us over and demanded an explanation. In a loud and whining voice, I protested that the big brute started it all. I had barely finished saying "he hit me first" when the padre slapped me in the face. He hit me so hard that my cheek turned red and began to swell up. It was the slap that exorcized the *devil* out of Totò. From then on, I never lied again and became a model student.

"What was it about this incident that caused the sudden change?" Vita asked. "Couldn't have been the slap. You had been beaten much harder than that and never bothered you before. Why now? Why here?"

Many a time I have asked myself the same question. To this day, I haven't been able to put my finger on anything specific. I just don't know. Perhaps I realized that I had entered a world where rules and regulations made no allowance for mischief. In our tightly controlled daily life, the smallest infraction was dealt with quickly and appropriately. Common punishments included paddling, kneeling facing the wall, and limited recreational activities. But a harsher treatment came from the other kids who tended to shun mischievous students; they avoided them in the schoolyard and in the mess hall. Undoubtedly, peer pressure was one of the main factors that led kids to adjust to the school's strict discipline. The impervious few were eventually expelled from the collegio.

"It sounds like what kids feared the most was being ostracized, no one to play with or talk to, always alone. Your parents should have tried it on you," Vita suggested.

She was probably right though she knew my home surroundings made such a punishment almost impossible. Like most of the kids I grew up with, I had little adult supervision and too much freedom to do what I pleased. In addition, there were many kids who found my shenanigans entertaining or were mischievous like me. In the Dominican school instead, there was strict observance of the rules and assured shunning by schoolmates. It was the appropriate setting for me to change my behavior and become an exemplary youth and an outstanding student. It was not unusual for the teachers to call on me whenever they wished to impress government officials who came to inspect the school periodically. Once, the county commissioner, a rotund old man with a large balding head and thick black-rimmed glasses, came to evaluate the school's accreditation status. The teacher, fully aware of the man's importance and visit, decided to showcase some of his best students. He called on me and another boy and told us stand on the opposite side of his large desk, facing each other. He then instructed us to challenge each other on our general knowledge of Virgil's *Aeneid*. We could ask only questions to which we knew the answers. The winner would be the one who gave the most correct answers. After about fifteen minutes, the contest ended with a tie. The commissioner was impressed with our performance and congratulated the teacher for such a *great job*.

The three years I spent at the *collegio* were perhaps the happiest years of my childhood I was popular with my classmates, and the padres liked me because they considered me a perfect candidate for the priesthood. But my plans did not include the priesthood. A few months after the performance before the county commissioner, I began to think about my future at the school and concluded I would leave at the appropriate time. I would soon be finishing high school, at which time I had to decide whether to commit to the priesthood and enter the seminary. This meant transferring to the *convento*, wear the Dominican habit, and begin my religious studies. That was a step I never intended to take, in part, because I never heard the call to religious life. I was sent there not to become a priest, but to shape up and get an education like most other kids. Another reason that contributed my decision to leave was the monks' behavior. Whatever they did to inspire religious fervor, they undermined their unseemly lifestyle. They lived in style and comfort, much against their vows of poverty and chastity. Some were rumored to molest students; others were allegedly entertaining women in their rooms, especially mothers who came to visit their sons. But what really hastened my resolve to leave was a sickening incident I witnessed on the schoolyard.

One Sunday afternoon, a boy accused the janitor of having stolen an orange from his desk. The father superior, a big and pockmarked man in his late forties with a dark complexion, bushy eyebrows, and long hawkish nose, confronted the janitor in the schoolyard in front of all the students. When the old man denied the accusation, the padre slapped him so hard that the poor wretch fell to the ground. We were all stunned by the violent gesture at the hands of the man who gave us Holy Communion every Sunday. On his knees, the janitor continued to maintain his innocence and with the palms of his hands joined together and raised in prayer, begged for his job. He had a wife and six children to feed; he cried pitifully. The priest hit him again and deaf to the man's poignant pleading, ordered him off the premises. Some kids were visibly shaken; others were in tears. I never forgot the dumfounded expression in the poor devil's blank stare as tears ran down his face. It showed the despair of a broken man wondering how he was going to feed his family. His anguish and the friar's cruelty touched me so deeply that I decided, there and then, to leave the school as soon as the semester was over. I didn't understand how a man of God could be so cruel. I still don't. His lack of compassion was unbecoming a man of the cloth as it debased everything they taught us at the school. Even if the janitor had stolen the orange, he surely didn't deserve the humiliation and the loss of his livelihood. "This place isn't for me," I remember telling myself.

And so I left the collegio that for three years saw me grow up into a mature young man. I didn't know then that I would always cherish the sweet memories of those formative years. Still today, I look back with nostalgia and gratitude for the place and the people that kept me out of juvenile institutions, set me on the right path, and gave me a good education. But emotional attachment aside, I never regretted my decision to leave. The time was ripe for me to leave Linguaglossa because among other reasons I was about to embark in the most significant adventure of my life. I was going to America. A few months after I left the Dominicans, the American Consulate in Palermo notified my parents that our long-awaited turn to immigrate to the US had finally come. We were now on top of the list of the immigration quota system. It had been seven long years since my father's older sister, Enza, who had been living in the US since the early twenties, petitioned the American Immigration Office for her brother Giuseppe and his family to join her in America.

CHAPTER 11

Before Leaving for America

Seven years was undoubtedly a long wait. People didn't understand why it took so long. Why we couldn't emigrate soon after our paperwork was filed and approved. The answer became clear when we started the mazelike process of navigating through the American immigration rules and regulations. At that time, immigration law was strictly enforced. It was based on a quota system that specified how many immigrants might come into the US from any given country in any given year. This created long lists of aspiring immigrants who waited years before their turn came up. My family waited for a long time even though sponsorship for family members had priority over some other classes of immigrants. The law was very specific regarding who might sponsor an immigrant and in what circumstances. Schools and businesses could request a visa for a needed expert in a given field, provided they showed they could not find such a person in the States. A high-end restaurant, for example, might request permission to bring in a specialized chef, just as a fashionable clothing store or factory might sponsor a master tailor. A basic rule was that the sponsor or petitioner had to be an American citizen or a business entity. In all cases, the law required the petitioner to assume financial responsibility for the material welfare of the immigrants during the first few months after their arrival. Naturally, it was in the sponsor's interest to help the newly arrived to find a job and get settled.

It went without saying that after the long wait, we were excited when we were finally notified that we had been cleared to begin the immigration process. But it was an excitement tempered by the certainty that we were about to leave behind everything we knew and by the uncertainty of what awaited us. My parents were especially apprehensive about uprooting the entire family and leaving behind the only world they knew. But they believed it was a risk worth taking for the sake of their children's future. After all, wasn't *lamerica* the land of plenty immigrant returnees talked about? My siblings and I, too young and foolish to be concerned about the chance we were taking, were thrilled to be going to the land of dreams. We were ready to share in the rich and glamorous lifestyle American movies projected on the screen of our local theater. Our friends, who wished they, too, were going to mythical *lamerica,* also bolstered our enthusiasm.

But after the initial celebration came the frustration of dealing with the Italian bureaucracy, the first challenge was to get our birth certificates. When my father went to the city's Office of Vital Statistics to request the documents, he was told that the employee issuing the certificates was on leave and wasn't expected back for at least two weeks. In short, it took a whole month and a half just to get the blessed papers. Certificates in hand, my father went to the police station to apply for our passports. He was turned away and told to return Thursday, the day of the week when passport applications were accepted. They didn't tell him that all of us had to go to the station so that a police officer might witness our individual signatures. Almost three weeks went by before the applications were finally completed and sent on to the proper authorities for processing. We were told the process would take about three months. And so we waited and waited.

After about five months we heard—through friends of friends—that the documents had arrived at the police headquarters and would be mailed to us in a few days. Weeks went by and nothing came in the mail. We grew anxious and began to wonder what could be the problem. No one in the family had a police record, which usually prevented people from obtaining a passport. Could the mailman have delivered them to the wrong address? That was unlikely because Beppe, the mailman, knew we were waiting for the passports. Also, a day didn't go by that my mother didn't ask him about our documents. Finally, my father decided to send me to the police headquarters in the big city and see what was holding things up. He sent me and not my older brother because I was the only one in the family educated enough to get answers from the self-important officials at the passport office. Also, I had studied in the big city and knew where the police station was located and which bus to take to get there. Anyway, the official I spoke with at the station assured me that whatever the holdup, the papers would be ready in a few days.

Sure enough, we soon received a letter telling us to come and get the documents. We were to pick them up at our earliest convenience and should bring along *this* notice. When I went back to the passport office for the second time, the same officer I had spoken with the week earlier handed me five passports instead of six. He didn't know why the other was *missing*. Immediately, I smelled a rat, not uncommon in those public offices. Pointing to the letter I held in my hand, I reminded him that it said all six passports were ready to be picked up. Raising his voice, he warned me against making libelous insinuations and threatened to have me locked up. Undeterred by his threat, I told him I was going to see the officer in charge. I didn't have to. His superior, a man with all sorts of ribbons and medals on his police uniform, happened to come by and having heard the commotion, came in and looked straight at the officer behind the desk.

Without demanding to know what was the problem, he ordered the man to give me *all* the passports. Sheepishly, the officer pulled the document from under a stack of papers on his desk and slapped it in my hand, saying, "There you go, get out of here." I didn't thank him, of course, and proud of having gotten what I had come for, went home with all the passports. My parents were delighted.

Although there were eight of us in the family— two parents, four boys, and two girls—we only needed six passports because my oldest brother, Francesco, had already immigrated to Venezuela, and the baby sister was too young to need a passport. She was added, picture and all, to our mother's travel papers as the law required. After we got the passports, we had another long wait, an interview with the American consul in Palermo. No one knew how long it would take the consulate to schedule an appointment. Before the meeting could take place, we were told, the consulate had to obtain a Certificate of Good Conduct—no criminal record—from the Delia police. In addition, it sought information about the family's social reputation and in particular, whether we belonged to the Communist party. These were the years of the still lingering Red Scare, a widespread fear of Communism, which Senator Joseph McCarthy had heightened and exploited through his committee hearings in the early fifties. For this confidential report, the police sought the views of local informants, including the parish priest and the head of the town's Democratic Party. Once the consulate received all the paperwork certifying that were an upstanding family with no criminal record and no Communist affiliation, it could call us to Palermo for a short meeting with the consul.

At the American Consulate

The long-awaited day finally came; the entire family was to report to the American Consulate in Palermo on Thursday, November 17, at 9:30 a.m. The happy news left no doubts that our departure was real and imminent. But as good as the news was, it caused a sense of subtle apprehension that gave pause to our enthusiasm. We were coming face-to-face with the uncertainties of the world totally unknown to us. The *what ifs*, *hows*, and the *wheres* began to crowd our minds and prick our balloons. And so with tempered excitement, the day before the interview, the family took the train to Palermo. Except for my father, it was the first time any of us had been on a train. It was thrilling to be on the train though it was noisy and dirty. We had to dust off the wooden seats, which were covered with the soot puffed up by the slow-moving, coal-fired locomotive. It took almost four hours to cover the roughly eighty-mile distance to Palermo. Those days, trains in Sicily didn't go very fast due in part to the poor conditions of the tracks and the broken-down locomotives. Also, trains had to stop at every town to pick up or drop off passengers and on occasion, replenish their water supply. The option of going by car was out of the question for several reasons. First, seven of us plus our baggage would have required at least two cars. Second, the few car owners in Delia had never ventured more than a few miles out of town and would be wary of driving in big-city traffic and getting lost. Thirdly, a car ride would likely take as long as the train since the road to Palermo was narrow, dangerously winding, and full of potholes. Last but not the least, it would have been very expensive. In fact, the two cars that took us to the nearest train station—Delia had no train station—cost a bundle. Besides, we didn't really mind the ride.

We actually enjoyed the novelty of it all though it took us almost the whole day. By the time we arrived in Palermo, it was getting dark and thousands of bright lights lit up the dark skies. Other than my father, none of us had ever been to a big city, and everybody was overwhelmed by all the lights and the many cars and horse-drawn buggies crowding the streets. Parked outside the train station were several taxis and horse-drawn carriages waiting for costumers. My father negotiated a good price with a coachman who took us to the bread and breakfast where we had arranged to stay. We were literally exhausted and went to bed after a light supper of minestrone, bread, and some dry fruit.

The following morning, we got up early, ate a generous breakfast, and walked to the consulate, about four city blocks away from the B and B. When we got there, the nameplate *Consolato Americano* on the side of the main entrance pointed us to a double door. We walked in warily, unsure of what to say to the woman sitting behind the desk. The receptionist, a distinguished-looking lady in her fifties, could tell we were anxious and did her best to make us feel at ease. She welcomed us with a reassuring smile and a warm *buon giorno*. Clearly, she had been at the consulate long enough to have greeted hundreds of nervous country folks like us. She asked my father to hand her our immigration papers and after looking at them through her thick glasses perched on the tip of her nose gave him a piece of paper with the address of a nearby medical clinic. According to the instructions, we were scheduled for a physical exam at 11:30 that same morning.

We were at the clinic a little over an hour, but the exam itself it didn't last long even though the doctor had to see all seven of us. It was a brief checkup meant to see whether we were carrying communicable diseases and were healthy enough to work once in the US. I found it strange that the consulate would require the exam to be performed at a clinic and by a doctor of its own choosing. It would have been easier to have a medical exam in Delia and bring the results with us in a sealed envelope. Only years later, was I able to figure it out; the Americans didn't trust the Italians. They wanted to make sure that would-be immigrants didn't choose a sympathetic physician or one who could be easily bribed. The doctor the consulate trusted and recommended was a friendly young man in his mid-thirties from a small town near Palermo. He joked with my father about our large family, and after a short visit—mostly checking our vital signs—told us to not worry and relax; we were all in good health.

Of course, this sort of checkup was much more convenient and reliable than the system in place years earlier in the United States. Up until the mid-fifties, American doctors performed a version of this exam at Ellis Island, the processing center for arriving immigrants. At that time, immigrants landing in New York were taken to the island for a series of controls, including a simple physical test. A typical screening had the newly arrived immigrants climb the long staircase leading to the main hall while doctors or other trained personnel, standing at the top of the stairs, observed their movements. The experts were looking for signs of exertion, especially heavy breathing, unusual gait, and other physical flaws. Those found in poor health were either quarantined or repatriated, depending on the severity of the illness. Clearly, repatriation was a much drastic outcome than being declared unfit to emigrate right from the start at the country of origin.

Of course, the old American way of determining the health of arriving immigrants would not have affected us since the consulate's doctor gave us a clean bill of health. The good news was not a surprise as much as an official proof that we passed our first and major test.

My parents, in particular, were so happy that I failed to see what the excitement was all about. We knew we were all healthy. So why the jubilation? Only later did I understand their relief. Failure to pass the exam would have resulted in the denial of our immigration visa, leaving the family in serious economic difficulties. Two years before our Palermo experience, a Delia family was denied permission to immigrate to Canada because a family member failed the physical. It was rumored that the doctors at the Canadian Consulate in Naples determined that the father showed signs of tuberculosis. Gossip spread like a wildfire, branding the family as diseased and thus to be avoided. They were regarded as social outcasts. Also, the trip to Naples—food, lodging, transportation—cost them so much money that they had to sell their small farm and the mule they worked the land with. In essence, they were left without the most important means of livelihood. The entire family was doomed to endure poverty and social ostracism.

Given the consequences of a failed medical exam, my parents' relief was more than justifiable, indeed. Being found in good health meant we were cleared to emigrate. But before going back to Delia and beginning our preparations, we had to stop by the consulate for a brief meeting with the consul himself, a mere formality. When we got there, the receptionist read the doctor's note my father handed her and with what seemed like a congratulatory grin on her face, invited us to follow her into the consul's office. The man who came around the large desk and greeted us was tall with reddish hair parted in the middle and a set of blue eyes framed by black-rimmed glasses. His distinguished look confirmed what we thought a *true* American looked like. Holding out his large hand for my father to shake, the big man said with a heavy American accent, "Congratulazioni, Signor DiMaria." My father nervously shook the man's hand and blurted out the only English words he thought he knew, "Gut moneeeink . . . Gut moneeeink," his version of good morning. Actually, it was late afternoon. After a few pleasantries between people who didn't speak the other's language, the consul slowly walked us to the door and again wished us good luck.

The next day, we took the train home and began making arrangements for our departure. My father proceeded to dispose of everything we had, selling some things and giving away what he couldn't sell or take with us. My mother bought nice clothes for everybody, mostly for the kids. I got a brown-striped suit, a white dress shirt, and a brown pair of low quarter shoes. It was the first time in my life I owned a suit and wore it with pride. Most importantly, my father made reservations on a passenger liner that was scheduled to sail for New York at the end of January 1961. We could have left earlier, but we needed time to come up with the money to pay for the trip. Passage for seven people wasn't cheap. A good portion of the money came from the sale of the house and the horse. Another big chunk came from what was left of the money my father had sent from Venezuela. The rest we borrowed from friends and relatives.

Saying Goodbye to Delia

Leaving behind the place of our birth wasn't easy. Delia and its people were all we knew. My parents had mixed feelings. On the one hand, they were happy to go to America; on the other hand, they had misgivings about what we found find on the other side of the ocean. Gnawing at them were the many questions about their children's future. Would their youngest be able to go to school right away? How would they get around without knowing the language? How well would they adapt to a new way of life? Also, there was the question of work. Would there be work for them and their older boys Pasquale and Totò? Without knowing the language, what kind of work could they find? These and similar doubts dimmed their enthusiasm. As for me, I had none of these concerns. I was eager to leave for the new world and live the life American movies glorified on the big screen.

The evening before we left, people came by to wish us *buona fortuna* (good luck). Some older folks, thinking that the US was something like a big city, brought letters for us to hand-deliver to one of their relatives who had immigrated a long time ago. One old lady, in particular, wanted us to tell her older brother that their sister had just died. We should have no problem finding him, she said, because he lived where everybody else lived in Broocculinu. Mostly others asked us to remind their immigrant kinfolk, when we saw them, to remember their sick and poor relatives in Delia. My friends had no such requests. They were plain envious of the fabled opportunities that awaited me in the fabulous land of girls and adventures—what of those pinup girls or those big and fast cars like the De Soto Rock Hudson drove! Though it was a joyous occasion for us and the well-wishers, the general mood was somber. Tears tempered the hugs and best wishes. My grandparents, especially, sensed they would never see us again. The next morning, we left for Palermo and that same evening took the overnight ferry to Naples where we were to embark for New York.

Those days, Italian immigrants going to the Americas left either from Naples or Genoa. Palermo's port was not deep enough for the huge passenger liners sailing the Atlantic Ocean. Often, a ship would start from Naples, pick up additional passengers in Genoa, and from there set sail for its destination across the Atlantic. Some of the older and smaller vessels would stop in the Canary Islands for supplies. Our ship was big and modern and would sail straight for America as we were told when we bought our passage.

Once in Naples, we didn't have to wait long; we sailed that afternoon. In the morning, when we arrived from Palermo, we walked around, overwhelmed by the crowds, the traffic, and the hustle and bustle typical of big cities. We stared open-mouthed at all the beautiful stores and the many cafés and pastry shops. We stood out as the wide-eyed country cousins we truly were. The way we dressed, the uncertain way we went about, and some of our old suitcases held together with ropes made us an easy target for the streetwise peddlers and hawkers that hung around the port. One of those swindlers took my father for 5000 lire, roughly the equivalent of $200 today but a considerable sum for us at the time.

My father thought he had made a good deal when he agreed to pay the money for a guarantee that no customs inspector would go through the family's belongings and trash our suitcases. He told my mother not to fret about any inspection because he had *fixed* everything. And in fact, no one inspected our luggage. When my mother pointed out to him that she had seen none of the passengers going through any inspection, he began to wonder about the wisdom of his *deal*. Two days into the voyage, he learned he had been duped. A fellow passenger told him there was no such thing as customs inspection when leaving the country. Inspection requirements were only for those coming into the country. Though my mother made it a point not to remind her *traveled* man of the big rip off, he could not shake off the embarrassment. How could he, a man of the world who gone and lived overseas, fall for such a scam? Didn't he know that Naples was notorious for its swindlers, especially around the port? Didn't he leave from Naples when he went to Venezuela?

Luckily, we were in Naples for only half a day. Around noon, we started boarding the *Leonardo Da Vinci*, one of Italy's newest and biggest ocean liners at the time. By four o'clock we were smoothly floating away from the port, from Italy. I never forgot the heart-wrenching scene as the ship began to drift away from the dock. Hundreds of people, who came to bid farewell to their departing relatives, were standing on the platform, weeping and wailing. Handkerchiefs in hand and arms flailing in the air, they were crying out their last goodbyes. Deep in their hearts, some of them knew they would never see their loved ones again. But as the ship picked up speed, the crowd began to disappear in the distance, the city faded into the horizon, and we were off to *lamerica*.

PART 2

Finally America

CHAPTER 12

Sailing to America

I had never been on a big ship before and had no idea what it was like to be on the high seas for days. The crossing lasted a full week, and it was an unforgettable experience. From the moment we went on board, we were wonderstruck by the ship's immense size and cleanliness as well as all the elegant furnishing and decorations. We entered a sophisticated world we didn't even know existed. Our sleeping quarters or cabins were particularly impressive. They were all on the same level or floor, just below the main deck. My parents and my baby sister had their own room. My younger brother and sister shared a cabin, and my older brother and I also shared one. Our cabins had bunk beds, bathrooms, and showers. Every morning, the maids, in white uniforms, came in to clean and make our beds. They were very courteous and never failed to remind us that if we needed anything we only had to ask. They treated us like royalty, which made us feel more awkward and totally out of place. Of course, *royalty* is a figure of speech, but for us wide-eyed country folks it came close to what we imagined royalty lived like. Just a few days earlier, we boys slept in one bed. My mother washed our sheets no more than four times a year. And no one in the family had ever seen or taken a shower, except me.

Showering was one of the first things they made me do when I first arrived at the boarding school. All students were required to brush their teeth daily and take a shower at least twice a week, every other day in the summer. Regrettably, I stopped taking showers after I left the *collegio* due in part to the lack of inside plumbing and chronic water shortage. Although by the time we left for the States we had running water in the house, it was hard enough to do the cleaning, let alone taking showers. Water ran only for about an hour a day, and frustratingly, sometimes it skipped a day. The problem was made more acute by the fact that no one knew when the water would be turned on again. To collect every drop, housewives left the faucet on with a large jar underneath. But however much water they collected, it was just enough for the most basic domestic needs. In addition, we used it sparingly because we could barely afford the water bill, just like most other poor folks. Second, even if we had enough water, we had no effective means of heating it. Our primitive stove, roughly an open kitchen hearth, could accommodate only one small pot at a time. That life of abject poverty was now behind us. Literally overnight, we were catapulted into a world of comforts and plenty: the modern world.

The amenities in our cabin were only a small feature of the elegance the ship had to offer. Just a flight of stairs or a short elevator ride and we were on the main deck where we mingled with other second-class passengers. We spent most of the day relaxing and participating in recreational activities, some organized by the ship's crew. When we were not eating in the mess hall or watching a movie at the theater, we were in the main hall playing cards, having a drink, or taking a walk on the promenade deck.

Passengers were friendly and willing to hang out with strangers. We were all on the same boat: strangers in need of fellowship and thus open to meet, dance, play, talk, and drink with others. It didn't take long, for instance, for us to bond with the Moro family, our dining companions. What started as a casual encounter at the dinner table between the two families soon evolved into a warm friendship. Lunch and dinner were served on the main deck in a large and beautifully decorated restaurant. I'll never forget the first time we went to eat. The tables, arranged for eight or ten passengers, were draped with white tablecloths, set with linen napkins, stainless steel silverware, and two or three bottles of wine. In general, meals consisted of several courses served on fine china. The waiters, all dressed in white four-button jackets, were courteous and ready to comply with requests for more food or drink or something not included in the day's menu. We shared a table with the Moros, a young family from Boston on their way back from visiting relatives in Calabria. They were second-generation Italians and spoke enough Italian, actually Calabrese dialect, to carry on a conversation without much difficulty. The two families enjoyed each other's company and spent time together outside the restaurant, either in the main hall or talking leisurely walks on the promenade deck.

The Moros gave us plenty of good advice about life in the States, what to expect and what to avoid. When Mr. Vince Moro learned we were going to Reading, Pennsylvania, he warned us about Pennsylvania's winters, which unlike the mild winters of southern Italy, could be very cold with lots of ice and snow. By the light clothes we were wearing, it was clear we had never thought about the cold weather we were about to experience. Definitely, we needed to buy heavy winter clothes as soon as possible. The good news, the Moros assured us, was that there were plenty of jobs to be had, and it would not be a problem to find work right away. "No need to worry about the language barrier," they said, "because in many factories there were first or second-generation Italians who were bilingual." Some of these people might even live in the same neighborhood where we would likely wind up living. It was reassuring to hear that these neighborhoods were like *little Italies* with at least one Catholic Church and several ethnic grocery stores. Certainly, if we didn't like the neighborhood, we could move as soon as we saved enough money to buy a house somewhere else. Many immigrants did just that.

Conversations at the dinner table or during strolls on the main deck was usually between the two couples though Pasquale and I often took part in it. We were eager to know what type of job we could find and how to get to it. Where there buses or trains? My brother, in particular, was interested in learning what it took to get a driver's license and buy a car. I wanted to know about education and how easy would be for me to enroll in school, seeing that I didn't speak English. My younger siblings got along well with the Moro's two children, each trying to teach the other how to play certain games. This they did in spite of the language barrier; the Moro teenagers, a boy and a girl, did not speak a word of Italian, and none of us spoke English.

There were other activities that filled our long days on the high seas. Together with our newly made friends, we engaged in a variety of recreational pursuits. During the day, we played cards, took walks, and talked about what we expected to find in America. After dinner, we usually went to the movies or took part in the nightly entertainment the ship's crew organized for the evening. Our preference was the dancing session to the rhythm of a live band. Before the dancing got going, a standup comedian lightened up the mood and got folks to loosen up. Some were already relaxed having had a drink or two. A lot of people, mostly older folk, took to the dance floor, especially when the band struck up a waltz or tarantella. Some nights, the entertainment crew organized games that assured the maximum passengers' participation, bingo being the most popular.

By the third day on the ship, I struck up an unusually close friendship with Gennaro, a young man from Naples. We spent a lot of time together, telling jokes, playing cards, and talking about women, a favorite discussion topic. One afternoon, Gennaro boasted about having an affair with a beautiful young lady on the ship. She was going to a small town in Ohio to meet the man she had just married by proxy. She was traveling in the company of her mother-in-law, the chaperon who never let her out of her sight. I thought my friend was just bragging and refused to believe him. To show he was not making stuff up, he asked me to go with him below deck to the young woman's cabin. When he knocked on the door and she heard his name, she opened the door wearing a skimpy, red negligee. As soon as she saw that her *friend* was not alone, she slammed the door shut. Gennaro turned to me and looked at me as if to say, "Do you believe me now?" I did. It didn't surprise me not to see the girl again for the rest of the journey, not even at the restaurant. Maybe she took *sick* and had her meals in her cabin.

Arranged marriages, such as this one, were common in those days. I could think of several girls from my hometown that agreed to marry strangers living in America or Canada. These men were usually much older than the women they sought to marry. They were immigrants who left Delia years earlier and relied on their relatives back home to find them a good, local wife. In most cases, the girl chosen for the match was pressured by her parents and relatives to give her consent even if she had never met the would-be suitor. She was reminded that the family's good fortune depended on her acceptance of the marriage proposal and go live abroad with her husband. By consenting to such an arrangement, she knew she was giving her family a chance to escape from their enduring poverty. Once she became an American or Canadian citizen, the country's immigration office would consider her petition to have her relatives immigrate and join her in the *promised land*. It was a price worth paying, at least as far as the family was concerned. For the girl it was the sacrifice of her life, to have to marry a man she had never met before. This does not exclude the possibility that some of these couples, in time, fell in love and led a happy life together.

Time on the ship was never dull. I was so busy that seldom did I go to bed before one o'clock in the morning. I was having the time of my life and wished it would never end. But it did end, almost overnight. Two days before reaching New York, we found ourselves in the middle of a raging storm. For a day and a half and a long night, hurricane-force winds and huge waves battered the *Leonardo*, causing it to pitch and roll dangerously. Tall waves cascading on the bridge gave the impression the ship was going to be submerged. In spite of the crew's assurances that the captain had everything under control and that the storm would soon blow over, most of the people were constantly on edge. No one was allowed out on the promenade deck. Indoors, ropes were tied to and between columns and doors for passengers to hang on as they moved about. Tables and chairs were anchored to the floor to prevent them from sliding. Once in a while, we saw an unfastened chair with or without someone sitting on it sliding across the room. In one instance, a passenger who had moved his chair and forgot to reattach it to the floor was thrown literally to the other side of the room. They took him to the infirmary to bandage his wrist and stop the bleeding from a small gash on his head.

But incidents such as this one were rare in part because of the safety measures and mostly because very few people were up and about. More than half of the passengers had become seasick and stayed in their respective cabins. They were truly miserable, cooped up in their rooms and unable to keep down the food the kitchen crew brought them. My entire family got sick. Even my father, who had seen it all when he went to Venezuela, had to take to his bed. As for me, I managed to weather the storm without getting sick; though at times, I had difficulty keeping my food down. Thank God, the hurricane didn't last long. Just as the ship's captain had assured us, by the second day the waves subsided, the skies began to clear, and the New York City skyline appeared on the horizon.

We were mesmerized at the sight of the city's size and skyscrapers. I knew that New York had the tallest buildings in the world; I just didn't know they were so tall and so many. I was also astonished by the huge chunks of ice floating in the New York harbor with some lumps bumping against the ship as tugboats nudged it up the river and to its designated pier. I had never seen ice before, except for the crushed ice or slush you find in a granita cone. The entire family grew more and more excited as the idea that we had finally arrived began to sink in. But our excitement gave way to a sense of bewilderment as we beheld an immense city literally covered with snow. This was hardly what we imagined *lamerica* would be like. As the ship neared the dock, our first reaction was to go out on the bridge, defying the bitter cold. Maybe we could see our sponsor among the people that had come to welcome the incoming passengers. But the freezing temperature made it impossible for us to stay out more than a minute or two. When the ship finally docked, we were allowed to disembark. The process was orderly and swift, as all immigrants had already been issued the necessary paperwork to enter the country.

A few hours before the ship entered the harbor, US Immigration officials came on board, processed our papers, and issued us the much-prized green card. This credit-card-size document—originally green—was still issued to all legal alien residents. It grants them the most rights and privileges enjoyed by a citizen. It does not give them the right to vote or the privilege to work for the federal government, especially in jobs requiring security clearance. There are some exceptions most notably in the area of national security, such as the FBI or the CIA. Anyway, green card in hand, the passengers were already cleared to get off the boat, gather their luggage, and be on their way. It took Pasquale and me some time to find and assemble the family's suitcases, which had been unloaded and scattered throughout the cargo-holding area, a huge warehouse. According to instructions, all passengers were required to stand by their belongings until they were cleared by a customs official.

We all gathered around our luggage and waited. After a short while, a uniformed officer came by. His nametag read Di Caro, obviously an Italo-American. In a mixed bag of broken Sicilian and Neapolitan dialects, he asked my father if we were carrying any plants, meats, fruit, or cheese. We were bringing only a small wheel of fresh pecorino cheese that Uncle Charlie had requested in one of his last letters. The cheese, which my father bought from a local shepherd, was not pasteurized and was immediately confiscated. After making sure the family was not bringing any other banned items into the country, Officer Di Caro told us we were free to go out and wished us *bona fortun*. We picked up our luggage and walked out of the restricted area. We entered a large hangar where hundreds of people were waiting to welcome the newly arrived. The place was a total zoo; some were scurrying about trying to get closer to the exit; others, yelling and waving their arms in the air, were hoping to get the attention of their friends or relatives. My family and I, numbed by the shouting and the shoving, looked lost and scared.

Where was Uncle Charlie, our sponsor? He had to be somewhere in the crowd. Would he recognize us? What really unsettled us was the woman and her two children near us who had begun to fear that no one had come to welcome them. The woman's despair had already given to pitiful whimpers, "Where is my husband? I don't see my brother. Where are they?" she kept saying. Fortunately for us, our growing anxiety didn't last long. Within minutes, my mother spotted Uncle Charlie and pointed him out to the rest of us. Except for my father and the little ones, we all recognized him instantly and began calling his name and waving frantically. We were relieved when he finally saw us and waved back with both hands in the air.

There was a reason why not everyone recognized Uncle Charlie. My father hadn't seen his brother-in-law since 1920, when he came back to Delia, married Aunt Enza, and returned with her to America. When Enza and Charlie came to visit in 1954, my father was already in Venezuela. My younger siblings were either too small to remember or not born yet. Anyway, seeing him waving back to us was a huge relief from the uncertainties that had weighed heavily on our minds. Although we didn't speak about our anxieties, it was obvious that we all had harbored unsettling what-ifs. What if Uncle Charlie could not come and send his sons instead? How would we recognize them? Did they speak Italian? What if nobody showed up to meet us? One can only imagine our happiness when he finally found his way through the crowd. We embraced, exchanged a few pleasantries about the voyage, and proceeded right away to a taxi stand for a ride to the train station.

Clearly, we couldn't all fit in a regular van; there were eight of us besides the luggage. Uncle Charlie was visibly irritated when he saw three suitcases, a huge trunk, and two sacks full of pots and pans and old shoes. He wondered what stopped my father from bringing along the kitchen sink. But sarcasm and frustration didn't help. He needed to stay calm and hire an additional van. That wasn't easy as taxis and vans were very busy near the pier at that hour. We waited almost a half an hour before a second van pulled up. The drivers seemed to get into a heated discussion with Uncle Charlie over the extra cost of the excessive luggage. In the meantime, it was already dark, and we were freezing in our loafers and lightweight jackets. Finally, with everyone and everything on board, the two vehicles drove to Penn Station.

The station wasn't very far, but it took forever to get there. The streets were covered with snow, causing the vans to move very slowly and slide dangerously at times. That particular week, Uncle Charlie told us it snowed so much that the city was under a state of emergency. New Yorkers had rarely seen so much snowfall at one time, neither had they experienced the bone-chilling cold that for days was gripping the entire northeast. People in the streets were wearing knee-high boots and fur-hooded parkas; they looked like the Eskimos we had seen in the movies. It was our very first impression of the new country, and we were confused. Was this *lamerica* we dreamed about? Where had we come to? Had we made a mistake to leave our beloved Sicily?

Our apprehension melted away when we saw the overwhelming size and grandiosity of the station with hundreds of people scurrying around all over the place. We had never seen anything so crowed and so awesome. Uncle Charlie asked us to keep an eye on the luggage and stay close to him so that we wouldn't get separated. We could go to the bathroom on the train; he told us. When the train finally arrived, we climbed on board following Uncle Charlie's directions. The scene reminded me of a schoolteacher taking his kids on a school trip. The ride was uneventful, as most of us fell asleep, weary of a long and emotionally draining day. We were awakened in Philadelphia where we had to change trains. It was past midnight and the station was practically deserted. An hour or so later, we boarded the last train for Reading, our final destination. We arrived at the house Uncle Charlie had rented and furnished for us around two o'clock in the morning and went straight to bed.

In Reading

When we first got up the following morning, we looked out the window and were dumbfounded to see columns of gray smoke coming out the chimneys rising above every house. The streets were blanketed with slushy, dirty snow. Cars, mostly old clunkers, were parked on both sides of the street; some men were scraping ice from their cars' windshields while others were attempting to start engines too cold to get going at first cranks. People, in knee-high boots and heavy coats, were trudging through the snow on their way to work or the corner grocery store. The sooty and frigid scene was truly disheartening. It was in this weather that my parents, in their lightweight clothes, went to the grocery store. Luckily, the store, owned and operated by Uncle Charlie and one of his sons, was only a block away. They were happy to find that the place stocked many of the food staples the family was used to, including Italian bread, olive oil, mortadella, fresh ricotta, cured black olives, and dried figs. After lunch, Uncle Charlie took us downtown to Sears so that we could buy the clothes we needed for the winter. He paid for everything with the understanding we would reimburse him once we started working.

That same afternoon, Uncle Charlie's family came by to meet their Italian cousins for the first time. They all spoke enough Sicilian dialect to make small talk and assure us to count on their affection and support. After all we were family. What was truly moving was to watch the encounter between my dad and his sister Enza. They hadn't seen each other for almost forty years since she married Uncle Charlie and followed him to the States. As soon as they saw each other, they ran into each other's arms, tears running down their cheeks. They remained embraced and speechless for some time. Then, drying their happy tears, they held hands and talked incessantly about their loved ones, especially their aging mother—their father had passed away years before. Sitting next to each other and still holding hands, they reminisced about their growing-up days in Delia. They talked about the many friends and relatives killed in WWI and those lost to the 1918 *Spagnola* virus, the deadly Spanish flu that claimed the lives of tens of millions worldwide.

They talked about how he, two years her junior, used to be protective of her and shooed away the many suitors he considered not good enough for her. Then, along came Uncle Charlie with his marriage proposal. The family deemed him acceptable in part because he was already an American citizen and implicitly, well off. But more important, it was hoped that through the marriage the entire family could eventually immigrate to America and join her there. But it wasn't going to be. All hopes were dashed in part because of the rise of Mussolini and the sanctions the US imposed on his fascist regime. In addition, fascist Italy began to encourage immigration to the African territories it had occupied and wanted to colonize. Soon after the fall of fascism in 1945, most of the family emigrated but not to America; some went to France, others to Venezuela, and my father stayed in Delia.

Aunt Enza's children found some of the stories interesting and wanted to hear more about their mother's life before coming to the States. They were especially curious about how she met and married their dad. But Uncle Charlie, clearly embarrassed by the suggestion that Enza married him for his money and his prized American citizenship, did his best to change the subject. He steered the conversation to the good fortune that awaited us, assuring us that we would have no difficulty finding work and feeling right at home. Our cousins, two women and three men, painted the same bright picture and offered us their unconditional assistance.

The afternoon was festive with both families happy to be in the company of their newly found relatives. Among other things, Enza asked her brother if he liked the house they rented for us.

"Was it comfortable?" She wanted to know though she knew it was. He replied enthusiastically that it was fabulous and took the opportunity to thank her and her husband for having rented and furnished it so beautifully. In the eyes of the culture-shocked newcomers, the house was more than just comfortable; it was a palace. It had three floors. The first floor consisted of a big living room with a huge bay window, a full-sized kitchen, a yard, and an outhouse just out of the back door. The upper floors had a large bathroom and four bedrooms. Everybody had his own bed. Uncle Charlie made sure the place was suitably furnished with sofas, tables, chairs, TV, refrigerator, washing machine, and other household appliances. I was so impressed with our new American home that in the first letters to my friends back home I described it as a mansion. In the basement, I boasted in one of those letters, there was a coal-fired boiler that provided hot water year-round and hot air for the entire house in the winter. I knew my friends would marvel at my comforts and envy my good fortune.

In my letters, I made a point not to mention an embarrassing incident that occurred on our third night in the house. I feared that it would make my family look like a bunch of country bumpkins pretending to live a life of luxury. The episode was indeed awkward. That night, before going to bed, my dad went downstairs to adjust the hot airflow. He shoveled enough coal into the furnace to last until morning as Uncle Charlie had told and shown him the previous night. But as one who had never seen a furnace before, he forgot that he was supposed to open, not close, the flue damper. With the damper closed, the house filled up with smoke, and we all woke up coughing and frightened. Immediately, we thought the house was on fire. It wasn't. Shaken and unsure of what to do, my dad went to get Uncle Charlie, who lived right around the corner above his grocery store. He was not a happy camper to be awakened in the middle of the night. Having instantly understood what the problem was, he came to the house, all the while chastising his brother-in-law for having failed to follow his instructions. Just the day before, he had told him not to forget to open the damper. But upon noting that the poor man was deeply embarrassed, he told him not to worry about it; in time, he would learn how to use modern conveniences.

We were already enjoying the novelty of domestic appliances, all thanks to Uncle Charlie. How could we ever repay our generous sponsor for all the time and energy he spent going to garage sales and checking newspaper ads for used furniture? Although the subject was never broached, it was understood we were expected to pay back all the money he had spent on our behalf. Some neighbors wondered whether he had taken a chance in putting up his own money without a guarantee he would get it back. The more cynical went as far as to insinuate that he was probably making a profit from his *investment*. After all, he was a *clever* businessman. They all doubted we would find work right away, considering that we had no skills, spoke no English, and my parents were too old. But as it turned out, we all found work within two weeks and began to repay our debt to Uncle Charlie and our creditors back in Delia.

Factory Work

Within a few days of our arrival, Uncle Charlie found work for my brother and me. A week later, both my parents were working. We all took manual-labor jobs that didn't require knowledge of the language. My parents worked in a clothing factory: my father as a janitor, my mother as a seamstress. My brother and I worked at a hosiery mill that steam-pressed ladies' stockings and pantyhose. In both places, there were several Italian immigrants with enough knowledge of English to translate whenever the foreman needed to talk to us. For my brother and me, the job was physically exhausting. Not only were we assigned the night shift or graveyard shift, as we called it, but we were also exposed to excessive heat. It's not as weird as it sounds that we would suffer unbearable heat in the middle of February and in one of Reading's coldest winters.

February was a very cold month indeed, but the heat had nothing to do with the outside temperatures. The steam released by the pressing machines was so intense that it turned the place into a steam bath. In addition, the leg-shaped forms pressing the nylons were so hot that we risked scorching our fingertips if we were not fast enough in removing the hosiery. But what was truly backbreaking for us short people was the machines' height. We had to jump every time we removed a stocking from its steel mold, which was every two seconds or so. Admittedly, we didn't work eight hours straight. We took two or three ten-minute breaks, usually to go to the bathroom or eat the sandwich we brought from home. We could take longer breaks if we wanted to, but we were on piecework, that is, we were paid on the basis of the number of stockings we pressed. So it was in our interest to go back to our work right away, hard as it was. When we got home in the morning, we threw ourselves on the couch, too tired to do anything, even to eat. My mother cried more than once seeing us so exhausted. She often regretted coming to the States, wondering if we shouldn't just go back home. But we had come to stay and to make a go of it.

Pasquale and I were so determined to make it and thus so eager to make money that we even volunteered to work Saturdays or Sundays. There was good money to be made on weekends as each piece we pressed was paid double. We were proud of our weekly paychecks in part because it was the first time in our lives we earned money. We were rich! But we were also thrifty. We gave our money to our parents, and pulling all our earnings together, we were able to repay Uncle Charlie in a matter of months. By the end of the summer, we had finished paying our debt to the relatives who had loaned us money for the passage. Also, for the first time in our lives, we set foot in a bank and opened a savings account.

I remember my father's uneasiness on entering the bank, a high-ceiling structure with ornate columns and balustrades. He was visibly intimidated by the bank's austere atmosphere: uniformed guards at the entrance, coiffed tellers standing by their respective windows, and employees dressed in suits and tie scurrying about the place. He was walking haltingly and speaking softly, almost in a whisper, afraid a security guard might take him for an intruder and throw him out. I told him there was nothing to be afraid of and that we were welcome customers. But my assurance wasn't enough for him to relax. All his life, he had believed that a bank was a place where only people with money were allowed to enter and do business. At least, that was how it was in Delia. It took the teller, a second-generation Italian lady who helped us set up the account, to convince him otherwise. In her broken Sicilian dialect, she made small talk and assured him the bank would always appreciate his business. From then on, he went to the bank to deposit our paychecks, confident *Signorina* Maria would be there to welcome him and enter the checks' amount into his savings book.

After our family paid all its debts, my brother and I were free to keep our money and open our own savings accounts. Instead, we continued giving our paychecks to our parents so that we could buy a nice house, which we did by the end of the year. Although we liked the house we were renting, it was time to move. As far as we could see, there was nothing wrong with the house. For us it was still a *mansion*. The problem was the neighborhood, which had decayed considerably since its heyday of early immigration. Originally, it had been home to a community of Italian immigrants. It had been Reading's *little Italy* with its grocery stores, barbershops, bakeries, church, notary public, sandwich shops, and other facilities that made immigrants feel at home away from home. Though most immigrants had already moved, and many businesses had closed, a few hung on. Uncle Charlie still had his grocery store, and Sabato's Bakery was still open. Mr. Jimmy was cutting hair at the same barbershop he opened after he came back from France in 1919. He proudly reminded his customers—mostly old immigrants like himself—that he and Uncle Charlie had been General Pershing's doughboys in WWI. The faded pictures on the wall attested to his war stories. Maybe because of lack of costumers or plain old age—he was in his early seventies—Mr. Jimmy worked only a few hours in the afternoon if he felt like it.

CHAPTER 13

Moving on Up

Leaving the community where we had originally found comfort and convenience was in keeping with the aspiring mentality of the immigrant: move on and up to better things. Typically, once they learned the language, most immigrants went on to start a new business, learn a trade, look for a better job, move to a nicer neighborhood, and be sure their kids got a good education. When they first arrived, they had no choice but to live in the same neighborhood where their sponsors resided and take whatever job they could find. Not by chance, we went to live near Uncle Charlie's house. The immigrant community there or what was left of the original *little Italy* made us feel at home and helped us adjust to our new life in America.

Two days after we arrived, for instance, Mr. Dominick and Mr. Frank, two of our neighbors who had come from Sicily at the turn of the century, stopped by to welcome us to *lamerica*. They offered all sorts of advice, ranging from the types of winter clothes we should buy to the best bakery in the area to the Americanization of our first names. They told us we should dress like Americans. To begin with, all of us guys, including my thirteen-year-old brother Fedele, should wear hats, bowler hats. We bought them but after a week or so discarded them; we looked ridiculous with those things on our heads. They also told us we should

Americanize our names. I (Salvatore) would be called Sam and Pasquale became Pat. We accepted readily their suggestions; after all, they were what we called the *vecchi americani* or old, acclimated Americans. They had been in the country for fifty-some years and knew everything there was to know about America, or so we thought. Little did we know that they were both illiterate and had little understanding of American culture, much less of the English language. I was not surprised when I later learned that the name Sam stood for Samuel, not Salvatore, and that Pat was short for Patrick, not Pasquale.

This does not explain why we left a community of people who espoused the same beliefs, observed the same traditions and most importantly, spoke our language. We were happy to be among other Italians, especially at the beginning when we needed all sorts of help and information—how to get to work? Which bus to take? How to register the children for school? Where to go to get the phone installed in the house? Was there a doctor who spoke Italian? Every time we went somewhere, be it to shop at a department store or pay a bill, we found someone willing to come along and translate for us. Usually, we relied on Uncle Charlie and our cousins, but we were careful not to abuse their kindness. Once in a while, we asked a neighbor for help.

A week after our arrival, for example, I went with our neighbor Michele to the AT&T local office to have a phone installed in our home. Michele had been in the country for over three years and had already Americanized his name to Mike. At the telephone office, I noticed the clerk had difficulty understanding Mike's English. When she finally thought she did, she filled out the paperwork, made me sign it, and gave me a copy. Only when we left the office did I notice the miscommunication—the lady registered the phone in my name, not in my father's name as we wanted and as it should've been since he owned the house. For the next forty-odd years, until my parents' death, the phone book entry read, Sam DiMaria. The phone incident made me realize that some of my translator's English was not as good as they claimed it to be or as I thought it was. It was not unusual for them to have to repeat a phrase or an entire sentence before they were understood or sometimes misunderstood.

The reason we moved away from our little Italy was simple and in some ways predictable. As we grew familiar with the culture and began to learn the language, the neighborhood started to lose its appeal. We had grown self-sufficient enough that we no longer needed to rely on the help of the community. At the same time, we had come to the realization that the place was essentially a slum. Many of its residents were welfare recipients or low-wage earners or unemployed. Of the original Italian immigrants still living there, most were like Mr. Dominick and Mr. Frank. They were simple people whose aspirations had never been higher than living in a modest home and drawing a small government pension. Unlike them, we had ambitions. My parents' recurring refrain was "We emigrated to give our children a better future." They left behind everything dear to them in the hope their kids would be given the opportunity to live the American dream. From this perspective, one might rightly say that buying a home in a better neighborhood was a step toward fulfilling the dream. Actually, at that time we didn't see the move in terms of *dreams*. We moved simply because we had saved enough money to buy our own place and didn't want to stay in that rundown area.

Perhaps it was natural for some neighbors, immigrants and Americans alike, to view our move with resentment and a dose of curious jealousy. They couldn't understand how it was possible that the newly arrived had already bought a house in a better neighborhood while they, after years of *hard* work, were still renting and struggling to make ends meet. A neighbor immigrant said it for everyone when he told my father, "I don't get it. It just ain't fair. I don't know how you did it. You just got here and already are doing better than many of us who have lived here most of our lives." Another expressed a similar resentment, noting that he, born and raised in America, felt cheated. If anyone deserved to have better things, it was him and not the foreigners who came to steal jobs from *real* Americans like him. The answer my dad was careful not to give was obvious, "Aspiration, hard work, and sacrifice, that's how we did it. You should try it."

The new house wasn't that far away from where we lived before. And although the area was not another little Italy, it was home to quite a few early-century Italian immigrants. But these immigrants' living conditions were higher than those of their counterparts from the old neighborhood. For instance, our next-door neighbors, the Mancinos, had four children all of whom were successful businessmen and professionals. Not a day went by without some of their children and grandchildren stopping by to check on the old couple. On Sundays, a whole bunch of them came for dinner, the women arriving early to do the cooking. They were all very nice to us, never failing to greet us in their broken Sicilian dialect. One of the grandsons, a cardiologist, would often ask my father about his heart condition. "Joe, you gotta stop *fumari*, smoking no good for you," he would warn my dad. There were other Italians who would often gather in the little park across the street for a game of bocce. At times, Dad joined them. Besides being safe and clean, the neighborhood was centrally located and well serviced by public transportation. Buses came by frequently, allowing us to move around town easily, be it going to work, school, or just shopping downtown at the big department stores.

Fun and Games

Those days, before shopping malls came into being, department stores such as Sears and JC Penny were usually located downtown and could easily be reached on foot or by bus. They consisted of three to five story-high buildings often a few blocks away from each other, at least in Reading. Shopping malls began to spring up in the suburban areas a few years after we arrived in the early sixties. For us, accustomed to just walking downtown for shopping, the malls' relocation out of the city created a serious inconvenience. We could get there only by bus. But that was quite a task because the bus came on the hour and only until

6:00 p.m. It all changed in 1962 when Pasquale bought a car and we no longer needed public transportation to go places. For my mother, in particular, the car was a godsend. She no longer had to take the bus to go shopping and lug home bulky grocery bags. For us young adults, it made it easier to go out in the evening, especially on weekends.

One of the first things Pasquale and I did with the new car was to drive to Atlantic City, then one of the most popular vacation spots on the East Coast. Its famed boardwalk and sandy beaches attracted thousands of summer tourists. We had never been to the beach before. We were excited. Once there, we went to find a hotel room for the night. Wherever we went, the desk clerks asked us if we had reservations. We didn't; we didn't know we needed one, not that we would have known how to book a reservation, much less look up the hotels' numbers in the phone book. Even if we had the phone number, I doubted our English would have been good enough to make the desk clerk understand what we were calling about. So one desk clerk after another took us for a couple of bumpkins fresh from the farm and told us mockingly to try somewhere else.

We were about to despair when we finally found a room at a boardinghouse a little out of the way from the tourist area. The landlady was a gracious elderly woman of Italian descent who greeted us in her limited Neapolitan dialect. She showed us the room and told us we could pay when we checked out. The room was small but clean and pleasant with a spectacular view of the ocean. Soon after we got settled, we went to one of the stores on the boardwalk, and we each bought swimming suits, sunglasses, and sunhats. Clad in our brand-new outfits, we walked straight to the beach, doing our best to look like typical beachgoers. The lodging, the money in our pockets, the beach full of seemingly well-to-do people, made us feel like millionaires living the life.

That was the only vacation we took during our first years in the States. We stayed at home and engaged in other fun activities, such as bowling and dancing. Bowling was one of the most common family sports at that time. Before huge Bowl-O-Rama centers became popular, there were small bowling venues everywhere in the city. My siblings and I, together with some friends, usually went to the one near our house. We got to know the owner, who appreciated our business and gave us a discount or a free Coca-Cola once in a while. Saturdays, we often went dancing at one of the many so-called nightclubs. Most of these establishments were no more than mere bars with a few tables and chairs, a dance floor, a live band, and a burly doorman. The label *club* was used mainly to allow the owners to deny admission to anyone they considered undesirable.

I felt the humiliation of this discriminatory practice one Saturday night when my brother, some of our friends, and I tried to get in a predominantly Pennsylvania Dutch establishment. A tall, beefy guy with a heavy Pennsylvania Dutch accent turned us away, shouting, "No vops allovood." Though at the time I didn't know what *wops* meant, I knew I just experienced blatant bigotry for the first time in my life. But it didn't deter us from finding other more inclusive clubs to go to on a Saturday night. In time, we grew out of this type of entertainment, especially when my brother got married. Also, our friends got their own cars and began to go their separate ways. From then on, our best entertainment was during the Christmas season when friends and relatives visited with us and played cards 'til late at night. Generally, on Christmas Eve about twenty relatives gathered at our house, bringing gifts and homemade dishes for the evening meal. The women got busy in the kitchen, cooking and setting the table, while the men played cards or watched TV. A few were outside grilling the sausages my father had made weeks earlier. When they brought in the meat, we all sat down to eat. The dinner was festive but never a relaxing affair. There was Christmas music blaring in the background, kids crying, and people talking louder and louder as my father's homemade wine started claiming their senses and their speech.

It wasn't clear if and how many of them went to church for the traditional midnight mass. Some of the older ladies wanted to go, but their half-hearted wish quickly yielded to excuses: the bitter cold, the strain of the late hour, and the need to stay behind and help with the children and around the kitchen. In the end, only my mother, Aunt Enza, and her older daughter usually went. The others joined the younger women in clearing the table, doing the dishes, and putting the children to bed. The men went back to playing cards over the objections of the women who wanted to dance. Little after midnight, soon after the women came back from church, we began to open our presents and sing Christmas carols. Afterward, some went to bed and many of us played cards until sunrise.

This was a typical Christmas at the DiMarias until it ended in 1972 when Pasquale died. He passed at the young age of thirty-one, leaving behind a wife and a six-year-old boy. With him gone, we stopped having festive get-togethers. He left a vacuum no one was able or willing to fill. Sadly, we often realize how much some people impact our lives only after they are gone! Whether it was a party, a picnic, or a card game, he was always there calling up people, organizing activities, and making things happen. He was especially good at smoothing over differences between quarreling relatives and bringing them together. His death was the most traumatic experience of my life; he was my anchor. His passing affected me so deeply that for years I couldn't bring myself to talk about him without tears spilling down my cheeks. Even now, as I write these words, I feel my eyes welling up and a knot tightening in my throat. We were very close, as close as two brothers could ever be. We were less than two years apart and looked so much alike that people thought we were twins. Though he was not book smart, he valued education and was proud of his college-kid brother. I never forgot his last request; he made me promise not to abandon my dream.

The idea that I was destined to get an education never faded from my view or from my parents' expectations. Though they seldom talked about it at home, the entire family took it for granted that I would go on to college once I learned the language. English would prove to be a major obstacle because it is a very difficult language to master. Unlike Italian or other Romance languages, it has fewer grammar rules to guide the beginner, not to mention the fact that living and working among people who spoke only Italian or broken English didn't help much. To really learn the language, I had to go to school. And I did, thanks to Uncle Charlie. I will always remember my immense gratitude to that man. Although or because he had very little schooling, he strongly believed in education. He was disappointed that none of his children went to college. At times, he regretted not pushing them hard enough though he was happy they at least finished high school at a time when the dropout rate was unusually high.

We had barely arrived in America when Uncle Charlie warned me not to give up on my education. In a way, he wanted me to accomplish what he had hoped for his children. Three days after our arrival in Reading, he enrolled my brother and me in an English course for foreigners. The class was taught in the evening and had about sixteen male and female adults from various European countries, including Greece, Poland, and Italy. Predictably, quite a few people dropped out by the end of the first month. Some were too tired to stay awake and pay attention after a long day at work. Others were disappointed that the teacher stressed grammar rather than the practical everyday speech they had hoped to learn. I appreciated the emphasis on grammar because, unlike most of them, I had a solid foundation in languages, Latin in particular. By the end of the semester, my written English had improved so much that I decided to enroll in the city's evening high school. The program offered school dropouts the opportunity to complete their education and receive the much-coveted high school diploma or its equivalent, the GED.

To my surprise the school had more than seventy returnee students, all in their twenties and thirties. I later learned that many had dropped out because they got married young, others had to go to work, and a few joined the army by lying about their age. Most girls quit school either because they went to work or got pregnant. At that time, it was taboo for an unmarried girl to be seen in public pregnant. Parents did their best to avoid the *scandal*. Some put pressure on the boyfriend to get married right away, in which case both students dropped out of school. Others withdrew their daughters from school and sent them away to live with a relative until they gave birth. In my class there were a couple of girls who had dropped out because they got pregnant in their junior year. Now they were back in school to complete their graduation requirements. In those days, we could not get ahead in the workplace without a high school diploma. Almost all Help Wanted ads stated in bold letters, **High School Diploma required**. One might say that back then employers' demand for a high school diploma was the equivalent of today's requisite for a college degree.

In my determination to further my education, I didn't stop and ask whether I knew enough English to attend high school. Was I biting more than I could chew? Did I think I could do the work that was challenging even for native speakers? That was exactly the secretary's question when I, accompanied by my friend and translator Mike, went to enroll at Reading evening high school. Noticing that we looked lost, the elderly secretary asked if she could help and invited us to her office. Speaking slowly and enunciating her words carefully, she politely asked what she could do for us. She never imagined we had come to register for classes. In his broken English, a nervous Mike explained the purpose of our visit. Thinking that it was Mike who wanted to enroll, she tactfully tried to discourage him, reminding that high school was very difficult for those lacking basic language skills. But when she finally realized that it was I who wanted to enroll, she was really confused. After a few seconds of shifting her puzzled stare from me to Mike and back to me, she said, "OK, I think I get it." Then, looking straight at me, she said with condescending incredulity, "So it's you who wants to enroll!"

"That's what I've been trying to tell you," said Mike meekly, embarrassed for his poor performance as a translator.

"This is a first!" she exclaimed, dropping the pencil she was holding in her hand. "How can he possibly do high school work if he can't even speak English?" she asked, convinced that the two us had no idea what it meant to take high school courses. Then, rolling her eyes and unsure of what to do or say, she called the principal who was in the inner office talking to some teachers.

Mr. Morgan was a distinguished-looking man in his mid-fifties. Slim and tall with thinning graying hair parted to the side, and a rimless pince-nez perched on his long nose, he cut a fine figure in his light-brown suit. After the secretary briefed him on the situation, he held up his hand to signal to Mike he wanted to hear directly from me. He wanted to see for himself how my English really was. In my best English, I told him I had gone to high school in Italy and was familiar with most subjects taught in American schools. I knew chemistry, math, zoology, and other subjects; I just didn't know the terminology in English. The principal tried to explain that high school would be unusually difficult for someone who hardly spoke English. It would be better if I came back in a year or two when I could speak the language. When I insisted—through my translator, of course—that I was able to do high school work, he gave up. Throwing his hands up in frustration, he turned to the secretary and told her to go ahead and enroll me. I registered for two courses: English and math.

School, I discovered, was truly challenging mostly because of the language barrier, just as Mr. Morgan had warned me. I was the only foreigner in both classes. Some students tried to interact with me, but their attempts didn't go beyond curiosity questions such as "Where are you from? How long have been in this country? Where do you work?" By their skeptical tone of voice and facial expressions, it was clear they wondered what in the world I was doing there. I could barely speak the language. What could I possibly get out of courses they themselves had difficulty with? Some students, especially those sitting near me, noticed I was getting good grades and were at loss trying to figure out how I was doing it. One student by the name of Carmen De Angelo began to seek my company. He was intrigued not by my good grades, he later told me, but by my accent and last name DiMaria. Somehow, this little Italian reminded him of his immigrant grandfather, a man he had loved very much.

Carmen De Angelo

Carmen was in his early thirties of average height with broad shoulders, thick eyebrows, and olive complexion. He combed his black hair straight back and plastered it down with a fair dose of hair cream. His voice was raspy and his speech slow and staccato. He dropped out of school when he was seventeen, ran away from home, lied about his age, and joined the marines. The military taught him self-discipline and skilled trade. He came out of the service as an accomplished welder. Now, he lived alone though his long-time girlfriend lived next door and the two were often together. When he first met me, he made it a point of describing himself as a *paisa*, a proud claim of his Italian ancestry. Within weeks, he started calling me *gumpa* the American version of the Italian *cumpà*. Some fellow students were startled by the use of a term that, as far as they knew, was commonly used in reference to mafia thugs, at least in the movies. For them, the word was often spoken as a stereotypical designation of Italo-Americans. I tried to dispel this derogatory implication by explaining to Carmen and friends that *cumpà* was actually an endearing word meaning *friend*.

In most dialects of Southern Italy, the term denotes a godfather, that is, a man who sponsors a child at baptism or confirmation. By this ceremony, the godfather and the baby's actual father become and address each other as cumpà, short for *cumpari* (roughly co-fathers). By the same token, their respective wives become and address each other as *cummà*, short for *cummari* (roughly co-mothers). In its common use, the term means friend, buddy. For Carmen, I embodied his Italian heritage, of which he was unusually proud. He exuded pride whenever he came to the house and had a chance to chat with my parents. Every weekday around seven o'clock in the evening, he came to pick me and take me to school in his 1951 Chevy. He enjoyed greeting my parents with the few Italian words he knew. My mother, in particular, loved to hear him speak some of the dialect phrases he learned from his grandparents, "Bona sira . . . Comu stai . . . Grazi . . . Saluh" (good evening . . . how are you . . . thank you . . . to your health). Sometimes, if we were not in a hurry, he would accept a glass of my father's homemade wine and some of my mother's cooking. He loved to hear my parents call him Carmelo, an Italian version of his name. So much so that he insisted I, too, call him Carmelo. And so, I took to calling him Carmelo. I still do.

Some weekends, the two of us went bowling or just for a drink. Once in a while, he would ask his lady friend to invite one of her friends, and the four of us would go dancing or just have dinner. But most of the time, it was just the two of us. One evening, we went to one of his favorite nightclubs, *The Playhouse*. The evening would have been fun were it not for an incident that gulled Carmen's ethnic sensitivity and drew out his explosive temper. When we arrived, the place was filling up. Some patrons were standing by the bar, nursing their drinks, talking, and watching young couples dance. Carmen and I sat at one of the few tables still available and after a few drinks Carmen got up to dance. Soon afterward, he urged me to ask one of the girls sitting across from us to dance. Shy and not a great dancer, I hesitated at first but then gathered enough courage to ask. The girl accepted. While we were dancing, her estranged husband approached us and putting a hand on my shoulder, pushed me aside, saying dismissively, "Get lost, you dago." He shouldn't have said that.

In a flash, Carmen pushed his chair away from the table and sprinted onto the dancing floor. Nostrils flaring and eyebrows scrunched downward, grabbed the man's tie, pulled it down, spat in his face, and grunted through clenched teeth, "Touch my friend again and I'll kill you." It didn't matter to Carmen that the man was twice his size and could have easily beaten him to a pulp. Luckily, a bouncer stepped in and defused the situation. I was scared and fearing the incident might flare up again, convinced Carmen to leave. He was still upset when we got to the car and insisted on waiting for the guy to come out. Sitting in car, he opened the glove compartment, pulled a handgun, and after making sure it was loaded, put it in his coat pocket. At the sight of the gun, I turned white as a sheet and begged him to take me home. Eventually, he gave in and we left. It was the last time I went out with him to a nightclub.

I didn't quite understand Carmen's reaction, other than the fact that he was trying to protect me from the big bully. I had no idea that he was reacting to the ethnic slur *dago*. In all honesty, I thought the man had said Diego, a common Italian name. But Carmen knew better, and the slur cut deep into his pride. But even after he explained the seriousness of the insult, I didn't think much of it. Where I came from, I told him on our way home, racial discrimination was hardly an issue. Italians were all of one nationality, one religion, and one race. If this helped him to understand my indifference toward the man's slight, it did little to soften his anger. As he drove, he talked about how all his life he had endured racist name-calling, and each time it hurt him more. Although I understood his resentment, I was concerned about his volatile temperament and tried to downplay ethnic slurs as mere empty words. I cared about the man and feared that his temper may one day get him into serious trouble. When everything was said and done, Carmen was a good man, and I was fortunate to have him as my *gumpa*. Among other things, he made it easy for me to go to school and get to work every evening.

We actually became lifelong pals though we went our separate ways. Carmen stayed in Reading, where he had a welding shop and a reputation as a crackerjack welder. I went away first in the army and then to college. But we stayed in touch. Whenever I went home to see my parents, we managed to get together for a drink and catch up with each other's lives. Carmen never tired of telling people how proud he was of his *gumpa*, the professor. Once, we called on Mr. Alyson, our English teacher from our high school days. Now retired, the old man was happy to see us and hear about my academic career. He never forgot his reaction when he first saw me in his class. What was this little foreigner, who barely spoke English, doing in his class? As time went by, he began to wonder how I managed to get As in his weekly exams.

I was proud of my grades, but some of my classmates couldn't figure out how a foreigner was doing so well. I soon learned that Mr. Alyson had that same doubt. One evening, during one of our ten-minute breaks, he told me he wanted to see me. I didn't know what to expect and feared the worst. Did he think my English wasn't good enough to stay in his class? Was he suspecting me of cheating? My fears dissipated when he said, "You are getting the highest grades in the class, yet you barely speak English. How do you explain that?" I told him that grammar and syntax came easy to me because I had studied French and Latin in Italy with the Dominicans. What a coincidence! He, too, had been in a Dominican school. This commonality aroused his interest in me and from then on he was especially understanding of my language limitations. During the second year at the school, he invited me to his house several times to help me with my English. It was during one of these visits that I learned that my *Americanized* name should be Sal, not Sam. Mr. Alyson explained that Sam stood for Samuel, hardly a substitute for Salvatore. But after years of being called Sam, I decided to just keep it. My siblings still call me Sam, so does my wife.

I was truly grateful for the interest Mr. Alyson took in my education, especially his advice on how and what to study for the college entrance exams, which I was planning to take that year. Did he honestly believe I could actually pass the Scholastic Aptitude Test? In retrospect, I doubt he thought I was up to the challenge, but he never discouraged me from trying. I was determined to take the test because I was told that without the SAT, I couldn't go to college. At the end of the year, I took the exams. It was a total failure.

No sooner had I begun taking the test than I realized I had bit off more than I could chew. The material was way over my head. It covered a variety of subjects, ranging from math to American history to English grammar to literature. In some cases, I didn't even understand the instructions, much less the literary passages we were supposed to analyze. Some topics were totally foreign to me. One of the questions in the culture section, for instance, asked whether a football coach was more important than an army general. I answered coach though I had no idea what football was. I didn't even get to finish the exams. I had barely started the math section when the bell rang, and I had to turn it in. Fully aware of my inadequacy, I left the test center wondering whether I would ever go college. Discouraged and demoralized, I didn't look forward to receiving the results. When they finally arrived, they confirmed my fears. I scored less than 600 out of 1600 in total. The sorry outcome dealt a devastating blow to my ego and my plans to pursue higher education. I was so embarrassed that I never told anyone, not even my parents. But not everything turned out that badly. That year, my shattered self-confidence got a major boost as I received my GED, my very first American degree.

Degree in hand, I left the grueling work at the hosiery mill and went to look for a better job. I soon landed a job in a shoe factory, boxing and stacking shoes according to style, size, and color—no more night shifts, no more unbearable heat, no more backbreaking work. In fact, the job was easy and the pay good. The fifty or so employees were a mixed bag of Americans and immigrants mostly from Greece and Portugal. We all got along and didn't hesitate to engage in small talk though the language barrier caused Americans and immigrants to hang out separately. The foreman, a grandfatherly figure with a thick Pennsylvania Dutch accent, was very patient when he talked to us foreigners. Looking back, the lack of Italian speakers on the premises was a blessing in disguise that it forced me to practice my English. I think I would've learned a lot more had I continued to work there. But after about three months or so, I received a draft notice from Uncle Sam directing me to report to the army induction center in Harrisburg, Pennsylvania.

CHAPTER 14

In the Army

The notification threw my plans out of kilter. It was the second blow to my college aspirations in less than a year. The order per se was not a surprise because Pasquale had been called up the year before when he turned twenty-one. People, including my own children, wondered how I could've been drafted in view of the fact that I was not an American citizen. I told them—and my students every time they asked—that draftees didn't have to be US citizens to serve in the military. All male residents, legally residing in the US, were subject to the draft the moment they turned twenty-one. All American males were required to register for the draft when they turned eighteenth. They could register at the local post office or at school. Most youngsters registered at their school during their senior year. In my case, a few days after the family arrived in the country, Uncle Charlie took Pasquale and me to the post office and registered us, as the law required.

When Pasquale was called up, friends and relatives suggested ways for him to avoid serving in the military. The most common advice was to start taking some medicinal herbs that would make him sick enough to fail the physical exam. But the more plausible and least harmful suggestion was for him to claim he didn't speak English. It worked. When he reported to the induction center, he played dumb well enough to convince the officials there that his English was too limited for him to function adequately in the army. They concluded he didn't understand basic instructions, neither could he read or write in the language. Whatever English he spoke with the officials consisted mostly of Italese, roughly a mixture of words borrowed from English and pronounced with an Italian inflection. For instance, the word fence became *fenza*, to push *pusciari*, car/*carru*, job/*giobba*, and so on. Actually, Pasquale's command of the language was better than he led to believe. He feigned ignorance not only because of our culturally rooted aversion to military service—Italians would even physically injure themselves to avoid conscription—but especially because he was planning to get married. He feared that a two-year stint in the military could derail his plans; he had just gotten engaged and hoped to marry the following year.

As for my situation, I, too, was looking for a way out. Besides my dislike of the draft, I was also afraid that two years in the army would further undermine my chances of going to college. As word of my induction notice spread through the Italian community, several people offered tips on how to avoid or postpone the draft, just as they did in Pasquale's case. After considering the various suggestions, I settled on the same excuse my brother had given the year before, don't *speakka ingles*. For added insurance, I took Mr. Dominick's advice. I wrote the army depot in Harrisburg requesting a deferment because I was planning to go to school. There and then, I failed to see the paradox. How could anyone who couldn't speak English pretend to go to college? The army people in Harrisburg surely saw through it right away. When I reported at the center and claimed I didn't know English, the officer in charge opened a folder and pulled out the letter I had written requesting the deferment.

Reading aloud from it, he pushed the piece of paper under my nose and asked in a sarcastic tone, "So you don't speakka ingles. Did you write this?" There was little I could say other than a meek, "Yes, sir." I was embarrassed and thought of Mr. Dominick's suggestion and all the other half-baked notions he held about American culture. I learned the hard way that the poor man had heard about a deferment or *deferin*, as he pronounced it but had no idea what it really meant. He didn't know that it was a postponement of military service, usually granted to those who were admitted to a college or already in school. By following his advice, I had effectively invalidated my no-speak-English excuse. And so it happened that I was promptly inducted into the US Army. After a hasty medical exam, I was sent home with instructions to report back at the depot within ten days to begin my military service. When on the prescribed date I reported for duty, I was issued the standard induction papers and was taken to the local train station. There I joined dozens of recruits awaiting transportation to an army-processing center somewhere in the South. I was in the army now and would be for the next two years.

Boot Camp

On the train, I was scared, lost, and all alone among a crowd of my peers. I didn't know anybody, and my English wasn't good enough to strike a casual conversation with anyone. Most worrisome was the uncertainty of the where, when, and what. Where were we going? When would we get there? What awaited me? The ride in itself was an experience that has never left my memory. For the first time in my life I felt alone and helpless. I was the outsider among scores of fellow recruits with whom I had nothing in common. Some knew each other from high school or had common interests to talk about: sports, movies, songs, people they knew, or plain youthful revelry. I sat there all by myself looking out the window, numbed by the crowd, the noise, and the anxiety about what was to come. One of the recruits, apparently curious about why I was sitting there in dazed silence, tried to start up a conversation. But the moment I spoke, my halting English made him realize that the conversation couldn't go beyond the usual "how are you . . . what's your name . . . and where are you from." It was already getting dark when we finally pulled into Washington Union Station, and the two sergeants in charge started shouting orders for everybody to get off the train.

Before we dispersed in the station, the sergeants yelled out instructions I didn't understand in part because of my English, in part because of the deafening noise. I became very nervous trying to figure out what was going on. My instincts told me to follow the other recruits. After all, I was going where they were going. Once inside the station, I was literally mesmerized by its vastness and marvelous architecture. It was huge with large arched windows and an impressively high vaulted ceiling. In a way, it reminded me of New York Penn Station, the train station I saw when we first arrived in America. I kept on walking around, staring in wide-eyed wonder at the beautiful decorations that gave the place an aura of intimidating magnificence. All the while, I stayed close to one of the sergeants for fear of getting lost among the hundreds of travelers rushing in all directions.

We were at the station for a couple of hours when a loudspeaker announced the arrival of our train. Unable to understand the announcement, I followed the sergeants and the recruits as they began to hurry toward the tracks and onto the train. There were no civilian passengers aboard, just army recruits, hundreds of them. Boarding was orderly as everybody looked and found his assigned seat. The train was full to capacity, it seemed. For the overnight ride, the seats converted into bunk beds screened from the aisle by a curtain. An hour or so after we pulled out of the station, the sergeants ordered lights out, and everybody prepared for bed. I climbed up onto the upper bunk assigned to me and went to bed. It didn't take long for the monotonous clickety-clack of the wheels to lull me to sleep. We were awakened early in the morning as the train started pulling into Columbia, South Carolina. We were told to grab our belongings and get off the train; we had arrived. The army trucks already waiting in the parking lot outside the station took us to Fort Jackson, our final destination.

Fort Jackson was a huge processing center where hundreds of inductees arrived and left every week or so. Here, draftees became GIs on the very first day they arrived; they were issued their first GI uniforms and got their first GI haircut. Almost immediately, our contingent was organized into groups or platoons of twenty men. Each group, led by a platoon sergeant, was marched to various *stations*, such as the barbershop, quartermaster, mess hall, and infirmary. Reveille, sounded by a recording, not by a bugler as is in the movies, was at 6:00 a.m. and roll call at 7:00 a.m. sharp. Each soldier would fall in with his assigned platoon, and after a quick headcount, the sergeants would take their respective platoon to the designated processing station. No recruit was allowed to leave the base. "You're in the army now," we heard over and over. In the days that followed, we were vaccinated against all sorts of diseases, including yellow fever, tetanus, and hepatitis. Most of our time was spent taking aptitude tests on a variety of topics, ranging from English to math to current affairs, logical reasoning, and foreign languages. In between tests, we practiced basic army drills, such as standing at attention, at ease, about-face, saluting and addressing officers, and so on.

What was the purpose of these tests? Didn't all recruits take all sorts of exams when they first reported at their respective induction centers? Certainly, I was given a series of tests at the army depot in Harrisburg, Pennsylvania. But there was a difference. The earlier tests were meant to determine whether individual inductees were mentally and physically qualified for military service. The battery of tests in South Carolina instead was aimed at establishing a recruit's Military Occupation Specialty or MOS, that is, the type of jobs they were best suited for. Not that the tests gave always an accurate indication of the draftee's aptitude, often they didn't. A recruit I knew, for instance, was sent to Military Police School even though he had worked in a pharmacy for two years and was better suited for medical training. I was assigned a medic MOS, though I had never taken an aspirin or used a syringe in my life. Being an Italian with a fair knowledge of French and Spanish, I thought they would send me to a language school to be trained as an interpreter or translator.

We were not sent to MOS schools right away. After being processed, we were individually shipped to various military bases throughout the country to begin basic training. The eight-week training, largely the same for all draftees, stressed getting in physical shape, using basic weaponry, and learning army procedures—duties and obligations, dress code, saluting, ranks and insignia, and so on. I was sent to Fort

Gordon, a few miles from Augusta, Georgia. There I joined hundreds of fellow recruits from all parts of the US. Some were twenty-one-year-old draftees like me; others were eighteen- or nineteen-year-old volunteers straight from high school. Though we dressed the same and drilled together, there was a marked difference between the two types. The conscripts tended to be laid-back with an I-don't-give-a-damn attitude. By contrast, the volunteers were full of enthusiasm and did everything with a gung-ho approach. They were the first to line up in formations and the first to volunteer. They spit shined their boots and belt buckles until they could see their own reflection as the drill sergeants demanded. They even rehearsed certain drills in the barracks after a long day of marching and drilling. Obviously, they wanted to emulate the soldier/hero romanticized on the big screen by movie stars in neatly pressed uniform. Some even tried to pull grenade pins with their teeth as in the movies; others talked about capturing dozens of enemy soldiers someday. But it wasn't long before they learned that the glamorous world of war fictionalized by famed actors such as John Wayne or Gary Cooper was nothing but fiction.

Draftees instead seldom volunteered for extra duties and did the bare minimum to comply with the instructors' demands. I was one of these. At times, I even questioned orders I considered gratuitous or excessive. I questioned why was it necessary to spit shine my boots and belt buckle. Wasn't it enough they were spotless? This defiant attitude once got me in serious trouble. One day, while on kitchen police or KP, a duty most GIs hated, I was told to wipe a section of the kitchen floor. I performed the task quickly and efficiently, using a mop. But one of the cooks, a corporal, ordered me to clean it again this time on my knees. I argued with the man, pointing out that the mop worked just fine and that there was not a speck of dirt on the floor. When he insisted, I threw down the mop and stormed out of the mess hall. The corporal lost no time in calling my company commander to report that I had gone AWOL or absent without leave.

AWOL was a serious offense and could result in a harsh punishment, such as forfeiture of pay, reduction of rank, and even confinement to the base. Fearing the worst, I went straight to the company's headquarters to complain about the cook's capricious order. Luckily, the company commander, a young captain from Minnesota, took no punitive action. He simply reasoned with me, insisting that in the army everybody had to follow orders. He, too, had to follow orders, just like anybody else. I reminded him that he, as an officer, volunteered for the job and all that came with it. I instead was drafted. In the end, he ordered me back and asked the sergeant in charge of the mess hall to assign me to a different supervisor. The rest of the day went without incidents though the corporal kept on looking at me with seething resentment.

There was clearly a streak of the old rebellious Totò left in me. In this respect, I hadn't changed much since my childhood days. Whether at home, at school, or with my friends, I always questioned why things needed to be said or done in a given way. Now as then, I seldom accept what I read or hear without first determining for myself its truthfulness or practicality. This trait of my personality surfaced in all its peculiarity one night during basic training. That night, our company was engaged in an exercise that required us to crawl on our hands and knees for about one hundred yards. In the pitch dark and unable to see more than ten feet in front of us, we were to cover the distance carrying our backpacks and cradling our rifles in our arms. The officer in charge warned us against standing up because a machine gun would be firing live rounds at about six feet aboveground. I found it hard to believe they would be firing at such a dangerous low level. "If a kid got scared and jumped up, he could be killed," I reasoned. No sane commander would allow such a dangerous exercise. His career would be on the line should something go wrong.

There was no question about the machine gun firing real bullets. We could hear the whizzing sounds of the red-hot tracers flying about our heads. Naturally, because of the dark, we couldn't tell how high the bullets were flying. But the way I figured, the gun had to be shooting at an elevation of over seven feet to avoid killing someone. So I got up, bent over a little and, cradling my rifle, slowly crouched to the end of the field. A few guys, mostly young volunteers, were already there. They were all dusty and sweaty, and a few had scraped elbows and knees. I remember one of them looked at me and then turning to the others, shouted, "Hey, y'all, look at this little guy here. He ain't got a scratch on hisself. He ain't even got no dust on him." When I explained that I actually walked, they couldn't believe it. They thought I was crazy. I could've been killed; they reminded me. But while some thought I took a foolish risk, others agreed with my way of thinking and wished they had done the same thing.

By this time, I felt I was getting along with most of the soldiers in the barracks, and once in a while they invited me to come out and drink a beer or two with them. But there was a big cultural divide between them and me. Though we all lived the same life in the same environment, it was difficult for me to find a sense of commonality with them. I knew little about their culture, and they knew nothing about mine. I had never heard of baseball; they had never seen a soccer game. I could not relate to their high school stories just as they couldn't appreciate stories about my life in the old country. Most of them had never heard of Italy, much less of Sicily. The few who had heard of Sicily tended to associate it with the mafia. "Sicily? Oh, yeah! Mafia, Al Capone," they would say. Some had never traveled outside of their state and knew little about faraway countries. A young recruit from Mississippi once asked me where I was from. When I told him I came from Italy, he naively asked if I had come by train. I didn't bother explaining.

But more than anything, my main problem was my poor knowledge of the language, especially colloquial and everyday language. Whatever English I knew was largely bookish, acquired through schoolwork and reading anything I got my hands on. Thanks to my knowledge of other languages, I found that reading was much easier than speaking. Obviously, at times I had to look up words in the dictionary in order to make sense of some phrases. But looking up words didn't always help me understand the idiomatic expression. Of the many such instances, I remember the first time I read the expression "hit the road." Though I knew what the individual words meant, the phrase didn't make sense to me. How can you "hit" (in the sense of smack, punch, strike) the road? It took a reading through the many expressions listed in the dictionary under *hit* to learn its actual meaning. But for the most part, I was able to recognize many English words, in particular those rooted in Italian or Latin, such as government for *governo*, credit for *credito*, study for *studio*, assassin for *assassino*, and hundreds of other similar words. I had been in this country for little over three years and had already read Margaret Mitchell's voluminous *Gone with the Wind* and several of Hemingway's novels. At that time of my induction in the army, I was reading Arthur Schlesinger's lengthy biography of President Kennedy, *A Thousand Days*. Did I fully understand everything I was reading? I seriously doubt it. But my vocabulary improved considerably and with it my understanding of the language.

Although my language skills were improving, I still had difficulty communicating with some of my fellow recruits. Their speech consisted of street talk colored with a lot of F words. Theirs was the kind of language you don't find in books, at least not in the books I was reading. In addition, I struggled to understand some Southern boys whose speech was couched in heavy local drawls. Expressions such as "bob war" (barbed wire), "Ida claire" (I declare), "rye-cheer" (right here) seriously challenged my comprehension. Unlike reading, speaking didn't afford me the convenience of a dictionary or the time to reflect on the meaning of some of these weird sounding expressions.

Once, when a fellow soldier was late for chow and I asked him where he had been, he said something like, "I been running all over hell's half acre." There and then I had no idea what he was talking about. It took me a while to figure out that he had been "very busy . . . all over the place." Even when I knew what to say, my foreign accent made it difficult for many fellow soldiers to understand me. It was not uncommon for people to ask me to repeat my words slowly. Some got a kick out of hearing my bookish English pronounced with a heavy Italian accent. Just to hear my reaction, they would often call me names like "Hey, you motherfucker . . . shithead . . . asshole." I learned quickly what these expressions meant, but I didn't know how to use them like they did. So I would typically reply with Italianate epithets such as "You eediott . . . you eembeceell." Of course, they laughed. It took me a while to realize they were not making fun of me. They simply got a bang out of my accent. Many of them had never met a foreigner before. In fact, I was a novelty to them, especially for the good ol' country boys straight from the hills. But their fun did not last long. Within weeks, I grew familiar with their slang and began to reply with the same insults they were hurling at me. That was when they lost interest in their silly game.

The upshot of this experience was that it improved my camaraderie with fellow trainees. But there was something else I could not stomach. I hated when they called me *shorty*. I don't know why it upset me so much. It took me a long time to come to the conclusion that I was short, indeed. What was interesting about this name-calling was that though I felt picked on and humiliated, it ultimately led to an awakening that influenced me for the rest of my life. At the beginning, I did my best to ignore those who took pleasure in calling me shorty by dismissing them as just eediots. However, there were times when I could not hold back my anger and would confront them, saying something like "Who the f— are you calling shorty, hah?" Of course, they laughed off my challenge to a fight. But one hot summer day, during an all-day march in full gear and over rough terrain, I lost it. While I was struggling up a sandy hill, sweat stinging my eyes, and mosquitoes buzzing all over me, the guy behind me yelled, "Move it, shorty." In a flash, I unslung my rifle and was about to hit him in the face with the butt of the gun when all of a sudden I stopped and standing still, heard myself thinking, I AM SHORT.

This acknowledgment, silly as it may sound, changed my life. Simply put, I was finally free of the inferiority complex that for years had inhibited my aspirations and stifled my self-confidence. I no longer felt inadequate about who I was or what I wanted to do. Whenever I thought I was too short to deal with a particular obstacle, I instinctively looked for alternatives that allowed me to overcome that obstacle. Once, during a training exercise, my platoon had to ford a stream. At the point of crossing, the water was about five feet deep. Though the depth was no problem for the big boys, it was too deep for me. So I walked about a hundred feet downstream, where the water was not as deep, and got across like everybody else. Some of the guys made fun of me, calling me chicken for not daring to cross where they did. But I didn't care. This newly found attitude led me to pay less attention to what others said or thought of me. I took pride and satisfaction in my self-assurance. For one thing, the boys stopped calling me *shorty* as I no longer reacted the way they expected me to. If anything, they began to see me less as a source of amusement or curiosity and more as a resourceful guy with a mind of his own. Some even began to seek my company.

My language skills continued to improve as I began to interact more with fellow recruits. My street talk, in particular, was getting better by the day. During my first years in Reading, whether at home or at work, I spoke mostly in Italian and didn't really have much of an opportunity to learn common, everyday English. Sure, I heard the *old americani* talk, but there wasn't much I could learn from the way they spoke. Their speech, a crude mixture of English and Italian, was often difficult to understand. For instance, one of their favorite expressions was "Whattah eck wah keh." Though they knew the meaning, they had no idea what were the actual words they were using. They were just repeating what they had been hearing for years. Only when I acquired a decent command of the language was I able to figure out that they meant to say, "What the hell do I care." I also learned that "seeckeeniyenzah" was their rendition of *second hand*, and that their *doworri* stood for "don't worry."

My ability to understand the immigrants' peculiar speech was in part due to my growing familiarity with street language while in the army. This familiarity also helped me to forge a sense of common identity with fellow soldiers. But it was an identity of sorts. Obviously, we were all GIs doing a lot of things together: slept in the same barracks, got up and went to bed at the same time, wore the same uniform, ate in the same mess hall, and spoke the same language. But one can be with others in school, at work or at a football game, and still feel alone, unconnected. This was pretty much my case with a lucky exception. I enjoyed the solidarity of several soldiers of Italian descent who were eager to identify with my *italianity*. They saw me as a living reminder of their own immigrant ancestors just as Carmen De Angelo did back in Reading. Soon, they were all calling me gumpa. One of them, Tony Angillo, a big man from the Bronx, took a special liking to me. Big Tony was curious about my background and often asked me about Sicilian life and traditions. His grandparents were from a town near Palermo—he didn't know the name of the town.

The two of us, Big Tony and Little D—DiMaria—were always together, whether in the barracks or out on the company grounds. In some ways, he reminded me of Carmen, especially because of his temper. Like Carmen, he made sure nobody messed with his little gumpa. Once, he scared the living daylights out of one of our cooks who tried to hit me. The incident took place in the mess hall a few days before the end of our boot camp. While we were in line getting our food, a young cook slapped a serving of soupy mashed potatoes on my tray. I told him I didn't like his concoction and preferred a serving of vegetables. When he insisted I eat his mushy, butter-laden potatoes, I threw it back at him, saying, "You eat this shit." Before he could strike me with the big wooden spoon he had in his hand, Angillo reached across the counter, grabbed him by the collar and pushed him back with a threatening "Don't you dare, *capisc*?"

My children found it odd that I never mentioned Tony Angillo in my army stories after this incident. Did something happen that soured the friendship? If so, what? Actually, nothing happened between us, I assured them. After basic training, we simply lost track of each other. We were assigned our MOS and were sent to the appropriate military base to start our individual training. Tony went to Fort Sill just outside Lawton, Oklahoma, for his field artillery school, and I was ordered to Fort Sam Houston for my medic training, a few miles southwest of San Antonio, Texas. Those days, before iPhones and social media, it was not easy to stay in touch. Also, though soldiers wrote letters to their parents and girlfriends, letter writing was not common between soldiers. Sadly, Tony and I never saw each other again.

Fort Sam Huston

I was ordered to Sam Houston because it was one of the largest military medical training facilities in the US. I wondered why they sent me by plane and not by bus, as in Tony's case. Whatever the reason,

I would never forget that frightening experience in part because I had never flown before. The flight to Dallas was not that eventful other than the unsettling anxiety common among first-time flyers. Not so the Dallas-San Antonio flight. Although short, this leg of the trip was terrifying. The plane, a small single-propeller aircraft, had less than a dozen passengers on board. Anxiety turned into fear the moment the plane lifted off and began to fight its way through billowing thick black clouds. The clouds, a light wind, and a fine drizzle all but guaranteed we were in for a rough ride. We were hardly fifteen minutes into the flight when pelting rain and strong winds began to buffet and toss the plane in all directions. My knuckles turned white as I tightened my grip on the armrests, too scared to let go. I truly thought we were going to die.

My fear was somewhat allayed by the pilot's casual manner. A big man in his fifties, he looked more like a cowboy out of a Western movie than a professional pilot. He wore jeans, pointed cowboy boots, and a large cowboy hat. From under his graying thick mustache dangled an unlit, half-smoked cigar. No sooner had we taken off than he began to tell stories. Once in a while, he would turn around to look at the passengers and referring to his tales would say something like "About that . . . as I done told you . . . Let me tell you. . ." He was totally oblivious to the nerve-racking turbulence. His laid-back demeanor had a calming effect on the terrified passengers. It showed he had flown in these conditions before and there was nothing to worry about. Despite his cavalier unconcern about the storm, I was greatly relieved when we finally landed safely in San Antonio.

Following the instructions detailed in my official army orders, I took a taxi and reported to the base's processing center. That same afternoon, I was assigned to Company B, 2nd Battalion and taken to one of its barracks. The following day, I began my MOS training, together with the other soldiers who, like me, had just arrived. MOS school was vastly different from boot camp. Here, there was no curfew, no lights out, and no drill sergeants screaming orders at nervous recruits—no more long marches, daily drills, firing range, and the much-hated bugle-blasting reveille at five thirty in the morning. Soldiering was no longer a 24/7 job but a ten-hour workday. Come five o'clock, we shed our uniforms for the relaxed, summer look of T-shirts, sandals, and shorts. We were free to do and go as we pleased. Our most common recreational activities were bowling and swimming. The base had a huge bowling alley and an Olympic-sized swimming pool. Many went to the USO to shoot pool, play ping-pong or a card game. In the evening, there was always the enlisted men's club, where we could mingle and dance with female soldiers, commonly referred to as WACs (Women Army Corps). Some guys would catch the bus to downtown San Antonio, about six miles away. On the whole, life at Sam Houston was paradise when compared to life at Fort Gordon.

MOS training lasted six weeks. The instructors were nurses from the base hospital and older medic sergeants with battlefield experience in WWII or Korea. Some sergeants relished telling horrifying stories about gruesome wounds they had seen and treated in combat. They taught classes on all sorts of first aid procedures from how to use a thermometer, apply a tourniquet, give shots, dress wounds, treat common colds, and recognize symptoms of common diseases. This last item consisted of long and tedious lectures and documentaries. A disease the instructors tended to emphasize over and over was syphilis and its devastating effects on the human body. The presentations included sickening images of warts, ulcers, and open sores on the victims' mouths and genitals. Clearly they kept on showing these nauseating slides to impress upon us the seriousness of the disease and the importance of diagnosing it quickly and correctly. Perhaps to underscore the disease's debilitating effects, the instructors chose to show the stomach-turning images just before lunch. We, medics-to-be, failed to see the instructors' purpose of the timing and called it sadistic. We would later learn that syphilis and gonorrhea were actually the most common sexually transmitted infections we would see in our battalion infirmaries.

I recall with nostalgia the time spent in San Antonio. My English had gotten much better, and I was having an easier time making friends and doing things with them. Within days, I befriended some kids who, like me, listened to classical music, read books, and liked to shoot pool. After hours, usually around five o'clock, we would hang around the recreation center to watch TV, enjoy some form of live entertainment, or shoot pool. But our preferred spot was the swimming pool, where we could socialize with female soldiers. Some evenings, we would go to town to get something to eat and have a few drinks at a popular bar. Almost every weekend, we went to Mexico. One of my buddies, Jim Mason from Redding, California, had a souped-up 1957 Chevrolet, and four or five of us would drive to Nuevo Laredo, less than three hours south of San Antonio. Though a small town with mostly unpaved streets, Nuevo Laredo had dozens of bars with attractive working girls ready to please the hundreds of American GIs that descended on the town every weekend, especially on payday. Like most other weekend *soldier-tourists* from bases around San Antonio and Corpus Christi, we would get to Nuevo Laredo on Saturday around noon. As far as I can remember, the few guards at the border crossing hardly bother to look at our papers. We had GI written all over us, and the guards knew where we were going and why. They usually made some sexually charged comments and wished us good luck with the ladies. It was the same kind of good-natured banter when we returned early in the evening, broke and exhausted.

Except for the young ladies of pleasure, the town was a dump. Most bars were filthy, many with dirt floors, broken chairs, and grimy drinking glasses. Street vendors offered food covered with flies and had no running water to wash their hands. The girls were so busy working they hardly had time to wash. The many *tourists* so overwhelmed the few sanitary facilities that some took to urinating against the walls in alleyways. But we were not really concerned with hygiene; we just wanted to have a good time bar-hopping, drinking, and visiting with the girls. Considering this total lack of hygiene, it is a wonder none of us caught a serious disease.

Being around my buddies and doing things with them gave me a genuine sense of fellowship. Perhaps unconsciously, I was already embracing some of their values and becoming more like them, American. It was around this time that a sense of belonging began to influence my thinking and made it easier for me to make friends and enjoy their company. We spent a lot of time together going places, playing cards, and talking about the books we were reading. When Bob Follone was around, we would gather at the recreation center and listen to him play the piano. He was an accomplished pianist who played popular music with the same deftness he handled Chopin or Mozart. Often, he played songs we knew and sang along. I still have a bunch of pictures taken with many of those guys in San Antonio.

Sadly, the time came for the group to break up as each of us, now officially as army medics, was sent to his permanent assignment. Some were ordered to military bases overseas; others were stationed here in the US. I was sent to Fort Bragg, North Carolina.

At Sam Houston

CHAPTER 15

Fort Bragg

Before reporting for duty at their new post, all MOS graduates were given a two-week leave. After almost four months, I was finally home. I had never been away for that long. Everybody was happy to see me, and they had all sorts of questions about my life in the army: the places I had seen, the things I had done. My father, in particular, was proud to see his boy in uniform. For him, his son had become an American through and through. For the two weeks I was home, I was busier than I thought I would be. During the day, when people were at work, I read. In the evening, my cousins came over to play cards or sit around, making small talk and reminiscing about the old country. Some evenings, I visited with friends and relatives. I saw Carmen a few times. I still remember the terrible scare my old gumpa gave me—or I gave him—when I first went to see him; he almost killed me.

At that time, Carmen was renting a small apartment. As he had no phone, I just went to see him unannounced. When I knocked on his door, I heard a raspy low voice ask, "Who is it?"

Thinking of spooking a guy who didn't scare that easily, I decided to play a prank on him. I didn't answer and foolishly knocked again. When I didn't answer for the third time, he swung the door open and thrust a loaded .45 pistol on my chest. His glassy stare, the sweat dripping from his face, and the gun-hand shaking uncontrollably said it all; the man was terror-stricken. Then, as if recovering from a hypnotic trance, he whispered in punctuated words, "Don't you ever do that again?" I stood, frozen, unsure of what to make of the situation. For a split second, I thought he was going to shoot me. Clearly, it wasn't the warm welcome I expected. He finally calmed down and we went inside. What was going on? I wanted to ask, but I didn't.

After double-locking the door behind him, he sat on the bed and put the gun down next to him. With his listless gaze fixed on nothing in particular and talking as if to himself, he muttered, "I think I'm cracking up." He went on to tell me that for almost a week the mob and the FBI had him under surveillance. A couple of months earlier, Federal agents raided a gambling operation at a *club* where he worked as a doorman. He was among those taken into custody. But because he was just a doorkeeper, the FBI promised not to charge him with anything if he testified against the mobsters arrested. The mob, in turn, warned him against testifying, period. To show me he wasn't imagining things, he called me to the window and pointed to a Cadillac with Massachusetts plates parked across the street. "You see that car," he said, "it just sits there for one to two hours every day. It's either the mob or the FBI keeping an eye on me." There was no question in his mind that the *surveillance*, regardless of who was behind it, was clearly meant to intimidate him. He was so scared to leave the house that he was not going to work and had his girlfriend bring him groceries. He didn't know what to do. But time was running out. In a few days, he was scheduled to appear before a federal grand jury in Philadelphia and needed to decide whether to be a witness for the mob or the FBI. Either way, he was toast.

After weighing several options, I suggested he should consult a lawyer about taking the Fifth Amendment. At first, he appeared to dismiss my idea. After all, what did a little immigrant know about the American judicial system? But in the end, he took the Fifth and was ever thankful to his *smart* gumpa. In expressing his gratitude, he said he was surprised that I actually knew about the Fifth. He didn't know I was a voracious reader and understood much more than I was able to express verbally.

A person who was not so surprised about my actual knowledge of English was my boss and future friend Sergeant Patterson. Within a few weeks after I was assigned to his aid station in Fort Bragg, Sergeant Patterson recognized that although I spoke with a heavy foreign accent, I knew English better than most of the medics under his command. Strange as it may sound, he would often turn to me for questions dealing with the proper way of saying something or expressing a thought in writing. Once, he received a letter from the IRS. With his thick, reading glasses on, he read and reread the notice for a good five minutes trying to make sense of it. Finally, in exasperation, he threw it on my desk and shouted, "What's this here shit, D? You read it!" The paragraph-long letter informed Sgt. Leroy Patterson that the IRS wished to talk to him about some tax deductions he had claimed the previous year. When I told him what the document was about, he hit the roof and launched into a string of profanities against the government, the IRS, and anybody or anything that interfered with his freedom and privacy. But in the end, he calmed down and began to think about his predicament.

When I told this anecdote to my children, they wondered why the sergeant called me D. I explained that in my days, soldiers were commonly addressed by their last name, which was sewn just above one of their shirt pockets. People who had difficulty pronouncing the name DiMaria simply called me D. But what really puzzled them was the old sergeant's inability to understand a simple letter written in plain English. It also struck them as rather odd that he would ask a foreigner to read and explain the notice. "Was he illiterate?" they asked. "Why not ask other soldiers in the aid station?" they wondered. At that time, I too was puzzled. I didn't know then that a great number of old-timers were barely educated. Thousands of young men had been allowed in the army during WWII when the need for fighting men often led recruiters to overlook education and age requirements. They even enlisted men who could scarcely read and write. Leroy Patterson was one of those. He was given a bare-bones physical, declared fit for combat, handed a rifle, and shipped to Africa to fight the Germans.

Regarding other medics at the station, there were seven of them, each with specific duties, such as ambulance driver and medicine dispensers.

I was the station's clerk, responsible for filing reports, answering the phone, and seeing to it that the battalion medical records were up to date. Sergeant Patterson was convinced somehow that my understanding of the written language was above that of the average man under his command and insisted that the little foreigner be the unit's scribe. There were times when I felt that the sergeant took a personal interest in me because he saw me as an underdog determined to overcome whatever roadblocks stood in my way. He took me under his wing and soon became my mentor and friend. Several times, he took me to his house for dinner and on occasion, to a bar for a drink.

I remember an incident that showed how seriously he took his role as a mentor and protector. One afternoon, we went to a bar that had just opened a few blocks from his house. We ordered a couple of beers and sat at a table. A patron sitting not far from us kept on making gestures and grunting noises in obvious disapproval of my presence. He finally blurted out something that sounded like "Whas tis white boy doin' heah?" Sergeant Patterson, who was about six feet four inches tall and close to three pounds, stood up, looked straight at the man, and in a loud voice for everybody to hear, said, "Hees with me, y'all heah?" Still standing, he looked around for a few seconds as if daring anyone to disagree. No one said a word.

At Fort Bragg

There was no question in my mind that the old sergeant really liked me. He was always there for me whether to defend me against a bully or get me out of a jam. Once he truly stuck his neck out for me. I had been at Fort Bragg for about six months when I decided to learn how to drive and eventually buy a car. I asked my friend George Smith if he would be willing to teach me.

George, a carefree nineteen-year-old from Arizona, was happy to oblige, and soon we started going out in a Jeep, with me at the wheel. Since I didn't have a driver's permit, we usually practiced on a side road not far from the barracks. One Sunday afternoon, when most soldiers were off duty and a lot of people were out and about, George got a Jeep from the motor pool and the two of us went for a long ride. Though I was confident I could drive on a busy road, we decided to venture out on a narrow dirt road that led away from the post.

Sitting next to me, George started talking about his girlfriend back home, paying no attention to the road. He showed little concern about my increasingly high speed or the hazard of driving on a sandy trail. I learned very quickly that driving on sand was as dangerous as driving on snow. As we came to a bend in the road, the Jeep began to slide left and right. George grabbed the steering wheel in the vain attempt to stabilize the vehicle. But it was too late; the Jeep was already out of control and was going up a steep bank to the right. At the top of the slope and on a flat surface, it careened past some bushes and came to a stop when it crashed against a big tree. The impact crushed the front fender and smashed one of the headlights. Thankfully, neither of us got hurt, but we knew we were in deep trouble. We were able to drive back to the base but were apprehensive about taking the damaged Jeep to the motor pool. What would George tell the motor pool sergeant? Didn't he check out the Jeep to go to battalion headquarters? What was he doing outside the post? Who was driving?

Although I tried to reassure a visibly shaken George, telling him not to worry about anything. I knew I, too, was in hot water. Not only had I wrecked the Jeep, I had also driven without a driver's permit. In addition, I felt responsible for having talked George into taking out the vehicle from the motor pool under false pretenses. But worrying and feeling sorry didn't help. It was getting dark, and we had to do something. But what? After discarding a number of half-baked options, I thought it was time to call Sergeant Patterson. The old sergeant was at home and answered on the second ring. When he understood what the problem was, he told me to stay put and wait for him. He came right away. After assessing the damage, he chastised us for having been so irresponsible. But seeing that I was really frightened, he told me not to worry, he would take care of things. And he did. He made a phone call and told us to return the Jeep without saying anything to anyone. A few days later, I learned that Patterson's pal, the motor pool sergeant, had the vehicle repaired, and the incident was never reported.

I wanted to continue taking driving lessons from my friend George though he was easily distracted and not a good teacher. But Sergeant Patterson wouldn't hear of it. "I'll be your instructor until you get your license," he told me in a tone that allowed no argument. A month after the accident, I was ready to take the driver's test. I had the option of taking it with the army or the state. I chose to go with the state because a state-issued license allowed me to drive any vehicle, civilian or military. Two weeks later, the sergeant drove me downtown to the North Carolina Motor Vehicle Department for the test.

My First Car

Now that I was a licensed driver I was allowed and at times required to drive the aid station's vehicles, which included a Jeep, a truck, and the ambulance. As my driving skills improved and I began to savor the freedom of going places without having to rely on others, I started thinking about buying a car. But I knew nothing about cars. Once again, I turned to my mentor who knew all about cars, at least that was what I thought. As it turned out, the motor pool had a car that had been sitting on cement blocks for about eight months. Sergeant Patterson told me, "We should go take a look." It was a white and red, two-door 1959 Ford left there by a soldier who had been killed in Vietnam. His family was now selling it for $350. The sergeant, after walking around the vehicle looking for dents and kicking the tires, raised the hood, checked belts and hoses, and declared it in great condition. He told me it was a bargain, and I should buy it. And I bought it. I was on cloud nine and drove my big Ford everywhere. I was proud of myself. I had done what my friends back in Sicily could only dream of doing. I sent them pictures of myself at the wheel of the huge automobile. My pride was such that, though lacking driving experience, I decided to drive home to my parents in Reading. I was eager to show everybody my new purchase and prove I could drive in heavy traffic on major highways. The decision was foolhardy, to say the least. For one thing, I didn't know the way and had to rely on maps and gas station attendants for directions. Also, I just didn't realize how exhausting it was to drive 500 or so miles.

My Ford

It was a grueling experience. A distance that a seasoned driver might cover in less than nine hours took me over eleven hours. I didn't realize that driving slow was more dangerous than it was cautious. In fact, I nearly got killed going at around fifty mph. On the interstate between

Washington DC and Baltimore, I almost wound up under a truck that was coming behind me at full speed. Luckily, the driver was quick enough to apply the brakes, skidding all the way to a few feet from my red-and-white '59 Ford. What a scare! It didn't dawn on me I needed to go faster to avoid winding up under some big truck. If anything, the near-accident made me more *cautious* and of course, more nervous. When I finally got home I was bone-tired but relieved I made it all in one piece. Everybody was happy to see me, especially my parents. They saw my adventure not as a reckless disregard for life, but as a sign that their son was going about life like a real American.

Their happiness was tempered by the awareness that I had to go back soon. In fact, I left after about a week. This time I was fully aware and apprehensive about the long drive back though I knew which roads and exits to take. As it turned out, the real problem was not going to be the drive but the car. Halfway to Fort Bragg, the engine overheated and steam began to hiss from under the hood. I stopped at a gas station, lifted the hood, and foolishly started unscrewing the radiator cap. I had barely loosened the cap when a burst of steam gushed out, spilling hot water all around. I was fast enough to jump back and avoid being scalded. The station attendant, a grandfatherly figure wearing a greasy overhaul and a dirty baseball cap, came out of the garage and suggested I wait for the engine to cool off before pouring water into the radiator. He also showed me how to unscrew the radiator cap correctly to avoid getting burned. Maybe because he took pity on me or simply because he was a very thoughtful person, he gave me a gallon full of water to take along, should the engine overheat again. His last advice was to keep an eye on the temperature gauge and stop the car if the gauge started rising toward the red line. I thanked the man and got back on the road.

Engine overheating was so common those days that it wasn't surprising to see cars stranded alongside the road while the drivers waited around for the engines to cool off. ~~Tough~~ Though antifreeze was available; it was not widely used perhaps because of the cost. People often carried a gallon of water in the trunk of their car, just in case. For me, overheating would soon be the least of my worries. More serious mechanical troubles awaited me down the pike. About fifteen miles before reaching Fort Bragg, I stopped to get gas and check the water level in the radiator. When I tried to get back on the road, I noticed the car started moving slowly and then stopped. After several attempts to get it going, I gave up. The gas station attendant, pointing to a large oil leak under the car, told me there was a problem with the transmission. I had no idea what that meant, other than I had no transportation to get back to the base. In the meantime, it was getting late and I needed to do something. I called Sergeant Patterson. As usual, he told me not to worry; he would come right away. And he did. After looking under the hood for a few minutes, shaking hoses, yanking cables, and kicking the tires, he conceded that he had no idea what was wrong. In the end, he agreed with the mechanic; the transmission was shot. We decided to call a tow truck and had the car towed to a garage in Fayetteville, little over ten miles from Fort Bragg.

The following day, the garage people told me that to repair the transmission would cost $280 plus taxes. It was almost as much as I paid for the car. I cussed and cursed the day I bought that damn lemon. Two hundred and eighty dollars was a lot of money! But what choice did I have? I had the money to cover the cost, but I couldn't get to it right away because I had it in my savings account in Reading. I decided to call Pasquale and ask if he could help. The money came and within days I was once again behind the wheel of my big, red-and-white lemon. But no more than three weeks went by before the transmission started acting up, again? The mechanic refused to accept responsibility, insisting that the problem was unrelated to the work he had done. This was a different issue, which he could fix for only $100. As much as I liked my old car, I feared it was becoming a bottomless pit. I had to get rid of it. And I did, swearing not to buy another used car again. I could get a Volkswagen for $1600. I was told. But where could I get that kind of money in such a short period of time? Bank loans were out of the question for a GI making roughly $1700 a year. So I called my parents and had them send me $1600, promising to repay them as soon as I went back to Reading and got the money out of my savings account. Cash in hand, I drove the limping piece of junk to a Volkswagen dealership and traded it in for a brand-new 1966 Volkswagen Beetle. It turned out to be a good deal and a great little car.

Sergeant Patterson approved of the new car though I suspect it hurt his feelings that his little friend didn't ask for his advice. He never said a word about the perceived slight, but he did wonder where I got that kind of money. I explained that after my parents paid off their mortgage, my brother and I kept our paychecks for ourselves and opened our respective savings accounts. By the time I was drafted, I had saved a little over $3500. By a soldier's standards, I was a rich man. It was not uncommon for fellow recruits to come to me for a small loan, even on payday, strange as it may sound. Actually it wasn't that strange. We were paid in cash every first of the month, early in the morning. By ten o'clock, there were poker and blackjack games going on in every barracks. Before the day was over, many troops were broke, having lost their entire paycheck. They had to have some spending money until the next payday or until they got an allowance from home. For some, it was a vicious circle. By the time they repaid their debt—usually no more than $30—they were broke again. I never charged interests, but I did have a strict rule. On payday, I expected the *borrowers*—typically the same two or three guys—to bring me what they owed. I just didn't want to chase people around and beg for my own money.

The sergeant found it hard to understand how the little foreigner could've put away $3500 in no more than three years. After all, as I had told him many times, I never took home more than $60 or $70 a week from my job at the hosiery mill or the shoe factory. In addition, I helped my parents pay off Uncle Charlie, the debt back in Italy, and the mortgage. In view of all this, again how could I have saved that kind of money? The old sergeant wanted to know. I reminded him that I was very frugal. Both my brother and I lived with our parents and didn't pay for room and board. We had no bills or expensive habits to speak of. Except for going bowling or dancing once in a while, we usually stayed home, playing cards or sitting around telling stories. I always enjoyed a card game and loved listening to my father's stories about the olden days. Frequently after dinner, we would sit under the leafy bower of grapevines in the back of the house and listen to him and his friends musing over their distant past. I enjoyed their tales because they told my story: where I came from and who I was. This was one of the many reasons I went home every time I had a chance. Thanks to my new reliable Beetle and my growing self-confidence behind the wheel, I drove to Reading at least every six weeks.

D, the Doc

Naturally, I didn't just take off work and drive home whenever I pleased. First, I made sure I finished all the paperwork on my desk, especially the monthly reports to battalion headquarters. Second, I always asked Sergeant Patterson if it was OK for me to take a day off, typically a Friday or a Monday. His reaction was always the same; he had no problem with me leaving early provided I had all my work done. The paperwork was only part of my job. Just like other medics assigned to the aid station, I gave out over-the-counter medications, such as aspirin, medicated creams, and common cold remedies. At times, I gave flu shots and other vaccinations required by army regulations. But I was mainly responsible for keeping and updating the immunization records of all the soldiers in the battalion, about a thousand men. In addition, when no other medic was available, I drove to the hospital to pick up needed supplies like Band-Aids, tongue depressors, gauze, syringes, antacids, and other items normally found in an army aid station.

Curiously, a remedy popular among our *sick* soldiers was a codeine-based syrup used to treat cough, colds, pain, and other minor ailments. Patients swore it was a cure-all drug and kept on coming back for more. Their praise of the syrup's effectiveness together with their frequent requests for more made me believe in the drug's medicinal benefit. As it didn't require a prescription, I gave it liberally. In so doing, I was following Sergeant Patterson's lead. I saw him dispensing the *miraculous* syrup rather generously to some of his old buddies who came in regularly with their little six-ounce bottles. Was he aware the medication was addictive and his friends were abusing it? Did he know they were getting hooked on it? I certainly did not. I had absolutely no idea I was facilitating a drug habit until the hospital pharmacist reminded me that codeine was addictive. Baffled by my request for an ever-larger amount of the syrup, he began to ask questions about how I was dispensing it. It didn't take him long to figure out what was going on and warned me to dispense it sparingly, given the risk of addiction.

From then on I heeded the pharmacist's advice. As to be expected, the habitual *patients* were disappointed. I told them they had to go to the infirmary or the hospital if they needed more than I could give them. Naturally, they didn't like the new restriction. Some tried to bribe me; others invoked our friendship. But I stood by the rule, with one exception, Jim Rose the company clerk. I gave him more than the regular dose and sometimes enough for him to take it to his lady friend. This special treatment was part of our unspoken agreement—the extra syrup for his not reporting my unauthorized absences from the company. Jim was an easygoing lanky young man from Michigan who tried to get along with everybody. Like all company clerks, he carried a lot of weight. Among his many duties, he was to report those who were absent at morning roll call. It was our understanding that he would not report me AWOL whenever I failed to return on time from my leave. This happened often, especially after Sergeant Patterson retired. But the arrangement had its limits. Once, I thought of remaining in Reading for three days beyond my authorized leave. When I called Jim to see if it was OK, he was very nervous and told me to return right away. He couldn't risk reporting me present any longer because the company's first sergeant was getting suspicious and had started asking questions. I went back that same day and to Jim's relief, I hollered, "Present" when he called my name at morning roll call.

My job was not just dispensing medications and clerking. I was also Sergeant Patterson's right-hand man when dealing with battalion headquarters. Whenever the battalion requested information about our unit's combat readiness, the sergeant relied on me to gather and report the requested data. I always accompanied him for the monthly meetings with the battalion command. Though I was the lowest-ranked man at the station, he preferred to take me along because I was the best prepared to provide the exact number of soldiers reporting sick every morning and not available for duty. I knew how many we treated at the station, how many we sent to the infirmary, and how many went straight to the hospital. I was also better informed to answer questions on whether we had everything necessary to keep the aid station running properly. Almost at every meeting, the colonel asked about the status of our medical supplies and our vehicles' readiness. He insisted that all the unit's soldiers be up to date with the immunizations required for overseas deployment. I guess he thought we could be ordered to Vietnam at any time and wanted the unit to be combat-ready. The officers appreciated my overall performance in answering their questions and often congratulated Sergeant Patterson on how efficiently he ran the aid station. It was at one of these meetings that a captain suggested I enroll at North Carolina State University in Fort Bragg. The school was offering university courses for military personnel at our base. "Would I be interested?"

CHAPTER 16

In College

At first, I was puzzled by the captain's suggestion. Certainly, being a good clerk at an aid station hardly qualified me for college work. Then, why did he bring up the NCSU program? Did he find it strange to hear my bookish English expressed in a heavy foreign accent? Was he making fun of English? Was he being sarcastic? As it turned out, his advice had nothing to do with these concerns. He thought of the NCSU program one day when he noticed I was reading Fitzgerald's *The Great Gatsby*. He was surprised that a recent immigrant like me would be interested in such an American classic. He asked me about my other readings and what I planned to do once I got out of the army. When I told him I planned to go to college, he encouraged me to look into the NCSU Extension Program. Naturally, I was interested. The opportunity rekindled the hopes that my SAT failure had dashed a year earlier. In a few days, I learned that NCSU professors came to Fort Bragg two evenings a week and offered a variety of college courses. I also found out that the army would pay for my books and tuition if I passed the courses I enrolled in. To my great relief, I was told that no SAT was required. I registered for elementary math and American history in the first summer session. Classes would begin in a couple of weeks, and I couldn't wait to start. I was so thrilled that I called home and told everybody I was going to go to college, after all. My mother ecstatic; my father simply said, "I knew you could do it. Make us proud, son."

I must confess that in all my excitement, there were moments when I wondered whether I was taking on too much and setting myself up for failure. I went through that experience when I took the SAT and feared a repeat of that humiliation. But this time I got it right. I did OK my first semester though my grades were lower than I had hoped for, B- in math and B in American history. I needed to learn how to study and improve my performance. And I did. Of the ten courses I took at Fort Bragg, my lowest grade was that B- I got in math. I was happy with my accomplishments, so was Sergeant Patterson. "My boy is going to college," he would tell his old buddies who stopped by the station from time to time. I took the sergeant's boasting with proud embarrassment.

I was thankful for the army's generous support and the advantage of being on a university campus, virtually of course. The school building was near the center of the post, within walking distance for most students. In my case, since my barracks were little over a mile away, I was authorized to use a Jeep out of the battalion's motor pool. Classes met after duty hours, twice a week from 6:30 p.m. to 9:30 p.m. with a short break in between. The schedule was convenient because it allowed students, including military dependents, to work during the day and go to school at night. Soldiers attending classes were normally excused from night drills or duties. Not everybody took two courses. Some took just the 6:30 p.m.–8:00 p.m. class either because they wanted to be home early with their families or because of a time conflict with their jobs, especially the civilians. The fifty or so students—most of them in their thirties or forties—were a mixed bag of enlisted men, officers, and military dependents. Many had been taking classes for a while and were working toward a BA; others wanted to beef up their resume and enhance their chances for promotion; a few were beginners like me, taking courses randomly without a particular degree in mind. Oddly, as far as I knew, I was the only foreigner at the school. I say oddly because there were hundreds of foreigners at the base, mostly Hispanics.

Though my English was still halting, it didn't prevent me from interacting with my classmates. Once people started talking to me, they realized that my vocabulary was far above what they expected from a foreigner. Among other things, they were eager to know where I came from and when and why I came to America. Of course, the moment I said I was from Sicily, they wanted to know all about the mafia. Did the mafia kill a lot of people? Was it safe to walk the streets at night? What were the chances of being caught in the crossfire between mobsters? I assured them that the mafia was a criminal organization just like many others. I also explained that today's *mafiosi* derive their power and influence more from bribing public officials than from the barrel of a gun. They resort to violence mostly against each other only when *civilized* means of persuasion fail. My explanation threw them for a loop because for them mafia meant indiscriminate murder and bloodshed. Al Capone came to their minds. They grew up watching *The Untouchables* on TV and the popular gangster movies at the local theaters. But besides my foreign peculiarity, our conversation seldom went beyond typical school-related questions, such as "What's your major?" or "When do you expect to graduate?" They lost me when they started talking about football or their wartime experiences. But on the whole, I must admit they were very friendly.

The new responsibilities that came with going to school forced me to learn how to make better use of my time. Within a few weeks, I fell into a routine that allowed me to do my schoolwork and manage to have a life at the same time. I tried to study during the day when there wasn't much to do at the station. Sergeant Patterson made sure that other medics didn't bother me in my little office. Sometimes, especially if I had a paper to write, he would give me the entire afternoon off. Also, I had his permission to stay at the station after hours, if I needed to. I was blessed to have such a good man as my boss. Unfortunately, he was just a few months away from retirement. As I said before, he was a good friend, and I knew I would miss him. When he announced he was turning in his retirement papers, I began to fear that whoever replaced him wouldn't be so approving of my studying while on duty. He would definitely put a stop to my frequent three-day weekends. I had heard that many sergeants, especially younger ones, ran their stations strictly by the book.

Last Days in the Army

It turned out that my fears were unfounded as Sergeant Patterson was not replaced. Soon after he retired, all of our medics were sent to Vietnam one by one, leaving me in charge of the aid station. I was my own boss. It was plain luck that I was not sent to Vietnam. At that time, I was just a legal resident, and according to regulations, noncitizen soldiers could not be sent overseas unless they shipped with their unit. Although I was the only medic left, the battalion commander Lieutenant Colonel Deutch refused to close the station. So there I was, manning the entire operation all by myself. I kept the place open without much difficulty, thanks in part to the colonel's full support. "If you need anything, just call my office," he told me. He was true to his word. Once when a young lieutenant rudely told me he was too busy to send some of his troops to the station for overdue immunizations, I called Colonel Deutch. Within twenty minutes, a very unhappy lieutenant showed up at the station with the troops I had scheduled for shots.

The problem with being the only one at the station was that I had to lock it up whenever I had to go somewhere. This irritated the company's first sergeant because there was no one there to take his calls. He also heard complaints from officers and enlisted men who found the place closed time after time. Why was the station closed? Where was D? Why wasn't he answering the phone? What really frustrated him was that he understood I needed to close the station in order to take medical records to the infirmary, go turn in monthly reports at battalion headquarters, or pick up supplies at the hospital. How could I be in two places at once? When he finally had enough of my *excuses*, as he put it, he decided to assign Private First Class Julio Martinez to help me. Julio was a nice young Puerto Rican who barely spoke English. His MOS was what his friends called *carbonero*. His work consisted of shoveling coal into the furnaces that kept the barracks' boilers running. Such a job did not require knowledge of English since he didn't have to interact with anyone.

For me, Julio's limited English was not an issue. I spoke enough Spanish to tell him what needed to be done: shelving supplies, keeping the place clean, and answering the phone when I was away. And there was the rub. Julio's spoken English was practically nonexistent. Whenever he answered the phone, which he always picked up on the second ring, he greeted the caller with a soft and protracted, "Alooh." Whatever he heard from the other end, he replied with his hardly audible *alooh* and kept on repeating it until the caller hung up in frustration. Soon the first sergeant realized that his solution was not working. Not only had he heard from complaining callers, he himself was also often on the receiving end of Julio's monotonous aloohs. A good thing that came out of this failed solution was that it got the sergeant off my back. But he had no other choice as he found himself between a rock and a hard place. The company was so understaffed that he could not replace Julio with someone more suitable for the job. He could only spare the *carboneros* who, because of their language limitations, couldn't do much else other than man the furnaces. As far as I was concerned, Julio was a real asset. His presence allowed me to keep the station open while I went away on errands, not always work-related, I must admit. Also, Julio kept the place clean and made sure people didn't walk out with medical supplies they were not allowed to have.

I must say that Julio, his language limitations notwithstanding, was of great help. To begin with, we became good friends. What facilitated our friendship was the fact that we were both foreigners, and I spoke enough Spanish to carry on a casual conversation. He soon introduced me to his buddies, mostly first- and second-generation Hispanics. They accepted me as one of their own, and before I knew it, we were a happy bunch. We usually went to the USO, a club for enlisted personnel. There we played cards or bingo, shot a game of pool, or saw a movie. Sometimes, USO personnel would organize live entertainment in the form of a comic skit starring fellow soldiers. More often, entertainment consisted of a makeshift band performing mostly country music. On weekends, we would go to a bar in town to drink and socialize with the waitresses. Often, we just sat around the barracks nursing a six-pack of beer and telling stories. A member of the group, Juan Martinez, was a born storyteller, and I loved to just sit and listen to his tales. We all spoke Spanish though my knowledge of the language was limited and largely bookish. But soon I became fluent in their street talk, a language laced with blasphemies and profanities.

Honorably Discharged

Sadly, just like all the other guys I befriended in the service, I never saw my Hispanic buddies after I left the army. But I never forgot them. Even years later, whenever I found myself in a crowded place, such as an airport or a stadium, I always looked around to see if I recognized someone from my army days. To my disappointment, never once did I meet someone I served with. There were times when I wondered—if for a split of a second—whether I really had been in the service. Of course, I had. I still have the photos, the memories, and the discharge papers. Yet I never stopped looking and hoping for an encounter with my army past.

Once, while taking a walk and talking with my son Pat about my army days, he asked me about life at Fort Bragg and my Hispanic friends. Did I know them long enough to call them friends? How long were we together? I knew them for little more than a year. I told him and we were together until I was discharged. I became a civilian in July 1966, after twenty-seven months of service, three months beyond the required two-year duty. The reason for the extension was that the battalion commander asked me to stay on for an extra ninety days. He needed that much time, he told me, to bring the aid station to full strength in terms of both supplies and personnel. During the previous months, he had been requesting additional medics and more vehicles, including a new ambulance. He repeatedly reminded me to make sure the troops' immunization records were up to date. The medical unit had to be fully staffed and equipped before the battalion could be classified as combat-ready. This classification would qualify the unit for combat duty in Vietnam, which was what the colonel wanted.

Was Colonel Deutch's eagerness to go to Vietnam a death wish? If not, why did he want to volunteer for such a dangerous assignment? Was he that gung ho about war? No! It was nothing like that. I told

Pat. The colonel's eagerness was not a death wish. And no, he was not a war fanatic. He was a professional soldier willing to risk his life for the opportunity to advance his career. Just like many other Vietnam volunteers, he was not inspired by patriotic fervor, especially at a time when the *real* patriots were not the guys at the front, but the antiwar protesters marching in the streets of America. People were denouncing the war as immoral and as a senseless sacrifice of human lives. Demonstrators routinely gathered in front of the White House, chanting antiwar slogans. A jingle that deeply affected President Johnson was "Hey, hey, LBJ, how many kids did you kill today?" Americans of all ages and backgrounds, men and women, college students, and even Vietnam veterans were staging frequent demonstrations in almost every major city in the country. But the protests, often violent, didn't change the minds of career soldiers willing to go to a war zone and risk a pointless death. For them, a tour of duty in a war zone was an opportunity to get combat pay, which added hundreds of dollars to their monthly paycheck. More importantly, it offered them the chance to secure the promotion that had long eluded them. Some even went back a second time. Our colonel was one of those.

For most soldiers, unfamiliar with newspaper reports or TV news about the war, the protesters were a bunch of peaceniks, restless college students, and commie agitators. As for me, I had no particular feeling about the war mostly because I was not aware, just like many of my fellow soldiers, of the actual carnage and the futility of the entire enterprise. Why then did I choose to remain in the army for an extra three months? To be sure, extending my stay was not my choice. The colonel gave me an alternative I couldn't accept. He told me that if I didn't volunteer to stay, he had the authority to delay my discharge for an additional six months. I didn't know if he could actually keep me in service, but the threat was too real for me to ignore. So I signed on the dotted line. Perhaps reading too much into my consent to stay, he tried to convince me to reenlist and become a career man. Not only would he see that I received a $5000 reenlistment bonus, but he would also recommend me for OCS, Officer Candidate School. After six months of rigorous training, I would be commissioned as second lieutenant. But he soon realized I was not interested in a military career and dropped the subject.

Nothing was going to disrupt my plans to go to college. I had to leave the army, period. I got out not a day too soon as the battalion was ordered to ship out for Vietnam the following month. Had I still been in, I would have been required to go with the unit and deployed to the front line, like most medics. Around this time, army medics were taking such a high number of casualties that they couldn't be replaced fast enough. The intensified TV coverage of the war with its gruesome footage had already seeped into the American living room, making people aware of the bloody price the country was paying for a conflict they didn't understand. Daily reports of staggering troop losses continued to fuel mass antiwar demonstrations throughout the country, especially on college campuses.

The impact of the protests hit home for me a few months before I was discharged, that is, when our unit began to train for crowd control. Every day we would line up in platoon-sized formations, carrying gas masks and rifles with fixed bayonets. For hours, the sergeants would drill us on moves and techniques that in the end were hardly appropriate for crowd control. Some gung-ho instructors told us we could use our rifles if the protesters turned violent. Luckily, we were never called to the task. It would have been a disaster worse than the massacre that would take place four years later at Kent State. That slaughter started when members of the Ohio National Guard were ordered to fire on the crowd, killing four students and wounding eleven others. News of the murders shocked the nation and led to more widespread demonstrations. Thank God I never took part in any bloodshed.

It was puzzling to some of us that they would include medics in crowd control exercises. Wasn't that the job of special units? A medic's role was to take care of casualties, not to inflict them. Our sergeants reminded us that whatever our MOS, we were first and foremost soldiers. Just like any other GI, medics were required to carry their rifles as well as perform all sorts of other tasks, such as guard duty or the despised KP. They had a point. But crowd control was not the role or the mission of regular troops. The job was better left to the police who were trained and equipped to deal with civil unrest. Also, it was an oversimplification to compare crowd control with a soldier's other duties. For one thing, these tasks did not require much training; anyone could walk a guard post or wash dishes and peel potatoes. Some duties, such as KP, even allowed for substitutes. KP was backbreaking and boring: peeling potatoes for hours on end, scrubbing and washing huge pots and pans, and mopping the floor over and over. You reported for duty at five o'clock in the morning and were under the cooks' whimsical orders until you were dismissed around eight o'clock at night. I detested kitchen detail so much that whenever my turn came up, I paid someone to take my place.

Guard duty, on the other hand, did not allow for substitutes. All those on the roster were required to report to the guardhouse at 8:00 p.m. and be on duty until six in the morning. While at Fort Bragg, I pulled guard duty at least four times. Although the task was not demanding, it was a drag having to get out of bed every four hours, following a schedule of two hours on and four hours off. But unlike the mindless KP, the experience could prove hair-raising. Whether patrolling empty buildings or ammunition dumps, it could be quite scary walking our post in the middle of the night. Any sound, even the snap of a twig or the rustling of dry leaves sent our blood pressure up. Needless to say, we were armed and could defend ourselves if we had to. We carried a rifle and a few bullets though we were instructed to keep the ammunition in our pockets. We might load the gun only if we felt our life was in danger. To make sure we followed the instructions and kept the rifles unloaded, the duty officer would come by to check on us and sometimes demand to see the bullets. But I am sure soldiers who got really scared didn't hesitate to load their rifles. I sure did.

Once, on a windy October night, I was assigned to guard a bank nestled in a wooded area near a small brook. The seclusion, the noises coming out of the streamlet, the ruffling of the leaves, and the dim lighting created an eerie scene. As the wind picked up, the lights started swinging from the lampposts, casting ghostly, shifting shadows. I was frightened. I heard voices and footsteps and saw armed thieves lurking in the woods. Of course, it was all in my head. I was so scared that I inserted the magazine in the rifle and loaded a bullet in the chamber. Soon, I saw the headlights of an approaching vehicle. Rifle at the ready, I called out, "Who goes there?" It was the OD or officer of the day making his rounds. He stayed long enough to ask me a few questions about my post and then drove away. I was relieved he did not get out of the Jeep to inspect my rifle. I would have been in serious trouble. Interestingly, his inspection had the healthy effect of snapping me out of the creepy world my wild imagination had dwelled in. The moment he left, I unloaded the gun and went on to walk my post, no longer seeing danger where there was none.

The next time I got really scared, the threat was not in my mind. Little over a month before I was discharged, I was assigned to guard an area the size of a football field full of vehicles assembled for shipment to Vietnam. The moon was almost full and its light glinted off the parked Jeeps and trucks, forming dark shadows between them. After about a half an hour of walking my post, I began to see figures moving rapidly, almost jumping from vehicle to vehicle. At first, I thought I saw ghosts. But I soon became convinced that actual people were out there. *Thieves*, I thought. Overcome with fear and hands shaking, I loaded my rifle. When I saw the silhouettes reappear from behind the vehicles, I pointed the gun in their direction and yelled, "Who goes there? Come out with your hands up or I'll shoot." That scared the *ghosts* to death and before I could repeat my warning I heard them cry out, "Don't shoot, D, it's us, don't shoot." I recognized the voices and was relieved to see that the whole thing was meant as a practical joke. Three of my barracks' pals, knowing when and where I would be on duty, decided to spook me. To make sure their prank would really frighten me, they draped themselves in bedsheets and began appearing and disappearing between vehicles. They succeeded in their intent, but their nervous laughter made it clear they fully understood how close they came to being shot.

The next day at the barracks, I didn't downplay how much they scared me, neither were they proud of their stunt. We all agreed on how their sophomoric game could have gotten them killed. They never thought of the danger they said; they just wanted to have a good laugh before I got out of the army. Perhaps their prank was an unconscious expression of mixed feelings of envy and betrayal. On the one hand, they wished they were the ones getting out; on the other hand, they felt I was betraying our friendship by leaving. They couldn't understand why I refused the colonel's offer to go to OCS school. Whatever their feelings, I would be out of the army in a few weeks. I had already joined the chorus of those who were about to be discharged. Among the soon-to-be civilians, it was routine to get up in the morning and shout the number of days they had left, "Twenty-nine days left, y'all . . . eighteen more days, five days and I'm f— out of here." They also made it a point to distinguish themselves from those who had decided to reenlist, calling them lifers, which for them was synonymous to *losers*.

But their eagerness to get out of the army didn't mean they had a clear idea about their future in the real world. Many, in fact, didn't know what was waiting for them outside. As for me, I knew what I wanted to do. I wanted to go to college. Though my plan was to enter NCSU-Raleigh right away, I had to wait until the following year because—out of pure ignorance—I failed to apply for admission. I thought I could just show up for classes.

But the delay wasn't a total waste of time as I was nearly broke and needed to make some money. By the time I left the army, I had gone through most of my savings and wasn't about to impose on my parents. So I got a job as a shipping clerk at Penn Iron Works, a small steel mill in Reading. I was responsible for keeping track of customers' orders, mostly pieces of heavy machinery. Every morning, blueprints in hand, I would go through the shop looking for items ready to be shipped. After tagging them, I would call one of the local trucking companies and schedule a pickup. Often I had to deal with irate customers who complained about late deliveries or defective orders. When my excuses weren't enough to calm them down, I would put my boss on the phone and let him explain or apologize.

I was with Penn Iron for a full year even though the job didn't pay well. Two dollars an hour wasn't a lot those days. But I lived at home and didn't have to pay for room and board. Also, I planned to stay at the job only until I started school the following August. Besides, the work was easy and the bosses were friendly. They were happy with the way I did my job and were more than accommodating whenever I asked for a day off or leave work early, usually on weekends. They even offered to pay for me to take courses in mechanical engineering at a local community college. I turned down the offer, explaining that I was going to college the following fall. They understood and wished me the best.

PART 3

College and Academia

CHAPTER 17

A Family Gathering

It had been a while since my grandchildren asked me to talk about my life. They had always seemed interested in my past and often asked me to tell them stories about my childhood. Vita assured me they were still interested; they were just too busy with their school activities lately. Whatever the reason, for a while, there hadn't been much talk around the house about Grandpa. But Vita was right, the kids had not lost interest in Grandpa and his stories.

 It was Thanksgiving, and as usual, all my three kids and their respective families were at the house. The food, the wine, and the loud talk added to the festive mood. As it often happened, when the siblings got together, they reminisced about their growing-up days. Vita's kids were particularly interested in some of the stories Uncle Pat and Aunt Jenna told and retold, always with a slight twist. Jenna never failed to recall the time I first punished her. She was about eight years old when she decided to take ten dollars from the family kitty. With money in her pocket, she went "shopping" at a garage sale down the street. She came back, proudly showing the souvenirs she had bought for everyone in the family. She did not expect my harsh reaction. I slapped her hard, warning her never again to take money without permission.

 "What if—" she said.

I shouted, "That was all the money we had and needed to buy food."

The slap on her face still stung, and she never forgot the lesson, she concluded.

Though I remembered the episode, I didn't recall slapping her. But I was not about to question her recollection. I knew Pat would. He usually found fault with his sister's version of the incident or any other incident she recalled. He pointed out that with the money she "stole," she bought a gift just for herself, at least that's how he remembered it. Clearly, he just wanted to ruffle her feathers, as he liked to do every time they got together. The contrasting recollections inevitably led to back-and-forth charges of poor memory and early senility. This brother-sister banter was short-lived but typical. Whenever one told a story about me or their own childhood, the other found ways to question its accuracy. And the bickering started. They often called on me to set the record straight, but I, as usual, refused to get involved. In a way, sparring typified their relationship. As long as I can remember, those two always argued about everything just for the sake of arguing.

An often-told incident, on whose accuracy they couldn't agree, had to do with my parents. It was their recollection of a story I told them when they were kids. As Pat remembered it, Grandpa Giuseppe and Grandma Vita had been married for just a few months when they engaged some cattle rustlers in a gun battle. One summer night, the story went, the young couple was sound asleep in their farmhouse when the furious barking of their dogs awakened them.

"Who could it be at this hour?" they wondered fearfully.

They were not expecting anyone. Obviously, strangers were prowling around. They had to be thieves, Giuseppe suspected with growing apprehension. But were they so daring as to attempt a robbery under the bright light of a full moon and with the owners on the premises? His suspicions were confirmed when he peered through the cracks of the bedroom window and saw three men driving the cows out of the barn and toward a waiting wagon. The young couple got their guns and from inside the house and began shooting at the thieves. The gunfight went on for almost a quarter of an hour before the rustlers fled, leaving the animals behind and carrying with them a fellow thief who had been wounded in the gunfight. The authorities were never called, but the thieves learned to stay away from Giuseppe's farm.

Now, it was Jenna who found fault with Pat's version, and again, they began questioning each other's memory. After a while, my granddaughter, Stella, asked them to stop quibbling and tell stories they agreed on. Pat started telling the story of the ghosts who tried to scare me while I was on guard duty, but the kids had already heard that one many times. They wanted to know what Grandpa did after he left the army. They asked me to talk about it. Though I was not feeling 100 percent, I gave in.

I began by telling them how excited I was when I first received the acceptance letter from the NCSU Admissions Office. The letter explained that I had been admitted as a sophomore and that the school classified me as a North Carolina resident. This meant I would be paying in-state tuition.

"What does that mean?" Stella wanted to know.

"Very simple," I said. "If you go to a public university outside your state, you have to pay out-of-state tuition. In most cases, that is nearly double what in-state residents pay. I hope you keep that in mind when you start applying for college."

"But even as an in-state resident, how could you afford college? It was not just tuition. There were also living expenses," Stella pointed out, eager to show that she already knew about college costs.

I explained that, besides the money I had saved working at the iron mill, I was getting the GI Bill. As an army veteran, I qualified for federal aid. The law, which dates back to WWII, provided a range of benefits for returning veterans, including financial assistance for those wishing to further their education. For some people, the draft squandered two years of their youth, not for me. For me, it was a blessing in disguise. It was no small matter that the government paid me about $150 a month for my first four years in college. It may not seem much by today's standards, but back then, it was a generous allowance. Tuition at NCSU was less than $200 a semester. But what I got out of the army was far more valuable than just money. Among other things, it gave me the opportunity to learn spoken English in a way I couldn't have learned had I stayed in Reading, living among other immigrants. In the army, I became familiar with a great variety of regional accents. I got so good at distinguishing types of speech that I could tell whether a fellow soldier was from Mississippi, South Carolina, or Massachusetts.

I also learned a lot about Americans. In particular, I was exposed to meaningful cultural peculiarities, such as the enduring friction between North and South. At times, you had the impression the Southerners were still living the Civil War. They were still bickering about the causes that led to the secession and its disastrous outcome. Even a hundred years later, Southerners talked with disdain about the well-armed, inept, and barbarous Yankee soldiers while speaking with pride about the poorly equipped and fearless Confederate rebels. They glorified their famed war heroes, especially the great Robert E. Lee and the staunch Stonewall Jackson while vilifying the Northern generals for the suffering and the devastation they wreaked on the South. They reserved their strongest animosity for William Tecumseh Sherman, whose scorched earth tactics earned him the infamous distinction of devil incarnate. The Northerners, for their part, teased the Southerners, calling them country bumpkins and incestuous hillbillies. They joked that Southerners were prone to have sex with family members and tended to marry their own cousins. I was not interested in their bickering though I found amusing and instructive the warring perspectives about a past Americans were still trying to define. But perhaps the most significant benefit I got from my military service was the opportunity to take college courses and enroll at the university. It was the only way I could have gone to college since I didn't pass the SAT.

At North Carolina State University

And so it happened that I, full of apprehensive excitement and with the money from the GI. Bill, began my pursuit of higher education. The moment I had wished all my life had finally arrived. In early August 1967, I packed up my belongings and drove to NCSU in Raleigh. Though I didn't have much stuff to take with me, my parents insisted on helping with the bags and the suitcase. My mother gave me a basket of homemade cookies and a large *'mpanata* (a type of pie filled with spinach), which she had made the night before. My father put two $20 bills in my hand, a token of his investment in his boy's future. After the final embraces and the drive-carefully exhortations, I was on my way. I knew the way, having driven the route many times while at Fort Bragg. Once I reached Raleigh, I stopped a couple of times for directions to the NCSU campus.

When I arrived at the dorm, some students were already settled in their rooms, others were unpacking, and still others were saying goodbye to their parents, who had helped them to move in. I must've looked lost because one of the students came up to me and, without asking what I needed, directed me to the office where I was to check in and get the key to my assigned room. The room was on the first floor and came with a bunk bed, two chairs, and two small desks. My roommate hadn't arrived yet, so I took the bottom bunk and placed my stuff on top of the desk near the window.

The atmosphere on the floor was friendly with students going in and out of their rooms. Some knew each other from previous years; most were new, like me. On the whole, they were in-state students though a good number were out-of-staters, largely from the northeast. I was the only foreigner. There were a few Cubans, who had come to the States in the early '60s, following Castro's takeover of the island. But they spoke perfect English and could hardly count as foreigners. The students' diverse backgrounds and the different speech patterns reminded me of my army days. Even the dorm reminded me of army barracks, especially the common bathroom and shower stalls. There was a common area with tables, chairs, and a TV. We all had a roommate. My roommate, who arrived a few hours after I did, was Joshua Clinton, a freshman from a small West Carolina town. Josh, a first-generation college student, was a shy, gentle soul who spoke softly and not often. In his thick Appalachian accent, he told me his hometown was about twenty-five miles north of Charlotte. Hardly a month into the semester, he was already missing his family and his mountains. Some days, he would stay in bed instead of going to class, and pretty soon, his grades plunged into the lower Cs and Ds. Sometimes, I tried to cheer him up by asking him to go for coffee at the student union or to the movies, but he usually declined, claiming he was not feeling well. Soon, he began to question whether he belonged in school and started going home every weekend. The last time I saw him was when he went home for Thanksgiving. He dropped out of school before the semester was over.

I missed Joshua's presence, but I understood his predicament—he felt like a fish out of water. Having lived all his life in a small community in the hills, all of a sudden, he found himself lost among hundreds of people, many of whom were from big cities and were well-traveled. Unable to adjust to the crowded spaces of campus life, he grew so lonely that he went back to the life he knew. He was happy back home; he told me when he came back with his father to pick up his stuff. I assumed the school would soon assign me another roommate, but it never did. I had the room all to myself for the entire year. It took me a while to adjust to living alone, but in the end, I liked it. I kept my door open, just like other students on the floor. It was an open invitation to fellow residents to drop in and shoot the breeze. Many of us didn't know anyone and were eager to make friends. In my case, being a foreigner turned out to be a blessing. Some kids had never met a foreigner before and were genuinely curious about my background. They were more than willing to show me around and proudly explain aspects of the American culture I was unfamiliar with.

It was here that I first learned about American football. When some of the students living on the floor learned that I had no idea what the sport was about and had never been to a game, they took me to a one. It was a warm and sunny September day, and the campus was abuzz with activities—lots of cars parked in the streets, on sidewalks, and even on well-kept private lawns. Hundreds of people, young and old, were all dressed up, as if they were going to a wedding. Many were parents and alumni in town for the game, a student explained. There were dozens of students in a marching band uniform, each carrying a musical instrument. They were part of the school band that would assemble at the stadium. That Saturday, NCSU was playing at home against its traditional rival, the University of North Carolina-Chapel

Hill. Dressed in Sunday clothes, we all drove to the stadium. One of my grandchildren, I don't remember who, wanted to know why we put on nice clothes; after all, it was a just game. I didn't know the answer. The only thing I knew was that, in those days, people went to a football game all dressed up. Up until recently, I said, football coaches showed up on the sidelines in a coat and tie and some even sported derby hats.

Another established tradition was to go to the game with a date. Did I have a date? Sort of! My friends asked a girl they knew if she would mind coming to the game as my "date." She agreed and sat next to me throughout the game. She was a sophomore like me, except I was about six years her senior. She was nice, and we were polite to each other, but it was clear she came along as a favor to her friends. That didn't bother me. My attention was focused on the huge size of the stadium and the crowd's deafening noise. I had never seen such a big place with thousands and thousands of frenzied fans rooting for their respective team. After a while, I too started booing or cheering, following my friends' lead. There and then, I didn't know what the shouting was about. I just joined in. But as the game went on and my friends kept on explaining the rules, I understood when and why it was time to cheer or jeer.

Although in my later years, I came to enjoy watching football, I can't say my interest in the game started while I was in college. In fact, in all my years in college, I went to see no more than three or four games. For me, it was a hassle to go to the stadium and fight the crowds. Frankly, at the time, the game interested me primarily as a cultural event: people formally dressed, big marching bands, pretty girls cheering on the sidelines, half-time entertainment, beer-drinking, and the loud cheering of the fans. What I found most peculiar was how everybody seemed to know the words to the national anthem, which they sang at the beginning of the game. Most Italians don't know their national anthem. They usually sing the first couple of lines and make up the rest with sounds like "Lararala, lararala." The Americans at the stadium, instead, sang proudly, standing, facing the flag, and placing their right hand on their chest. It was the first time I witnessed such a significant aspect of American patriotism. True, I had seen Americans sing the national anthem when I was in the army. We sang it so often that I learned it by heart. But there is a difference between a military convention and civilian flag-waving. For us in the military, it was a routine exercise; for most civilians, instead, it was and is an emotional expression of loyalty to their country.

Another important American tradition I came to appreciate while at NCSU was Thanksgiving. I had no idea how earnestly Americans observed this holiday. I knew about its historical significance and that it was a uniquely American tradition. But for us immigrants, at least in Reading, Thanksgiving was just a day off work and an opportunity to get together with friends and relatives. We did eat turkey, mainly because it was usually on sale, and my mother never missed a sale. For Americans, celebrating Thanksgiving was an act of patriotism. Generally speaking, I think immigrants begin to observe American holidays after they assimilate the culture and become fully Americanized. Clearly, I wasn't there yet though I was an army veteran and had recently become a naturalized American citizen.

The question of citizenship came up several times with my children. They, like many of my students, assumed that I had become a citizen by virtue of my military service. In their view, you serve your country, and in recognition, you're granted citizenship. It's plain common sense to award citizen status to one willing to risk his life for "his" country. Not so! Military service had nothing to do with the requirements for citizenship. Foreigners serving in the military, whether veterans or still on active duty, had to apply just like anybody else. There was a process all petitioners had to go through. First, they needed to be green card holders—legal residents— for at least five years before applying. When the immigration office reviewed and accepted their applications, they had to take a civics test consisting of a basic understanding of the three branches of government. In addition, they had to be acquainted with American history, especially the names of some of the Founding Fathers. To pass the test, they had to know enough English to at least be able to fill out a job application and get a driver's license. If they satisfied all the requirements, they were called on to swear allegiance to the United States of America. The swearing-in ceremony usually took place before a federal judge. Following the oath, they were declared naturalized citizens and given their naturalization papers.

But it's one thing to know the answers for a test and be declared a citizen and quite another to assimilate and actually live the culture. Such was the case regarding my first Thanksgiving at NCSU. For me, the holiday was just another long weekend and a good opportunity to stay on campus and catch up on my studies. When Jeremiah Parker, the student across the hall from me, heard about my plans to stay on campus, he wouldn't hear of it.

"It's Thanksgiving, man!" he said, confounded by my indifference toward such an important holiday.

Dismissing my excuses, he invited me to spend the weekend at his house with his family. I was literally taken aback by the unusual invitation. I had never been to someone's house for dinner and, more unusual for me, overnight. After a brief hesitation, I accepted, and together we drove to his house, which was in a small town on the North Carolina coast. I didn't bring anything. I didn't know I was supposed to bring a token of appreciation, such as a bottle of wine or a bouquet for Mrs. Parker. But they didn't seem to mind and, most likely, attributed the lack of etiquette to my being a foreigner.

What an experience it was! The family was very nice and welcomed me with open arms. I had hardly stepped into the house when the mother asked me if I was hungry. Would I like something to drink? The father told his younger son to put my stuff in the bedroom where I would be sleeping. At one point before dinner, I witnessed something I couldn't have imagined in a million years. Jeremiah's younger brother got into a wrestling match with his father, who ended up pinned down on the floor. Coming from a culture where you treated your father with the utmost respect (or fear) and called him "Sir," I was flabbergasted. When the horseplay was over, the father told Jeremiah to start the grill and the younger boy to go wash the car. They both obeyed with a polite and prompt "Yes, sir!" For me, it was an indelible lesson in parental authority and camaraderie at the same time. The experience inspired me to change my relationship with my own father, that is, reduce the distance—typical of the old country's culture—that defined our rapport. I succeeded. In a few years, my dad and I became buddies, often teasing each other.

College was quite an adjustment, as I was trying to strike a balance between school and social life. Academically, the first semester was not as easy as it had been at NCSU-Fort Bragg. Now I was taking five courses and wasn't pleased with the grades I was getting. What kept my grade-point average, or GPA, lower than I expected was the course in British literature, From Beowulf to Shakespeare. I spent so much time trying to get through the archaic language of these authors that I had little time left for the other courses. It was pretty discouraging at times when, after the professor went over the assignment in class, I realized I had misunderstood part or most of the text. There were times when I feared I might flunk the course. But in the end, I was relieved to pass it. The C+ I got in that course was the lowest grade I would ever get in college. I soon honed my study skills and began to get good grades with plenty of time left for some fun. At the beginning of the second semester, I had made quite a few friends and my social life improved considerably. A week hardly went by without me catching a poker game or going to a party. In the end, my year at NCSU was one of the best years of my college life.

But it all came to an end. Toward the end of my sophomore year, I made a choice that upended my social life and brought into focus the course of my future studies. I decided to transfer to the University of North Carolina at Chapel Hill, about twenty-five miles northwest of Raleigh. The move was emotionally stressful for me. Not only was I heavy-hearted about leaving my buddies at NCSU, but also I was anxious about the new campus. Where would I live? Would I make friends? Would the UNC professors be more demanding than the ones at NCSU? I expected to do well in school, as I would be taking mostly language courses for which I had a natural gift. But I was still torn about leaving the place and the people I had come to know and was fond of. But in the long run, the transfer turned out to be a smart decision, for which I was thankful to my friends in Raleigh.

When some of my buddies learned that I wanted to major in French, they suggested I transfer to UNC. Unlike NCSU, they said, Chapel

Hill was more of a liberal arts school with a well-known department of foreign languages. The teachers I spoke to confirmed that UNC was indeed a good school with an excellent reputation and advised me to apply. I did, and in less than a month, I received a congratulatory letter informing me that I had been accepted. It went on to specify that I was classified as an out-of-state student and should receive additional information regarding tuition and fees. I was thrilled and wasted no time in sharing the good news with my friends. But the excitement was short-lived. When my friend Jeremiah saw the letter, he called my attention to the out-of-state classification and reminded me that my tuition would be almost double what I was paying at NCSU. That cooled my enthusiasm, and I began to wonder whether I could afford the cost. The next day, letter in hand, I went to talk to one of my professors, Dr. Pollard. After agreeing that the out-of-state designation was a serious financial burden, he suggested I request a meeting with the admissions office at UNC. Within days of my request, I received a letter informing me that Mr. Polly from admissions would see me the following Thursday at 3:30 p.m.

I got to the admissions office just a few minutes before the appointment. The receptionist, a young lady on a work-study program, verified my appointment and told me to go in, gesturing toward the open door of Mr. Polly's office. Jack Polly, a heavyset man in his forties, was sitting at his desk, going through a file, as if looking for a specific sheet. He asked me to sit down and, having found the paper he was looking for, my letter requesting the appointment, proceeded to explain that my out-of-state classification was based on the fact that I was officially a resident of Pennsylvania. That's where I got my GED, and Pennsylvania was the residence listed in my application. He was sympathetic toward my financial situation and wished he could help, but there was nothing he could do.

"My hands are tied, I'm sorry," he said apologetically.

He went on to suggest I take a semester off, get a job in the area, and in this way, establish North Carolina residence. I could then reapply as an in-state student. I was incensed.

I stood up, leaned over the desk, and politely but firmly asked, "Sir, do you know how old I am? I am seven years older than your average freshmen. I cannot afford to take time off from school. In addition, I have been in North Carolina longer than I resided in Pennsylvania. We immigrated to Pennsylvania, my parents live there, but I did not choose to live there, nor am I my parents' dependent. I am twenty-six years old. I served in the army in this state, started college in this state, made friends in this state, and have made my choice to live in this state."

At that point, he asked me to please, calm down, and left the office, saying he would be right back. A few minutes later, he came back and told me that the admissions office would review my application and inform me of its final decision. The letter arrived the following week. "Congratulations!" it began. "We are happy to inform you that you have been admitted to UNC-Chapel as an in-state student." I didn't read further. I was ecstatic. The following year, I entered UNC as a junior.

I went back to UNC some thirty years later. When Jenna was a senior in high school, I took her to visit several college campuses. Chapel Hill was on top of the list, of course. I wanted her to go there and made the extra effort to convince her to apply. Besides the campus tour organized by the university, we spent a good hour touring the place on our own, just the two of us. I took her to Carmichael Residence Hall, the dorm where I stayed during my junior year. I showed her the Wilson Library where I spent countless hours studying and trying to meet people. I also made it a point of showing her Dey Hall, which housed the Romance languages department. It was an excellent department with dozens of first-rate professors and hundreds of students, I told her with pride. It offered undergraduate and graduate degrees in many languages, including Italian, Portuguese, French, and Spanish. I insisted on going inside. I wanted to walk through the hallways and take a look at the classrooms where, decades earlier, I had come to class almost every day. I was somewhat disillusioned; the place was no longer how I remembered it. Renovations and technology had turned the old classrooms into high-tech lecture halls with sophisticated projectors and wheeled chair-desks for students to move freely around the room.

"It just isn't the same anymore," I said as if talking to myself.

My face mirrored the letdown in my voice. Jenna understood my disappointment and tried to distract me.

"Dad," she said, "this is the best campus tour I have had so far. But let me ask you. Do you think it would be easy to make friends in a place like this? Was it easy for you back then?"

When I first came here, I had difficulty meeting people, I told her. I saw fellow students only in class. Also, the courses were taught in such a way that there was little interaction among students. It was not unusual for kids to be in the same classroom and never learn each other's names. After class, we all went our separate ways, some going to their next class and others back to their respective dorms. In the dorm, at least in my dorm, it was not that simple to interact with other students. Our rooms, unlike the layout at NCSU where rooms faced each other, had private entrances and were built like mini apartments. You never saw guys coming in and out of their rooms. In addition, there weren't that many out-of-state students eager to make new friends as there were at NCSU. Here a lot of kids were in-state, and many knew each other from high school back home. Unlike out-of-staters, they didn't need to make friends; they already had their buddies. This atmosphere tended to further isolate outsiders like me and was the primary cause of my dreadful loneliness. I dreaded evenings, and especially weekends, because there were no classes, and I didn't have a place to go.

Maybe had I had a roommate, someone to talk to, I wouldn't have been so lonely. But whoever was assigned to my room never showed up. I guess he chose to go to a different school or simply decided at the last minute not to attend. So I had the room all to myself, just as I did at NCSU. Eventually, I got to know Paul Fernesi, a graduating senior from my English class. Paul was a proud, third-generation Italian from Philadelphia. Perhaps because of his heritage, he made it a point to get to know me, and once in a while, usually on weekends, he would ask me to go out for dinner or to a party with his buddies. I really appreciated his invitations and enjoyed his company. Sometimes, I even waited by the phone for him to call and pull me out of my depressing evenings. Sadly, the "friendship" lasted until I began to sense that Paul and his buddies invited me along because I had a car. As the semester wore on, I became convinced they included me only when they needed transportation to go somewhere, a party or a restaurant not within walking distance. The realization that they were not interested in me as a person was devastating. From then on, I looked with suspicion at their invitations, and at times, I refused to join them, claiming I had other things to do.

I compensated for the dullness of my weekends by driving to NCSU once in a while. Raleigh was less than thirty miles away; and my buddies, Jeremiah, Jim Crowe, and Pat Clinton, usually had something going, like a party or a poker game. Once in a while, they came to Chapel Hill, especially when there was a basketball game. At the time, UNC basketball, coached by the famed Dean Smith, was one of the most competitive college programs in America. Jim, a diehard UNC basketball fan, never missed a game. He would come around noon—sometimes with Pat, sometimes alone—and we would hang out for a good part of the day, going out for lunch and stopping by the student union for a game of pool. At game time, Jim would go to the basketball arena using my student ID. As I told him repeatedly, I didn't know much about the sport and had no interest in going along. Whether it was a game or a party, the four of us got along well and enjoyed a special camaraderie. But just like the friends I made in the army, this friendship too came to an end when we all went our separate ways; they graduated and went to work somewhere, and I went to study in Lyon, France, for a whole year.

Many were surprised to hear that I was going to France. How come he is going? Some asked. The more curious wondered where I got the money to go live in France for a year. They knew my parents were in no position to help since they were both retired and living on meager pensions. I explained that I was a French major and met all the requirements to be admitted to the UNC Junior Year in France. As for the money, I had plenty. I assured them. I had funds in my savings account and was still receiving monthly checks from the government. In addition, during the summer, I had a great job, making good money and saving most of it. I had no major expenses, as I lived with my parents. They were happy I was staying with them, and it would've been unthinkable for me to offer to pay for room and board or for them to ask.

Summer Job

Since my first year of college, I had a summer job at a paper mill in Reading. The factory operated twenty-four hours a day, seven days a week. I was making $2.50 an hour with time and a half on Saturdays and double time on Sundays. My job description was what they called general help—I swept the floor; ran errands for the boss; I got coffee for employees who couldn't leave their workstations unattended; and once in a while, operated a piece of equipment if the man assigned to it didn't show up for work. All in all, it was an easy job except for the long hours and the humidity. The high humidity generated by the huge steamrollers that turned the stinking pulp into brown heavy-duty paper was unbearable. To escape the sticky and muggy air, I grabbed any chance to work outside the plant. At times, the boss would send me to the local hardware store to buy whatever supplies he needed, usually paint, screws, or a can of grease. Occasionally, he sent me out of town to go check on a customer's complaint about a bad shipment. One summer, he needed someone to dig a trench along the wall just outside his office and asked me if I would do it. I jumped at the opportunity to work in the open air though I had never used a jackhammer in my life. The project consisted of breaking up a concrete sidewalk and digging a trench about two feet wide, three feet deep, and fifteen feet long.

I enjoyed working outside, away from the steam and the stench inside the place. But the task I volunteered for was a real challenge. The pneumatic hammer was more grueling than I ever imagined. Its deafening noise and uncontrollable vibration so racked my body that I had to stop every few minutes, my arms shaking. I was too small to apply enough bodyweight on the hammer to prevent it from bouncing all over the place. Whenever I turned it off to reposition it, I could feel a quiver and a slight pain in my legs and wrists. But in the end, it was worth the fresh air and the freedom of working at my own pace with no one telling me what to do. Some of the guys in the shop were genuinely surprised by my work and took to calling me Jackhammer Sam. I did a good job, and the boss was pleased with my work. I just wished he had more outside stuff for me to do.

Unfortunately, I had to get back to working inside and putting up with the humidity and, at times, with outright boredom. A thing I couldn't stand was the humdrum routine that typified most Sundays. Typically, the foreman would tell me to sweep the floor and pick up the debris around the steamrollers, and the guys would ask me to go get them the usual coffee or snacks from the vending machines. The rest of the time, I sat there listening to the men bragging about their womanizing and drinking exploits while the clock ticked ever so slowly. The day never ended it seemed. But I had no reason to complain since I wanted to work on Sundays. When I grumbled about being bored and wished I had stayed home, the guys told me to stop whining, reminding me that we were getting double pay for just sitting around.

There was another aspect of my job I didn't like. Every year, for the first two weeks in July, the plant shut down for its annual maintenance, and we all worked ten hours a day, including weekends. We overhauled machines, greased equipment, and cleaned the entire plant top to bottom. I and another college kid, also a general help like me, were tasked with cleaning the plant's furnaces—two brick-walled ovens each about the size of a small SUV. Wearing dust masks, we would climb inside the furnaces and scrub clean the hot water pipes encrusted with asbestos residue. Inside the furnaces, or boilers as we called them, it was so hot and dusty that we had to come out every fifteen minutes for a ten-minute break. When the pipes were thoroughly clean, we would open sacks of asbestos, a soft white powder, and mix it with water. As soon as the mixture reached the desired consistency, we would climb back inside the boilers and insulate the pipes with it.

The heat, the dust, and the cramped space inside the boilers made the work backbreaking and exhausting. Only years later did I learn the work was not just grueling but also dangerous. Asbestos, public health announcements warned, was a cancer-causing agent. Although it had been known since at least the 1920s that asbestos was a hazardous chemical, most people didn't know until the 1980s that exposure to it increased the risk of lung cancer. Luckily, I worked with it only once a year, during the plant's annual maintenance. But even now, every time I see those TV announcements about mesothelioma victims, I am reminded I could be one of them. Thank God, so far I haven't had any problems and continue counting my blessings. But looking back, I'm glad I had that job. The money I saved working long hours and getting double-time pay made it possible for me to enroll in the UNC Junior Year in France program. The savings plus the monthly check from Uncle Sam's GI Bill made me a rich student. Without exaggeration, I had more spending money than most of the thirty-four kids in the program.

CHAPTER 18

Junior Year Abroad

We left for France on August 28, 1969. The group met in New York and boarded the transatlantic *Le France*, the pride of France. At the time, *Le France* was one of the biggest, newest, and most elegant passenger ships sailing the Atlantic Ocean. I recall my amazement when, while standing on its bridge, I saw the *Leonardo da Vinci* docked next to it. I couldn't believe how small the Italian vessel was in comparison. And to think that this was the same "huge" ship on which I had sailed a decade earlier.

The evening before I left home, friends and relatives came by the house to wish me a safe journey and to remind me to write. They were all proud of me, especially my father, who kept on telling people that his son was going to study at the big *università di Parigi*. I suspect he said Paris because he knew that nobody, including himself, had the slightest idea where Lyon was. The following morning, Pasquale drove me to New York. The ship would be ready for boarding early that afternoon. As my brother and I were about to leave, my father wanted to give me some money for the trip, though he knew I had plenty. I told him to keep it; I didn't need it. After insisting in vain that I take it, he slowly put it back in his pocket, the gesture indicating a hurtful rejection. Only months later did I realized that his offer of money was a mere token of his pride, his wish to be part of my "success." How could I have failed to see his offer for what it really was? How could I have been so insensitive to deny him his desire to share in his boy's achievements? The image of his humbled expression remained so impressed in my mind that, even today, I feel a gnawing sense of guilt for not allowing him to share in my dream.

The three-hour drive to New York was uneventful. We got there around noon and, after asking for directions, arrived at the pier where *Le France* was docked. My brother helped with the baggage, stayed around a little, and then drove back to Reading. Before leaving, he teased me about watching out for them, the French ladies, and encouraged me to write or call if I needed anything. Soon we started boarding. Once onboard, the professor directing the UNC program gathered all the students and gave us a long lecture about behaving on the ship and during our stay in France. Among other things, he reminded us that inappropriate behavior, such as too much drinking, reflected negatively on our school's reputation and on America in general. We had heard that before and were anxiously waiting for him to finish his briefing. We were eager to start looking around and exploring the huge ship. None of the students, except me, had ever been on a big ship. Everyone was in awe of the boat's elegant furnishings, from its big chandeliers to the soft leather chairs, from the glitter of the gift shops to the richly decorated dinner menus. The deck crew was all elegantly dressed in blue pants, white jackets, and red ties, the colors of France. We sailed late that afternoon, and five days later, we docked at Le Havre, France. That same day, we took the train to Paris where we stayed for two days at a hotel near the Champs Élysées.

Except for our professor, none of us had been to Paris. But we had read about its history and monuments. After supper, some of us went out, itching to see the City of Lights. We walked in the direction of the Eiffel Tower, which we could see from our hotel. What a sight! Its sheer size and the beautifully illuminated structure was a marvel to behold. Some of us wanted to go up to the observation deck, but it was getting late, and we had to go back to the hotel. The following day, we got up early and, in small groups, went all over the city on foot, by bus, or on the metro. When we met for dinner that evening, everybody was talking about the awesome places they had seen, Eiffel Tower, Louvre, Arc de Triomphe, Notre Dame, etc. Some of us even took a bus to Versailles, about an hour southwest of Paris. We wished we could stay longer even though we quickly learned ~~though~~ that Paris was one of the most expensive cities in the world. But the program had a limited budget and a schedule to follow. In fact, the program's French assistants were expecting us in Lyon the following day. They had already made arrangements for our temporary lodging and the bus to take us there. On leaving Paris, I promised myself I would be back while in Lyon. And I did, several times.

The train ride to Lyon was long and many of us slept. When we arrived, a bus was waiting to take us to a university dorm. We would stay for a couple of days until they took us to the family each of us was assigned to live with. It was at the dorm that I first met Bob Stone, a returning student from Charlotte, North Carolina. Bob was a good-looking young man about six feet tall with a pencil-thin mustache, bushy black hair, brown eyes, and an easy smile on his square face. Two years earlier, he had dropped out of UNC to come to live and work in Europe. Now, taking advantage of the UNC-in-France program, he decided to return to school as a junior. Perhaps because we were both older than the other students, there was good chemistry between the two of us right away. We soon became good buddies and enjoyed each other's company. Bob had a beat-up old car, and the two of us went out almost every evening, riding around town, going to movies, or stopping at a café to enjoy a cognac or a cup of coffee. His familiarity with the city and the language—he spoke French better than anyone in the group—made it easy for us to get around. Sometimes, we ventured to nearby towns to visit a museum or chateaux. Once, we even drove to Spain. What a trip that was!

Fall break was coming up, and Bob suggested we drive to Spain. It was late September, and the weather was warm enough for us to enjoy the famed beaches on the Spanish coast. He asked three other students to come along, mostly to help defray the cost of gas. We reached Barcelona early in the evening, and since stingy Bob didn't want to spend money on a hotel, we spent the night at the beach. Bob and Brittany slept in the car, the rest of us out in the open under a blanket. The next day, we drove down the coast to Alicante where we stayed for two days. Since it was off-season, the beaches were not crowded, and the two-star hotel we stayed in gave us a good price. We were actually planning to enjoy a few more days in Alicante when Brittany suggested we go to the island of Majorca. We did. The following evening, we boarded the overnight ferry to the island and got there early the next morning. For the three days we were in Majorca, we had a blast—swimming and sunbathing on the beach or having a drink on the terrace just outside our rooms. We even tried to tour the island on motor scooters. But we realized how dangerous those little machines could be when Kevin lost control of the one he was riding and fell. Miraculously, he was not hurt except for minor scratches. The scare was enough for us to give up on the tour idea.

We stayed mostly in Palma, Majorca's capital, enjoying the beach just outside the hotel and exploring the city's old town. We visited the old Arab and Jewish quarters but were particularly impressed with La Seu, Palma's majestic cathedral and one of Spain's largest Gothic churches. The day before we left the island, an incident happened that still amuses me. That evening, we decided to sit out on the terrace and relax over a glass of wine. After a few drinks, Bob suggested we go skinny-dipping. Except for him, we all knew that Brittany, the only girl in the group, would never agree to take her clothes off in front of the boys. To please him, Brittany played along, and we all "promised" we would go in if he went first. But instead of following him down the rocky path and into the water, we stayed up on the terrace, laughing at him. I can still see him naked, standing knee-deep in the water, pleading with us to join him. He finally came out of the water and got dressed before coming back up on the terrace. He had been played and was embarrassed. But he knew he had asked for it and took it in stride. Anyway, the incident was soon forgotten, and we hardly mentioned it when we got back to Lyon.

Driving to Greece

Bob was fun to travel with, always upbeat and ready to tell a joke or a funny story. Unfortunately, I didn't take other long trips with him, mostly because he was on a tight budget and could barely afford to live in Lyon, much less travel. But I did go on several trips with other students. A memorable one was the adventure to Greece, a 1,600-mile drive from Lyon to Athens. During Easter vacation, three other kids and I decided to go to Greece. Squeezed in an old Renault, which one of the students had bought for a few hundred francs, we traveled over the snowy Alps, drove through Northern Italy, and stopped in Venice overnight. It was the first time we had seen a city literally built on water and crisscrossed by over a hundred canals. We were in awe of the beautiful San Marco's Basilica and the magnificent buildings surrounding its famed square. But we were uneasy about the hundreds of pigeons flying over the tourists' heads and eating peanuts out of people's hands.

The following afternoon, we drove down the Dalmatian Coast on the Adriatic and, to save hotel money, decided to sleep in the open by the roadside somewhere near the ancient city of Dubrovnik, Yugoslavia. All four of us tried to sleep in the car, but it was so uncomfortable that I offered to sleep out on the ground if they gave me their blankets. It was a foolish attempt, as I soon discovered. In just over an hour, I woke up freezing to death and went back in the car with the others.

The next day, after stopping at a small town for gas and breakfast, we drove almost to the Albanian border before coming to a halt. As much as we wanted to continue driving along the panoramic coast, we had to turn around when we came across a huge road sign that warned all, in big red letters, against crossing into Albania under penalty of imprisonment. A few yards away from the sign stood two border guards with rifles slung over their shoulders. They were looking at us, wondering what we were up to. Would we dare to cross? Of course, we didn't. We didn't know why, but as I learned later, at the time, Albania was under a Communist regime and was on our State Department's Do Not Travel list. Anyway, the threat was real enough for us to turn around and take the first road into the hinterland. The detour was as scenic as it was desolate. The narrow road was curvy and dotted with potholes. The terrain was hilly and rocky with patches here and there of wood and vegetation. Huts, some with smoking chimneys, punctuated the landscape. Women, draped in long black dresses and black scarves tied under their chins, stood in front of their homes. Some looked at us with the curiosity of people unaccustomed to seeing cars go by; others made a slow waving gesture as if trying to imagine the faraway places we were coming from or going to. Along the way, we encountered a few herders leading their goats to pasture. Otherwise, there was hardly any traffic, and for long stretches, we were the only ones on the road. With no road signs and no cars going by, we were getting nervous and beginning to wonder whether we were lost.

It was a relief to finally see a road sign indicating we were about to cross into Macedonia. That day, we stopped in Skopje and checked in a nice hotel downtown. The next morning, as we prepared to get on the road for the last leg of the trip, the car wouldn't start. One of the hotel employees, seeing us standing helplessly around the old Renault, came over and immediately noticed the problem, the alternator belt was loose and badly frayed. It was a Sunday, and with our luck, all auto repair shops were closed. What to do? The employee, a polite young man in his late twenties with a happy face and big smiling eyes, remembered he had an extra belt in his car and went to get it. Though the wrong size, the belt did the trick. We were grateful for his help and offered to pay, but he refused to accept anything and wished us good luck. Before we drove away, he reminded us to get the right size belt as soon as we got to Athens.

Athens did not have the beautiful buildings and the marvelous architecture we saw in Venice. But it had the Acropolis with its magnificent Parthenon perched on the hilltop overlooking the city below. After two days in Athens, we took the overnight ferryboat to Crete. The small island was especially known for the mythical labyrinth where King Minos held the voracious, man-eating Minotaur. According to the myth, which all four of us knew well, the no-dead-ends maze was meant to disorient and ensnare the part man, part bull Minotaur.

It was the first thing we wanted to see. What a disappointment! The ruins were just an open space, the size of a large room featuring a short course of zigzagging corridors that we negotiated in just a few minutes. It was a maze, to be sure, but hardly the complex labyrinth that trapped the man-eating monster.

The highlight of the Crete venture was our chance encounter with Mr. Thanos Anastas, a local store owner who happened to speak English. Upon hearing we were Americans, he started telling us how much he loved American movies, especially Westerns. Someday, he said, he hoped to visit his uncle, who owned a Greek restaurant in Chicago. He was so eager to talk and be with us that he closed the store and invited us to his house for a late lunch. It was a feast. When we arrived at the house an hour or so later, his wife had already set up the table, and his brother-in-law was skinning a lamb that was dangling from a tree branch just outside the house. The multi-course meal lasted several hours with people talking over one another and in several languages. We left after taking pictures with everyone and expressing our hopes of seeing each other again. Mr. Anastas insisted on taking us to the seaport to board the ferry for Athens. The following morning, we were on our way back to France. This time, we drove straight through, stopping only for gas and food.

Back in Lyon, we couldn't stop talking about our vacation, telling everybody how great an experience it had been. We showed pictures of the Anastas family and the sumptuous meal they prepared for us. Our adventure aroused envy and curiosity among fellow students who had never been to Greece or seen some of Europe's most primitive areas. I never forgot that trip. In my memory, it stands out as one of the most fulfilling trips I took while in France.

Once, when I told my children about my European travels, they wondered why I never went to Italy. Actually, I did go. I told them. During Christmas break, a fellow student and I went to Italy by train, visiting major cities, including Florence, Rome, and Naples. But what really puzzled them was why I never went to my hometown. Had I forgotten about the friends and relatives I hadn't seen in almost ten years? No doubt, I wanted to see my friends. I just wasn't ready to go back. But I did make it a point to let them know that I was studying in France and brag about my travels through Europe. I sent them pictures of myself in front of famous landmarks—Coliseum, Eiffel Tower, Acropolis. It was my way of showing off, a way of telling them I was living the life. But it was a façade. In reality, I was embarrassed to face them because I felt I hadn't achieved anything to be proud of. I hadn't even graduated from college yet! I was not going to go back home without having first achieved the success they expected of me. After ten years of America, what has he accomplished? I feared they would ask.

One of my friends wanted to come to see me in Lyon, but I nixed the idea, telling him I was too busy studying. I admit the excuse was lame and inconsistent. On the one hand, I was bragging about my travels; on the other hand, I was claiming to be too busy with my schoolwork. Frankly, studying hardly took up much of my time; the teachers were lenient and the courses were easy. True, we had to take challenging university classes alongside French students, even though our language skills were hardly adequate to do the work. But the professors were understanding and nice enough to cut us some slack—extra help, simplified assignments, shorter term papers, and extended deadlines. Some even accepted papers written in English. We fared much better in a course designed for foreign students just like us—the material was watered down and the teacher easygoing. In this course, I had an experience that, though not quite the *shorty* awakening I had in the army, made me believe I had the ability to succeed in anything I chose to pursue.

Amelja

Thanks to my friend Bob, I was thrown into a situation I never thought I could handle. At the time, he was dating a beautiful Norwegian girl, and the three of us were often together, sitting at a café or going to the movies. It was not an ideal situation to be a third wheel. I needed to find me a girl. Bob thought so too and began pressuring me to do something about it. But I was too bashful and insecure to yield to his prodding. It all changed after we came back from our vacation in Majorca. One day, Bob pointed to a Polish young lady, one of the most beautiful girls in our class for foreigners, and dared me to ask her out. Just like most of the boys in the program, I had had my eye on her for some time but never got up the nerve to talk to her. That day, she was sitting next to me, and perhaps yielding to Bob's goading, I slipped her a note asking for her name. Of course, I knew her name. Everybody in the class knew her name, especially the boys. I didn't expect her to even read it. Instead, she penciled in her name, Amelja, and asked for mine. We continued exchanging notes until she agreed to go for coffee after class. It was the beginning of a great relationship that lasted until I returned to the United States and she went back to Poland. Bob hated to eat crow, but he did. He thought I was too chicken to ask her out, he admitted. He also assumed I didn't stand a chance since there were several other students vying for her attention. But he was happy with my success because now we could hang out as two couples.

The incident that led to this passionate romance was not just a conquest, as Bob called it, but a tremendous boost to my ego. I started wearing trendy clothes, speaking up with self-assurance and slowly shedding my shyness. More significantly, the episode allowed me to overcome a deep-seated feeling of inadequacy, leading me to believe that I could achieve anything I went after. When I returned to UNC, I was a changed man. I was no longer the lonely little foreigner who spent most evenings in his room, waiting for the phone to ring, studying, or listening to operas. I was now popular with my classmates, had many friends, and was frequently invited to parties. I also made a lot of friends through the job I took with the university.

The job was part of a work-study program that required me to check on the canteens throughout the campus. Located on the ground floor of most dorms, the canteens—some called them stores—sold all sorts of stuff, from snacks to school supplies to rainwear to sports paraphernalia. Some even provided recreation facilities, such as foosball and pool tables. The job didn't pay much, but I didn't have to do much. I was allowed to choose when to work and keep track of my own hours, which were limited to no more than ten a week. The job consisted of my casually dropping in on a store and, passing for a regular customer, look for irregularities and report to my boss. I was expected to pay special attention to the place's cleanness and any suspicious behavior on the part of the students working behind the counter. In particular, I was to watch the people at the cash register to see whether they rang up every purchase.

In essence, I was a spy, though not a good one. My casual visits became a game between the employees and myself. It didn't take long for them to catch on. The moment they saw me walk in, they would start mopping the floor and wiping the tables. In some stores, they even cleaned more than once the table I sat at as if to say, "We know who you are and what you're doing here." Sometimes, an employee would offer to bring me coffee. The offer was clearly made with tongue-in-cheek humor. The student-employees were so obviously accommodating that I found it hard to refrain from giving them a sly, conspiratorial smile as if to say, "I know you know, but I got a job to do."

One of the job's hidden benefits was the opportunity to get to know students from different dorms and expand my circle of friends. In spite of my unmistakable foreign accent, or perhaps because of it, I felt very comfortable talking to strangers and initiating conversation, especially with the girls. My soaring self-confidence was definitely one of my life's most important changes. Among other things, it helped me to rationalize and deal with my shortcomings. If I didn't do well in a particular course, I did not accept the possibility that I may not be as capable as the next guy. Instead, I convinced myself that my interests happened to lie somewhere else. I could do as well as anybody if I put my mind to it. If a girl turned me down, I dismissed the rejection by telling myself that she wasn't worth my time. My attitude was that of the fox who justified his failure to get to the high-hanging grapes by telling himself the fruit was too sour and, therefore, not worth his efforts to reach it.

Who was I kidding with such a snotty view of myself? Deep down, I knew it was arrogant on my part to presume I could attain any goal I set out to reach. But this self-assured outlook helped me to downplay my flaws, keep a can-do attitude, and aim for higher goals. The conquest had not been a mere romantic escapade; it was the discovery of my potential to do better than I had ever thought I could. In fact, when the time came to apply for graduate school, I had no doubt I would be accepted and do well in it. The only question was which school should I apply to. Following the advice of one of my professors, I decided to stay and do my MA ~~master of arts~~ at UNC. Why not? The school had an excellent graduate program, and I already knew most of the students already enrolled in it. After hearing them talk about job prospects, I decided to change majors, thinking it may be easier to find a teaching job once I got out. So since I had a BA in French, I opted to do an MA in Italian with a Minor in French.

Graduate work was not as grinding as I had imagined. I was required to take only three courses. Such an easy schedule left me plenty of time for a well-balanced social life—here and there a party, a date for dinner and a movie, or a game of poker. In some ways, the classes were easier than some of the undergraduate courses I had struggled with. No longer did I have to deal with the challenges of *Beowulf* or Shakespeare's archaic English or take sciences courses, for which I had little aptitude. All my classes were now based on Italian and French literature, topics I enjoyed and in languages I was comfortable with. Also, I had a lot in common with the students in the program, some of whom were Italians or of Italian descent. The environment was such that I made plenty of friends and had a lot of time for socializing. I stopped working at the canteens but continued to see my old friends at NCSU though several had already graduated and left the university.

CHAPTER 19

Pasquale's Death

Pasquale died the year I finished my MA degree. His death was not a surprise, as his cancer had already metastasized to other parts of the body. Nonetheless, the evening my sister called to tell me to come home if I wanted to see him alive, I was devastated. I left Chapel Hill right away and drove the whole night, praying he was still alive. I went straight to the hospital to find him barely conscious. The entire family was there, all crying. Sobbing uncontrollably, I held his hand and felt his slight grip. And then he drew his last breath. We slowly walked out of the room except for my mother, who stayed behind. I never knew why. I was so grief-stricken that I couldn't bring myself to attend the funeral though I made all the funeral arrangements, from the type of casket to the church service to the gravestone. At the cemetery, I watched from afar, unable to look on as my brother was lowered into his grave. For a time, I couldn't get him out of my mind; everything around me reminded me of him—photos of us children, his six-year-old orphan, my mother's tears.

I thought the best way to cope with my grief was to get away from everything that reminded me of him. About a week after the funeral, I decided to go see some of my old friends who were living in Toronto at the time. But it was hardly the escape I was looking for. Everybody wanted to talk about the very thing I was trying to avoid. Their heartfelt condolences and childhood memories of Pasquale thrust me deeper into my sorrow. I had to leave. I drove to Quebec City where I stayed all by myself at a friend's apartment for two weeks ~~all by himself~~. The distraction helped, but the painful memory never left me. For years, I refused to talk about him or look at pictures of him. Whenever his name came up, my face took on a somber expression, and I either changed the subject or walked away in sullen silence. Almost twenty years went by before I could actually talk about my loss without welling up in tears. When I finally began to open up, I understood why I refused to attend the funeral; it would've been the closure I couldn't bring myself to accept. I simply refused to face the fact that Pasquale was forever gone. It explained why I continued to think of him as still there, alive. I kept on recalling how close we were, always keeping in touch even when I was away in the army, in college, or in France. We even looked alike to the point that some people mistook one for the other. When he passed, I felt like I lost something deep inside of me. I lost my zest for life. It was then that I decided to give up my carefree lifestyle and think seriously about getting married, raising a family, and settling down for good.

PhD Program, UW-Madison

Hardly a week had gone by since my return from Quebec when I had to pack up my Volkswagen for the two-day drive to Madison. The University of Wisconsin had accepted me into its Italian PhD program, and I needed to find an apartment before the semester started. My decision to go to UW baffled some of my UNC friends. Though they knew Wisconsin had one of the most prestigious Italian programs in the country, they thought it was an odd choice for someone who grew up in a warm climate to opt for the cold winters of the Badger State. Frankly, I had never thought about Wisconsin weather or its location on the map. Only after I was accepted in the program did I bother to find out where it was located. At first, the prospect of the place's harsh winters dampened my enthusiasm, but the school's academic prestige and generous financial package helped to bolster my spirits.

Once I got to Madison, I was happy to learn that I was not the only Italian in town. The city claimed a large community of first- and second-generation Italians. In the area once known as Little Italy, there were still stores that looked and smelled just like they did in the old country. In a grocery store with the faded sign, DiSalvo's Alimentari, I found all sorts of Italian foodstuffs from mortadella to dried fruits, cured olives, anchovies, and other staples typical of Italy.

Mr. DiSalvo, a little man in his early seventies, bald, and with a set of bushy eyebrows that accentuated his clean-shaven fat face, lamented that the area had lost its character as immigration dwindled and the early immigrants slowly moved away. Business was not what it used to be. Some days, hardly a customer came in. But he didn't care. The store gave him a reason to get up in the morning and look forward to seeing and talking to somebody, anybody that happened to come into the place. He sure was happy to see us college boys! I got to know Mario DiSalvo rather well, as I and several of my classmates routinely stopped by for a good espresso and listened to his stories about the old days in Madison. He never charged us for the coffee.

Although we met at DiSalvo's quite often, our meeting place was usually my apartment, which I shared with Steve Giardina, a second-year PhD student from Chicago. I met Steve and the other students enrolled in the program—eleven in all—within days of my arrival on campus. Some were Italians fresh off the "boat," others were of Italian descent, and a few others were plain Italophiles. I felt right at home. Two of the newly arrived Italians were from Sicily, not far from where I grew up. Some lived in small studio apartments, two stayed at the dorm, and another lived in a university family housing with his wife. Steve and I were the only ones with a large apartment, which soon became the place to gather, listen to music, and talk shop. At times, we played cards but never for money. Occasionally we had a party that usually consisted of a *spaghettata* or spaghetti dinner and cheap wine.

During the day, we normally met at the student union, the bustling center of student life. The place offered a variety of educational and social activities in keeping with the size and diversity of the school's student body. UW had almost twice as many students as UNC, and a large number of them were from out-of-state, mostly from Illinois and New York. There were also many foreigners, especially from China. The Memorial Union, which some called the university's living room, was located right on the shore of Lake Mendota. For me, it was a mesmerizing novelty to live near a big lake. In the winter, the lake froze and became a white wasteland punctuated by a myriad of fishing shanties and motor vehicles parked next to them. I had never imagined it possible that people could drive cars over the ice without fear of falling through. In the summer, the water offered all sorts of recreational activities, from fishing to sailing to swimming. Some evenings, live bands played on the large patio overlooking the water. It didn't take me long to adjust to the new environment. Soon I began to prepare for the notorious Wisconsin winter. I bought heavy winter clothes and had a block heater installed in the car to make sure it started in freezing temperatures.

As the semester went on, the group began to bond, and strong friendships developed. Steve and I became so close that I asked him to be the best man at my wedding, which took place at the end of my first year at UW. My wife, Lynn, had told the children the story about the first time we met, how I proposed, and her family's reaction when she first invited me to her house. Her parents were pleased to hear that I was pursuing an academic career but were hesitant about the fact that I was nine years older than her, a little guy, and a foreigner to boot. Eventually, they welcomed me into the family, convinced that I would be a loving husband and a good provider. Lynn and I were married on the first of June 1973. But the kids, ever suspicious of their mother's selective memory, wanted to hear my version of the events that led to the marriage. I assured them that Lynn's story was accurate. But Jenna was especially interested in the reason why we got married so soon, barely nine months after our first encounter.

I couldn't think of an easy explanation. I could've said we were madly in love and couldn't wait to get married. However true, that was not the only reason. My brother's death the previous year was a big factor in my determination to get married as soon as possible. His passing traumatized me more than I had imagined. The deep grief had catapulted my carefree youth into responsible adulthood. By the time I went to Wisconsin, barely two months after Pasquale's death, I had already made up my mind to settle down and start a family. On the very first day of school, I noticed this attractive girl sitting in one of the classes I was teaching as a graduate student. Was it love at first sight? I don't know. But I remember thinking, "She could be the one," and made it a point to get to know her. She was the one.

Marriage and Honeymoon

We saw each other often, and soon we were in love. But we were careful to keep the relationship under wraps because I was her teacher and could get in trouble with the school. The following semester, when she was no longer my student, we got engaged and set the wedding date for early June. We held the ceremony at her parents' house with a few invited guests, mostly close friends and immediate relatives. Soon afterward, we left for our five-week-long honeymoon in Europe. It was a whirlwind tour of Europe's major cities. We rented a car and drove all over the place, from Holland to Sweden, Sicily, Spain, France, and back to Holland for our flight home. Lynn, who had never been outside the State of Wisconsin, found the experience overwhelming and breathtaking at the same time. As the kids were growing up, she never missed the opportunity to pull out the photo album and show them our honeymoon pictures—here we are in front of the Louvre, here your dad is "supporting" the Leaning Tower of Pisa, this is the *Little Mermaid* in Copenhagen, and so on with the rest of the pictures.

Looking at the honeymoon's photos always led to all sorts of questions by the kids. They wanted to know what kind of hotels we stayed in, whether we traveled by car all the time or ate at restaurants every day. The question that required some explaining had to do with our ability to pay for all that traveling. I was no longer getting the GI Bill and had not worked at the paper mill the previous summer.

Where then did the money come from? They wanted to know. Was it a wedding gift? Did our families help pay for the trip? Did we take a loan?"

They were speechless to hear that we used our own savings. Part of the money, I told them, came from a $500 wedding gift from my parents and another $800 from selling Lynn's life insurance policy. Also, the university's assistantship paid me for my teaching. The rest of the money came from our work at a local restaurant. After about a month in Madison, I got to know Pino, a Sicilian immigrant who owned a pizza restaurant in the old Little Italy neighborhood. We became good friends, and before long, I was working at the restaurant as a cashier. When he needed an extra waitress, I suggested he hire Lynn. Soon, both of us were working, eating for free at the restaurant, taking home a free pizza, and saving our money.

We had to be careful not to let our jobs cut into our studies. I worked part-time, mostly weekends, and Lynn averaged less than twenty hours a week, including weekends. At times, especially when I had to finish a research paper or prepare for an exam, I did not go to work. School came first always. Although I was doing well in all my classes, I caught some flak for working at a pizza joint. Some of my classmates felt that a PhD candidate should spend his free time hanging out with his peers, talking about classes, research papers, and other academic stuff. In their view, my menial job ran against the lofty ideals of graduate school. In plain words, my working at a restaurant embarrassed them. Even one of my professors chided me though I was one of his best students. He reminded me that working at a pizza shop was unbecoming of a future university professor. When I tried to explain that I needed the money because we were expecting our first child, he suggested I apply for a loan. I had never borrowed a penny in my life and wasn't about to start now.

Though heedful of the disapproval, I didn't stop working. Instead, I got another job. I joined the army reserve, which paid $5 an hour. It wasn't much, but it paid the rent. The Reserve met a weekend a month and 15 days in the summer for field maneuvers. To avoid adding to my peers' displeasure, I took care to keep my new job a secret. It was easy to conceal it since I served one weekend a month from 8:00 a.m. to 5:00 p.m. To make sure nobody noticed, I didn't put on my uniform until I arrived at the armory and took it off before going home. In July, when I had to report to a nearby army camp for the two-week training, I didn't have to worry about being seen in uniform since most students had gone home for the summer. To those still in town who wondered where I was, I told them I went to see my parents in Reading.

The more I talked about my jobs, the more my kids thought I was obsessed with money, what with the teaching assistantship, the restaurant job, the army reserve. Did we really need that much money? They wondered. They had never thought of us as money-hungry people, nor the types that lived beyond their means. Then why this concern with money? They wanted to know. I had never asked myself that question. I knew I had plenty, at least more than any of my classmates who were always strapped for cash. In fact, I was the only student in the program with a savings account. The most obvious reason for my impulse to make and save money was that we were expecting a baby and wanted to be able to provide the necessary care. But when my kids' questions eventually forced me to delve deeper into my relentless drive for more money, I began to understand that the drive was rooted in my upbringing. Perhaps, subconsciously, I was driven by the deep-seated fear of falling on hard times. I guess I never managed to blot out the haunting memories of my childhood poverty.

But the ghost of poverty, persistent as it might have been, never got in the way of my education. Although I worked three jobs, I got excellent grades. In addition, I was awarded a scholarship that exempted me from teaching for an entire year, allowing me to concentrate on my studies. I took the PhD prelims by the third year in school as required. Not only did I pass the exams at the first try but also went on to finish the dissertation within a little over a year. One of my professors once reminded me that, out of a beginning class of eleven graduate students, I was one of the two that earned the PhD in Italian and became university professors. Of the others, a few flunked out, others dropped out for reasons, ranging from death in the family to getting married. But the main reason was the dwindling job market. A market that, when we entered the program promised sure employment, was now beginning to dry up. Many students, seeing how PhD graduates were struggling to find work, left the program, or changed careers. Some enrolled in other programs, such as law school and MBA; others took whatever job they could find either in government or the private sector. A few even worked as cooks and cab drivers until they found something more befitting their education. I almost became one of those.

CHAPTER 20

At the University of Alberta

The job market spanning the decade between the mid-1970s and the mid-1980s had reached its lowest level in years, especially in the humanities. Throughout the country, there were very few teaching position openings. Facing a slumping economy, state governments were slashing education budgets, forcing schools to freeze all hiring or reduce it to the bare essential. Universities, especially state-funded ones, were not replacing retiring teachers largely because of budget cuts. With meager funds available, they preferred to hire in the sciences. The academic and social prestige the humanities enjoyed during the '60s had given way to the more practical sciences, such as chemistry and engineering. Also, it was not unusual for schools to post job openings in the humanities subject to funding approval. In most cases, the approval never came, leaving scores of applicants with the bitter taste of disappointment and dejection.

Another contributing factor that made the already shrinking job market very competitive was the growing attention to the gender gap. This was the time when women, championed by the growing women's liberation movement (MLW), began to demand their rightful place in the job market. So the few schools with openings in the humanities were under pressure to hire women. There was no doubt that women were badly underrepresented in the professions. When I left UNC, for instance, there was only one female teacher in the entire department of Romance languages. In the Italian program at UW, all five professors were male.

Just like others in my situation, I applied everywhere, even at schools that posted no job offerings. Some of them acknowledged my application with a cold, bureaucratic, "We regret to inform you . . ."; others didn't even bother to respond. I grew so discouraged that I seriously considered giving up on my dream and looking for a different line of work. I had a family to feed, and couldn't do it on hopes and dreams. I needed a job. One day, an auspicious phone call pulled me out of my deepening depression. It was one of my professors. He knew of an opening at the University of Alberta, and I needed to apply. A friend of his was going on a one-year sabbatical and the university was looking for a substitute. I applied immediately and within two weeks I received the offer and the necessary papers to work in Canada as an immigrant. It was a one-year appointment at the assistant professor level. For the first time in my life, I was referred to as Professor DiMaria. I liked it. Lynn and I were both happy that I was staying in the profession and began to make preparations for the move to Edmonton, Alberta. It didn't matter that I had never heard of the place. I started dreaming again. On August 5, 1977, I loaded my little Fiat and left for my new job.

I was shocked to discover that Edmonton was about four hundred miles north of the Montana border. But that's where the job was, and I was determined to hang on my dream. I drove three and a half days to cover the 1,500-mile distance from Madison to Edmonton. It was the first time I found myself face-to-face with rural America. For long stretches of highway through most of North Dakota and Saskatchewan, I seldom saw a car go by. Once in a while, I saw a farmhouse a few hundred yards on either side of the road. More than once, I wondered what would happen if my car broke down. I was literally in the middle of nowhere. What appeared to be a sizable town on the map turned out to be just a village with a gas station, a diner, and a church. Every town seemed to have a Cracker Barrel or IHOP, the town's hub where people gathered for breakfast, lunch, or dinner. On the first day of my journey, after driving for almost eleven hours, I decided to stop and checked in for the night at a Motel 6 in Bismarck. I slept like a log. I got up early and after a cup of coffee and a couple of doughnuts, I got on the road again.

Just before dark, I stopped at a motel just off the road. A small sign had the word, VACANCY, handwritten on it. I followed a cardboard sign with the word, "Office," scribbled on it and asked for a room. The lady at the desk greeted me with an air of distracted indifference and, without taking her lit cigarette out of her mouth, told me I had to pay in advance. I paid, and she gave me the key to the "room," as she called it. The motel consisted of three small trailers nestled into the woods and parked next to each other. The trailer/room cost little and offered less—the bathroom was dirty, the mattress lumpy, and the door had a flimsy lock. After putting my stuff away, I went to get something to eat at the bar, just outside the trailer. The joint, which was an extension of the office, had a dirt floor and a horseshoe-shaped counter. Three men in overalls, baseball caps, and long beards sat staring silently into their half-empty beer glasses. They appeared to be listening to a country Western tune coming out of the jukebox. When I placed the order, I felt their scrutinizing eyes turned on me. My accent must have startled them. Their probing stare seemed to demand to know who was this foreigner and what was he doing in their neck of the woods. I was unnerved. I took the food to my room and locked the door, praying nobody would try to push it open. The unsettling surroundings and the uncomfortable bed kept me awake for most of the night. I was glad when daylight began to filter in. I got up and, without bothering to stop at the bar for a cup of coffee or something to eat, set out for another day on the road.

After a long and uneventful drive, I stopped for the night at a roadside motel. The place was clean and the receptionist cordial. After a good night's sleep, I got up, eager to get to Edmonton though I was worried about where I would be staying. Perhaps, I could stay at a hotel until I found an apartment. But that would be expensive, I thought. I arrived at the university on Monday the eighth early in the afternoon. The people in the department were expecting me and gave me a warm welcome. They had already asked a graduate student, Gianni Arnolfo, to help me find an apartment. Gianni was a polite and generous young man, originally from Naples. Speaking in Italian, he assured me that it would not be difficult to find a place. For the night, however, I could stay at his house, where he lived with his wife and their two-year-old boy. The next day, we went apartment hunting, and by early afternoon, I had rented a place a few blocks away from the university.

About a week later, Lynn, with our baby, joined me. She never forgot that nerve-racking, white-knuckles flight. No sooner had they gotten in the air than strong turbulence began rocking and rolling the plane. The baby never stopped crying throughout the flight. When I picked them up at the airport, Lynn was so stressed out that she handed me the baby and started crying. We did our best to furnish the apartment with the furniture we bought at the local Salvation Army and St. Vincent de Paul Thrift Store. Within a week, we had everything we needed and were comfortably settled in our apartment. I must say that, though people were nice to us, our time in Edmonton was not our happiest—the salary was low, the winter forbiddingly cold, and we sorely missed our friends and relatives back home. Bad as it was, I accepted the offer to return for a second year to substitute for another professor scheduled to go on a sabbatical. The school obtained a work visa for me, and I returned the following August.

Years later, when I told my children about my decision to stay in Edmonton for a second year, they were thrown for a loss. How could I go back to a place I had called a hellhole? They wondered. The city, I explained, was dreadful only to the extent that we were cold and lonely. We didn't make many friends and had no social life. At least, once a week, Lynn called home, complaining to her mother how much we missed Madison. But Edmonton in itself was everything but a hellhole. It was a thriving and multicultural metropolis with many first-generation immigrants, mostly from Southern Europe and Southeast Asia. It was home to the Edmonton Opera; the professional football team, the Edmonton Eskimos; and the famed hockey team, the Edmonton Oilers. It also offered a great variety of ethnic restaurants and huge shopping malls featuring brand-name merchandize from Gucci to Armani, Pierre Cardin, and Calvin Klein. But though the city was modern and the people were friendly, Lynn and I never felt like we belonged. We were outsiders on a temporary work permit and living with our suitcases half packed. As for accepting the offer to stay an extra year, I had little choice. It was the only job offer I received. There were simply not many job openings anywhere in the United States.

Perhaps better than the other two of my children, the youngest, Jenna, understood what I went through at the time.

"You must've felt like a beaten man," she once said to me. "Here you were with a highly-educated PhD and no work."

No question. I was dispirited. But I didn't stop looking for a teaching job, temporary or part-time, close or far away. I even applied to schools as far away as New Zealand. I wasn't ready to give up on my dream though I began to fear that it was just a dream, a pipe dream. But if I was discouraged, I was not beaten. I could still show my mettle, especially if I felt I was wronged.

It was around this time that I took on the State of Wisconsin, which accused me of trying to avoid paying income taxes. The dispute centered on a tax matter arising from my work in Canada. After I left the University of Alberta, the State of Wisconsin wanted me to pay taxes for my Canadian income. Although I worked in a foreign country, I was still a Wisconsin resident and should, therefore, pay state taxes, they argued. For the $24.000 I made in the two years I taught in Edmonton, they sent a bill for $1,440. I pointed out to the revenue official handling the case that, since at the time the Canadian dollar was worth only seventy American cents, I owed taxes on 17.000 seventeenAmerican dollars in taxes, roughly the equivalent of 24 Canadian dollars. When the revenue office refused to see the logic of my argument, I decided to take the state to court. On the day set to appear in court, the state sent two of its lawyers, and I showed up alone. The judge asked me to present my case, and seeing that I was unfamiliar with court procedures, she instructed me to begin by stating not arguing my case. After I made my position clear, the judge became visibly annoyed with the two lawyers.

"What are you gentlemen doing here, wasting the court's time? You should be embarrassed," she told them in disgust and walked out of the small room, having found in my favor.

I looked with pride at the two lawyers who, with their heads down, were busily putting their papers back in their briefcases.

At the University of Minnesota

After Alberta, I was again without work and returned to Madison, not knowing what to do or where to go next. I was down in the dumps when a friend from the University of Minnesota called to tell me that the language department was looking for someone in Italian. I called, and after a short phone interview, the chairman offered me the job. The position became available, I was told, because one of the Italian professors had accepted a three-year post in the administration, and the program needed someone to replace her. I would be hired as an assistant professor on a three-year contract. I was happy to accept and, without delay, moved my family to Minneapolis. As with the previous job, the position was temporary and the quality of life was not much different—low pay, finding and furnishing an apartment, no social connections, and the alienating status of being not a member of the faculty. Just like in Edmonton, the transient nature of the job made it difficult for me to make friends. It discouraged my colleagues from investing in a friendship that was destined to fizzle out at the end of my nonrenewable contract. However, Lynn and I didn't feel as lonely as we did in Canada. Now we were just a few hours' drive from Madison and could go see family and friends anytime we wanted. At times, some of them came to Minneapolis and stayed with us for the weekend. Lynn's brother came up every time the Green Bay Packers came to play the Minnesota Vikings.

Although my situation was hardly ideal to engage in serious study, I never gave up on my scholarly research. I knew I had to write and publish if I wanted to stay competitive in a profession that was defined by the mantra, publish or perish. I didn't study as much as I wanted to when I was in Edmonton, in part because the library lacked an adequate collection on the Italian Renaissance, my primary area of research. But in my three years in Minneapolis, I was able to publish several scholarly articles in major academic journals, both in Italy and the US. However, even with my good publication record, I couldn't find steady work or, as they say in the profession, a tenure-track position. Things went from bad to worse when, at the end of my contract with the University of Minnesota, I found myself without work again. With nowhere to go, I moved my family back to Madison and accepted a part-time, no-contract position with the University of Wisconsin. I was offered the opportunity to teach one or two language courses, depending on the program's needs and enrollments. The job paid by the number of courses I taught. But whatever I earned was hardly enough to live on. To make ends meet, I went back to work at night as a cashier at the old pizza place. But despite my friend Pino's generosity, I was barely making enough money to meet the needs of my growing family. Unfortunately, Lynn could not help out, as she had to stay home and take care of the children. By this time, we had three children all under the age of seven.

We were poor. The familiar specter of poverty that lay dormant in my subconscious since my early childhood reemerged, looming as a dreadful possibility. On more than one occasion, we didn't take the kids to the doctor because we couldn't afford it. I had no health insurance since I was a part-time employee both at UW and at my friend's restaurant. Depressed as I was, I never stopped applying for a job, even at schools where there were no openings. Some universities invited him for on-campus interview, but these invitations were not always extended in good faith. Often, they had already decided on an internal candidate, and the interviews were a mere formality meant to fulfill equal opportunity requirements. The rejection letters I normally received never gave an explanation for the polite brush off. But whatever the reason, they added to my sense of frustration and hopelessness. Once, after receiving one of those "We regret to inform you" letters, I went to the park near our apartment and broke down, crying uncontrollably.

I did my best to hide my despair from Lynn though I suspected she knew all along the strain I was under. I was more successful in hiding my despair from my parents. It would have broken their hearts and crushed their pride had they known that their son, the professor was unemployed and barely scratching out a living. More than ever, I felt the mounting pressure to do something. At forty-three, I was unemployed with a growing family and no prospects. Out of desperation, I decided to expand my search and applied for a government job, at least, I wouldn't have to worry about job security and feeding his family.

At the FBI?

My kids were stunned to hear about my struggle to find a job and my intent to work for the government. They could not believe how close I had come to seeing my rose-colored expectations smashed against the crude reality of making a living. It was difficult for them to picture me, their undaunted father, on the verge of total despair. Did the man they had always seen as the very essence of wisdom and inner strength really consider walking away from his lifelong dream? they asked themselves. And if he had left the profession and taken a job with the government, what would have happened to them? Would they have moved around the country like military families? They also wondered what kind of work could I do for the government. As far as they knew, I had no other skills besides teaching Italian.

But I did have other skills. I knew several languages and could work as an interpreter or a translator. Naturally, I had to brush up on my Spanish, which I hadn't spoken since my army days. And I did. With a dictionary by my side, I started reading Spanish novels, and soon I got to the point where I seldom needed to look up words. By the time I decided to look for a job outside academia, I had read at least a dozen Spanish novels and a bunch of newspaper articles. As the spring semester was coming to a close at UW and there were no openings for teaching positions, I applied for a job with the foreign service and the FBI. I never heard from the foreign service, but the FBI showed interest.

They wrote, inviting me for a preliminary interview at their office in Milwaukee. The letter brought a great sense of relief and a fresh dose of high hopes. At least, I could provide for my family, I thought. Although I knew little about the bureau and the opportunities for advancement it offered, I began to envision the possibility of a career in government. With my education, I could conceivably rise to a secure and respectable position in the agency.

In high spirits and full of hope, I showed up for the interview as instructed in the letter. The receptionist's greeting, "Oh, Mr. DiMaria, we were expecting you," shored up my self-confidence and expectations. Mrs. Linden, that was the name carved on her nameplate, was a heavyset middle-aged woman with short silver hair and a reassuring smile. She asked me to sit down and offered me a cup of coffee, which I was too nervous to accept. Within minutes, Paul Di Genova, a large, balding man in his fifties came out of the inner office and greeted me cordially. He briefly talked about his Italian origin, recalling that his grandfather came at the turn of the century from a small town in Sicily. The town, it turned out, was just a few miles away from Delia. About the interview, he explained that the first phase consisted of a written /audio exam. If it went well, a second interview would follow at the FBI headquarters in Washington. The test was very easy, and I finished it in less than an hour. It consisted of listening to several conversations, mostly in the Sicilian dialect, and translating them into English.

I was somewhat disappointed to find out that they were interested only in my knowledge of the Sicilian dialect, which I spoke fluently. It was clear from the exam that they wanted me to listen in to the mob phone conversations and translate words or phrases typically used by mobsters. If they had other assignments for me, I didn't know. But I wasn't going to ask at this stage of the interview. The exit conference with Mr. Di Genova and one of his colleagues was brief and reassuring. They said my test scores were excellent, and I should hear from them soon. I left the office confident that a job offer would be tendered in a few weeks.

As I drove back to Madison, my mind was all over the place with questions about my future with the bureau. How much would they offer? Where would they relocate me? Did I have to be away from home a lot? Was the work dangerous? What about my dream career in academia? By the time I got home, I was all at sea, pulled by mixed and conflicting feelings. On the one hand, I was glad that I might get a steady job and stop living under the specter of unemployment. I wouldn't have to uproot my growing family so often, chasing one temporary job after another. On the other hand, I couldn't wrap my head around the idea that I was about to give up on the dream of my life. All those years in school just to sit in a van or a hotel room or an office, listening to mobsters talking about crimes they committed or were about to commit. What was happening to me and my dream? How would I explain it to my parents? When I got home, I talked with Lynn about my dilemma, and to her credit, she told me she would support me whatever path I chose to take.

CHAPTER 21

At the University of Tennessee

At the time, I didn't seem to have much of a choice. Nonetheless, while waiting to hear from the FBI, I continued to look for college jobs. I didn't stop applying even after Mr. Di Genova called to tell me that soon I should receive an invitation to report to the FBI in Washington for a final interview. "A mere formality," he said. By chance or providence, it was around this time that the universities of Missouri and Tennessee invited me for on-campus visits. I went to the interviews in Columbia and, a week later, to Knoxville half-heartedly, convinced that, in the end, I would receive the familiar "We regret to inform you" letters.

This time, the rejection letters never came. Instead, I received the most gratifying phone calls of my life. Both schools telephoned to offer me a job and requested my written acceptance within two weeks. I could hardly contain my excitement. After years of humiliating rejections, I received not one, but two offers. Lynn was overjoyed and immediately called her parents with the happy news. The first thing I did was to withdraw my application from the FBI. Mr. Di Genova understood and wished me the best. Then I called Tennessee to accept their offer and tell them my acceptance letter was in the mail. The following day, I wrote to Missouri to inform them that I had accepted another position at another university. I also called my parents. But they didn't seem to appreciate the full extent of my good fortune. They thought I was already successfully employed, as I had led them to believe.

Naturally, at the UW's French and Italian department, everybody was delighted, especially my professors who prided themselves on placing their graduates. My thesis director invited other professors and some of their students to his house to celebrate the good news. To the curious, who wanted to know why I chose Tennessee over Missouri, I gave two reasons: money and weather. When I went for the interviews, the Knoxville campus was green and the temperature was in the low forties; in Columbia, instead, the ground was covered with snow and the temperature was in the low thirties. I was tired of the frigid, Northern winters and looked forward to the more agreeable climate of the South. Moneywise, UT offered me the opportunity to supplement my salary by allowing me to teach in the summer. In addition, the department would recommend me for promotion in three years, bypassing the customary six-year probationary period. Lynn and I couldn't be happier with our choice and soon began to look at the logistics. We had to figure out when and how to move, which pieces of our used furniture to take and, most importantly, where to live in Knoxville.

Summer teaching meant that I had to leave for Tennessee as soon as the spring semester was over at UW. That didn't leave me much time to look for a house and move in with the entire family. Once again, providence provided. I met an elderly couple that had recently moved from Knoxville. The husband was a chemistry professor who transferred to UW; the wife was an Italian, who was looking for a part-time teaching job in the Italian program. When I told them I was relocating to Knoxville, they offered to rent me their house. Their older daughter was still living in it, they said, but she would be out by the end of the month. The rent was reasonable, and the house was big enough for the family's needs. Lynn and I planned our move to coincide with the arrival of the moving van, which was scheduled to arrive a week before the summer session started at UT. That gave us plenty of time to stop in Reading for a short visit with my aging parents. When my father asked why I left my "job" in Wisconsin to move to Tennessee, I saw no need to tell him the real reason. I simply said that UT had offered a better teaching position, a promotion I couldn't pass up. He and my mother couldn't be happier; their son was climbing the ladder of success. Though my father was ill and barely able to move around, he was excited to see his "truly" American grandchildren. He wanted them around him, petting them affectionately and telling them not to forget their Italian grandpa.

He knew the kids didn't understand a word he said, yet he talked to them anyway. Did he fear he would never see them again? His anxiety reminded me of the time when the family was getting ready to leave for America. My grandfather came by the house every day, wanting to be near his grandchildren and reminding us to always remember our roots. Before we left, he gave each of us boys an old family picture, telling us to carry it in our wallets. Deep inside, he knew he would never see us again. He died two years later. But now, as then, the young were intent on looking forward to a life of fun and adventures and could hardly be aware of, or concerned about, the forlorn resignation of their grandparents. They were already wondering what life would be like in the Volunteer State—the house they would live in, the schools they would go to, the friends they would make. When the time came to leave, we said our goodbyes, vowing to keep in touch and to come back to visit very soon. But those promises didn't stop the flow of tears welling up in the old folks' eyes. At their age, the future was the moment.

The house we rented in Knoxville was a detached, split-level structure located in a quiet neighborhood, close to a major thoroughfare and the kids' schools. It was bigger than we expected, and by the end of the week, we were settled in. The children were happy to have their own room and make use of the basketball court next to the garage. Within a week or so, they were already riding their bikes down the street and shooting hoops in the backyard with some neighbor kids their age. For the first three days, we had no major home appliances in the house. It took Sears that long to deliver the refrigerator and the washer and dryer we bought as soon as we arrived in town. In the meantime, Lynn had to take the wash to the laundromat. Also, until they delivered the refrigerator, we ate out a lot. Needless to say, the children were thrilled to eat at McDonald's or Burger King, which were everywhere.

We couldn't get over the countless eateries and the many brand-new cars on the road. How could such a presumably poor region of the country display so much affluence? It didn't take us long to figure out that the South was not as impoverished or backward as some Northerners made it out to be. Another peculiarity that caught our eyes was the great number of churches. They appeared to be on every corner. No wonder the people who came to welcome us to the neighborhood typically asked, "What church do you belong to?" The other common question was, "What do you do for a living?" They were pleased to hear that their new neighbor was a UT professor but slightly disappointed to learn we were not particularly religious. From all appearances, Knoxvilleans took their religion very seriously. Come Sunday, the town went to church. It was Lynn who noticed that on Sunday mornings the streets were practically deserted.

"Where are the people in this town? I hardly saw a car go by," she said one Sunday morning.

"I don't know," I said. "I guess they tend to sleep late around here. Come to think of it, I also noticed that, on some Saturdays, there aren't that many people in the streets or in the stores."

One day, one of my new colleagues, who had come to the house for dinner with his wife and children, explained that the streets are empty on Sundays because most people go to church.

"But as soon as services are over," he told us, "they dart out from the churches' parking lots and, like a swarm of angry bees, speed in all directions toward their favorite Shoney's or IHOP.

"You will also notice," he added, "that there is hardly any traffic on the Saturdays the Volunteers play at home. Around here, people follow their football with religious fervor. When the Tennessee Volunteers play, most Knoxvilleans are either at the stadium or, at home, watching the game on TV.

"Incidentally," he noted, "Neyland Stadium is one of the largest in the country with a seating capacity of well over 102,000."

I couldn't help noticing that my colleagues at the university didn't share the general population's religious fervor, nor did they show much enthusiasm for football. There were several reasons for their indifference toward UT football or the sport in general. Some came from different parts of the country, and their loyalty was to the team of their home state; others were foreigners and, like me, did not grow up playing or watching the sport. A number of them were too caught up in their scholarly research to appreciate such a pedestrian sport.

Although the department consisted of professors from different parts of the country and the world, they all got along rather well. I noticed a prevailing sense of collegiality when I attended my very first faculty meeting. They discussed the issues before them passionately, at times, but always with respect for each other even when they disagreed. To be sure, there had been some disagreeable colleagues, mainly in the Italian program, I was told, but they were now gone. Toward me, they were friendly, and soon, I felt like I was one of them. Some were naturally curious about their new colleague. They wanted to know all about my educational background, where I had taught before, how old was I when he came to the States, and similar other curiosities. They wondered why I, a professor of Italian, was also teaching Spanish. Wasn't I hired to teach Italian? My explanation was that I was offered the position because I could teach several languages besides Italian. At the time I was hired, I once reminded Michelle Pasteur, a French professor, that the Italian program was on its last leg with only thirty-four students. Because there were so few students, I told her, I was assigned to teach Spanish while working on revamping my program.

She didn't know it was that bad. But she admitted she was not surprised since the previous two Italian professors spent more time bickering with each other than caring about their students. At times, their squabbles played out in the campus newspaper where they smeared each other's reputation.

"I just didn't know they left the program in shambles," she said as if blaming herself for not knowing or doing something about it. She encouraged me not to hesitate to call on her if I needed help and wished me good luck.

I needed more than luck. I had to find ways to increase enrollments and improve the program's image both within the department and the campus community. One of the first steps I took was to introduce and lead a six-week-long summer study abroad—students could earn college credits by going to study in Italy with me. Eager to begin right away, I got in touch with an already existing consortium of several American universities that had a summer program in Urbino. The group had, for years, taken students to Urbino and was closely associated with the university there. Each school sent its own professor, who taught courses open to all students in the partnership. My proposal to join the consortium was met with skepticism by some of the department's older faculty.

"It has never been done before here at UT," some cautioned.

"What guarantee do we have our students are taught by certified teachers and not just by some local talent hired on the spot off the streets?" others asked.

I tried to alleviate their concerns by assuring them that the instructors were all professors from American universities. I also pointed out that many well-known universities, including Wisconsin, UNC, Indiana, and Michigan had been taking students abroad for years with excellent results. In the end, they gave me their approval to proceed though some were not fully convinced it was a good idea.

The initiative proved to be most effective in boosting student enrollment. By the third year, there were more than eighty students enrolled in the Italian program. This outcome made converts out of the skeptical colleagues who, incidentally, began to set up their own summer programs abroad. It soon became clear that I alone couldn't teach the growing number of students. I needed help. On that account, I asked the department to allow me to hire part-time instructors directly from Italy. This request too found its skeptics. Concerned colleagues questioned how these instructors could be properly vetted and whether they were qualified to teach at an American institution such as ours. In the end, they relented and agreed to let me try it for one year. The trial was so successful that it became a hiring practice for the next twenty years. That year, the department recommended me for tenure.

The day the faculty met to vote on my tenure, I stayed in my office, nervously biting my fingernails. The wait was killing me, as I imagined all sorts of negative scenarios. I didn't leave the office, not even to go to the bathroom, afraid I might miss the crucial phone call from the department head. But the news didn't come over the phone. It was Diego Gallegos, a Spanish professor, who came to congratulate me immediately after the vote. I wanted to call Lynn right away, but Diego kept on talking about an article or book he was writing.

As he got up to leave, he congratulated me again and said, "Oh, by the way, I almost forgot to tell you, the faculty voted unanimously in your favor, a rare occurrence in our department. Even the naysayer, Julia Petosky, voted for you. It should've been a short meeting," he went on, "but some colleagues wanted to know why you came up for promotion after only three years instead of the usual six. The head explained that his support for your early tenure was based on the excellent work you have done for the program and on your substantial publication record. He told everyone that you had published more than some of us senior professors."

Diego was hardly out of the door when the tension that had been building up during the months leading to the tenure decision gave way to tears of joy. Tears rolling down my cheeks, and barely able to speak, I called Lynn.

"Honey, we made it!" I managed to utter.

"I knew you would," she said, though she too had been under a lot of stress.

With the assurance of job security and pay hike that came with the promotion, Lynn and I decided to buy the house we had been renting since we moved to Knoxville. We liked the location and had already made friends in the neighborhood. Soon after buying the place, I became Mr. Fix It. I replaced old or broken fixtures, cut down some small trees, laid out a vegetable garden, built a shed, and moved the fishpond away from the house. We also bought a piano for our older girl to practice her music lessons. But the best purchase was a pool table, my favorite toy. It gave me the opportunity to entertain guests and, more importantly, teach my kids how to play while enjoying quality time with them. Often, when they came home from school, I would interest them in a game of pool and casually coax them to talk about their day. It was the least intrusive way for me to keep an eye on what was going on in their lives. I also bought a second car, which made Lynn's life much easier. She felt liberated, she said. Now she could go shopping or take the kids to the doctor without having to wait for me to come home from work. Life was beginning to smile on the DiMaria family.

My Parents Come to Visit

It was around this time that I finally convinced my parents to cast off their fear of flying and come to visit. The flight was short and direct; I assured them. My sister put them on the plane in Philadelphia, and I picked them up an hour and a half later at the Knoxville airport. I was proud to have them in my home and take them around. On the second day of their visit, I took them to the UT campus to show them my office and introduce them to some of my colleagues. Professor Gallegos, hearing that Mr. Giuseppe had worked in Venezuela for several years, greeted him in Spanish and told him, in Spanish, how much he admired his good friend, Professor DiMaria. But my pride and joy was the work I had done in and around the house, especially the screened-in porch and the brick patio next to it. I even dug a drainage system that diverted rainwater away from the house.

"Did you build this patio all by yourself?" my father asked, incredulous.

"Where did you learn to lay bricks like this?" my mother wanted to know.

They were amazed at their son's ability to do all that work and all by himself. But at the same time, they couldn't reconcile to the notion that a professor was doing manual labor. In their culture, it was unthinkable for an educated professional to stoop down to the level of bricklayers or ditch diggers. Physical labor was far below their distinguished social standing. What kind of professor was their son? I told them that their view, though common in the old country, didn't make much sense here. For centuries, their belief had been conveniently encouraged and promoted by a classist society interested in asserting their privileged status over the lower classes. I don't know if I convinced them that such a practice had no place in liberal America, but I could tell they were proud of me, and I delighted in their pride. Once back in Reading, they couldn't stop talking about their visit. They told people their son, the professor, lived in a mansion; had a huge office at the university; and was well-liked by his colleagues. The bragging embarrassed my sister, who did her best to minimize their boasting.

The promotion to associate professor didn't change in any way my commitment to teaching and scholarly research. I continued writing and publishing with the same intensity as before. Lynn had hoped that, once I was tenured, I would spend less time at work and more at home.

"You don't stop writing simply because you're tenured," I once told her, trying to convince her that research is a passion, not a chore. "It is a gross misconception to think that professors, once tenured, lose the drive to publish," I pointed out. "Those professors don't just lose the drive, they never had it to begin with. They shouldn't have been tenured in the first place."

Lynn began to realize, much to her chagrin, that I would never give up my studies, and that my ambition was to reach the heights of my profession. She also had to adjust to being alone with the children while I went to Italy to direct the summer program. The Urbino program, as it was called, was an integral part of my job. Not only did it contribute to the growth of Italian at UT, but it also boosted my salary. An invaluable dividend I had not foreseen was the beneficial impact that the renewed contact with Italy had on me and my career. When I first started the program, I only thought of increasing enrollments and promoting Italian on campus. I never foresaw that it would also give me the badly needed opportunity to reacquaint myself with the changes that had taken place since I left. Thanks to my yearly trips to Urbino, I acquired enough firsthand knowledge of modern Italy to make me feel confident in my role as a professor of Italian.

My colleagues valued my scholarship on the Italian Renaissance, and my students praised my teaching, especially my courses on Dante and Machiavelli.

They didn't know how seriously lacking my knowledge of contemporary Italy was. I was painfully aware of this shortcoming and did my best to hide it. The country had changed considerably since I emigrated more than two decades earlier. My position as a professor and as an Italian was truly ambivalent. On the one hand, I was the campus authority on all things Italian; on the other hand, I was barely familiar with the country's latest sociopolitical developments. Most of what I knew came largely from secondary sources, such as textbooks, videos, and social media outlets. In class, when discussing aspects of current Italian culture, such as politics, health care, or how to get around at an airport, I adhered as closely as possible to the textbook. I tried to avoid answering questions not covered in the course material, for fear that the students might notice my Achilles' heel. Mine was a balancing act that soon or later, I feared, would be exposed for what it was. I was equally apprehensive when I went to a professional conference. I was always careful to limit my scholarly presentations only to literary topics and, whenever possible, avoid mingling with fellow participants. In a word, I saw myself as a fraud.

Urbino

Then came Urbino. It was water in the desert. No sooner had I landed at the Rome airport than I began to quench my thirst for the cultural and linguistic novelties that had come to define modern Italy during my long absence. I was eager to get the real picture of the things I read about in the textbooks—baggage claim carousels, ticket counters, gates, bars, duty-free shops, newsstands, fast food outlets, and other facilities typically found in airports. On the bus from Rome to Urbino, I couldn't stop looking out the window at both sides of the road, taking in the changing landscape and the farming villages on the slopes of the Apennines. At times, I would ask the bus driver or a colleague about this or that castle perched on the hilltops along the road. For the first time in my life, I saw acres and acres of sunflower fields. I didn't know until then that the big yellow flower moves from east to west as it tracks the sun's movement across the sky. My interest in everything Italian was equally intense whenever the program took the students on weekend-long excursions. I wanted to see everything the big cities had to offer—museums, churches, ancient monuments, archeological ruins, and whatever else aroused my curiosity.

Years later, Professor Antonio Cervi, one of my colleagues from the University of Florida, recalled how insecure I was when he first met me on the bus to Urbino.

"Man, I'll tell you. I'll never forget your curiosity when you first joined our consortium," he once told me. "You wanted to know everything about everything. You were asking all sorts of questions even about everyday stuff, such as highway driving, store hours, which store sold what, health care, politics, and other common stuff. You were like a sponge, absorbing everything in sight."

For the next thirty summers, I returned to Italy, ever eager to rediscover and absorb—like a sponge— its evolving culture. Without a doubt, this direct experience with my old country gave me back my true and rightful identity. With my identity and professional self-confidence fully restored, I could finally claim to be the campus authority on everything Italian.

I remember well my sudden immersion into modern Italian life after being away for almost three decades. When I first landed in Rome, I felt at home right away. The din of regional accents, the smell of espresso, the stench of cigarette smoke, and the long lines—three abreast—at the ticket counters made me feel at home. These were my people, and soon I started acting and talking like them. For a moment, it was like I never left. But only for a moment, for there was a lot I had shut out or simply didn't know. But the sense of belonging was so instinctual that I began to think about my friends and relatives back home and the possibility of reconnecting with them and my past. Now I had something to be proud of and could go back home with my head held high. I was now living the dream I set out to chase when I first left Delia. I was a successful university professor, respected by my peers and my students.

Sadly, I had lost contact with all my friends, even with my best buddy, Nino. After so many years without hearing from each other, I wondered what he would say when and if we got together. All sorts of questions crowded my mind. Was he married? What kind of work did he do? Did he move?

CHAPTER 22

Nino

The more I thought about Nino, the more I wanted to know what became of him. I finally decided to try to get in touch with him. But how? I didn't know his address or telephone number. One summer, while in Urbino, I looked him up in the phonebook, just in case. Those days, most phone centers had the phonebook of every Italian county or province. I found three entries with the same name. I dialed one of the numbers, and the man that answered said he was not the Nino I was looking for. He was sorry he couldn't help. He had just moved there and didn't know anyone by that name except his own.

The lady that answered my second call was more encouraging.

"I think you are looking for my cousin, Nino," she said, happy to help. "He doesn't live in this town anymore, but I think my husband has his number. Let me ask him. Please wait."

A few minutes passed before a man came on the line. "Hello. Who is this?" he asked in a gruff tone as if he had been rudely awakened from his nap.

"My name is Salvatore DiMaria. I come from America, and I am trying to get in touch with an old friend of mine by the name of—"

"Are you by any chance Totò?" he interrupted.

Startled at being so readily recognized, I was speechless for a second or two. Then happy to have finally gotten a promising lead, I answered, "Yes! That's me."

"What a coincidence! A couple of weeks ago, I saw my cousin Nino, and among other things, he talked about Totò, his *Americano* friend. Let me give you his number. I bet he will be thrilled to hear from you."

The number he gave me was the same as the third one listed in the phonebook. The prefix didn't show that Nino had moved to a town about an hour away from where he grew up. I dialed the number, missed a digit, and dialed a second time. I was nervous, trying to think of what to say, and imagined what he would say. Would he reproach me for all those years of silence? For having forgotten my best buddy? That was possible, but the reproach would apply to him as well, I could argue. He too had been silent and was equally at fault. But I knew I couldn't really make that claim, as he had no idea where I lived in the US. I was both relieved and disappointed when there was no answer. I called repeatedly in the following days without ever getting an answer. I tried again the following summer, again no answer. Each time I called, I felt the same conflicting feeling of hope and anxiety. On the one hand, I wished he answered; on the other hand, I feared that, if he did, I wouldn't know what to say. How would I start the conversation? What kind of questions should I ask? What would he say? While these and similar questions were roaming in my mind, the phone kept on ringing.

"Maybe he doesn't live there anymore," Antonio Cervi tried to explain away my failed attempts.

I dismissed Antonio's suggestion out of hand. Nino's cousin had given me his current number, which happened to be the same as the one listed in the phonebook. And besides, the phone rang every time I called. That meant that the account was active. Why would Nino pay the bill if he were no longer using the phone? A more plausible explanation instead was that, in July, the month when I was calling, he was somewhere on vacation with his family. But I never gave up trying. Sooner or later, somebody had to answer the phone. One afternoon, during the Christmas holidays, I decided to call from the States. On the second ring, a young girl answered.

"Hello! Who is calling?" she asked in Italian, naturally.

Disregarding her question, I told her I was looking for Nino Vaccaro, and asked if he was her father and whether he was at home.

"He is in bed," she said haltingly, trying to figure out who was calling at that late hour.

I realized then that because of the six-hour time-difference, 4:00 p.m. in Knoxville was 10:00 p.m. in Italy. But it was too late for apologies.

"Get him up," I told her with the decided tone of someone she shouldn't question.

In less than two minutes, Nino was on the phone. Before he could speak, I asked, "Do you know who I am?"

"Yes, Totò! I think and talk about you all the time."

My end of the line went dead for a few seconds, as I tried to hold back my emotions. I couldn't believe what I just heard, and worse, it made me feel lousy for my long neglect of my dear friend. Actually, I had never forgotten Nino. I had simply stuck to my decision not to go back until I could return, proud of what I had achieved. We talked nonstop for almost an hour, one asking questions about the other's life, work, and family. I was also eager to hear about some of our childhood friends. We mulled over the strange coincidence that we each had three children, a boy and two girls, all of about the same age. We ended the conversation, pledging to get together the following summer. And we did.

Return to Sicily

In July, I took a long weekend off from the Urbino program and flew to Sicily. When I walked out into the airport's waiting area, I began to scan the crowd, looking for Nino, who had come to pick him up.

I kept on searching until he, arms flailing, called out, "Totòoo . . . Totòoo . . ."

After we embraced and kissed on both cheeks, he said, "I recognized you right away, but you didn't recognize me. Did you?"

"No, I didn't. You have changed a lot, put on a few extra pounds, and lost much of your bushy jet-black hair," I said in my usual direct but congenial tone.

My unceremonious observations made Nino feel like nothing had changed between the two of us. This was the Totò he knew, affable and unreserved. As we drove home, the familiar rolling hills, at times green with vegetation and often barren and rocky, brought me back to my youth. Those were my hills! This was my land! When we arrived at his house, the family was ready for the big welcome. Nino's wife and kids were waiting in front of the house to greet me, and the dining table was already set for a late lunch. After the customary hugs and kisses, Maria, Nino's wife, expressed her delight to finally meeting the Totò of Nino's boyhood stories. Nino's mother, though in her late eighties, remembered me very well and thought I hadn't changed a bit. She was being nice, and I told her so. I had lost most of my hair and gained a few pounds. Eventually, we sat down for a lavish lunch, which Maria and her two daughters had spent the morning preparing. The familiar smells, the taste of foods I hadn't eaten in years, and the conversation in the Sicilian dialect reinforced the sensation that I was indeed among my people. They were impressed with my command of the local dialect, admitting that it was as good as theirs.

Even Nino's mother complimented me, "Totò, you never forgot our dialect. You speak it so well."

I proudly reminded them that my dialect was actually more genuine than theirs. Unlike theirs, mine was not contaminated by the growing tendency among Southerners to mix dialect with Italian, the national language. In a peculiar way, I saw my command of the local language as the undeniable credentials of my roots and identity. But such a feeling was undercut somewhat whenever people referred to me as *lamericanu*, a subtle reminder that I was not really one of them. At first, I resented this distinction, but then, I sensed that, more than a distinction, it was an honor for them to claim my friendship. They spoke with pride about their American friend.

My impression was confirmed the next day when I went to my hometown, about half an hour away. Friends and relatives were excited to see me after so many years. In a cacophony of competing voices, they wanted to know everything about me—family, profession, life in America, and my summer program. Some of the neighbors, claiming familiarity with me, tried to stir my memory with hints, such as, "Do you remember me? I am the son of so and so . . ." or "We lived down the street from you . . ." or "My father was a friend of your father's . . ." All seemed eager to be acknowledged as friends of *lamericanu*. This justified, at least in part, the people's overwhelming participation in the reception the city mayor organized in my honor.

Two days before the event, the city distributed pamphlets, inviting the townspeople to come to city hall for a formal ceremony honoring Delia's distinguished son, *Il Professore* Salvatore DiMaria. The audience found in their seats, a flyer that listed the titles of my published books and essays, which someone had apparently copied from my webpage. The mayor and other city officials took turns praising their Totò and expressing the town's pride in my "great" achievements. The mayor made it a point to remind the audience that the Italian Consulate of Detroit had conferred on their favorite son the title of *corrispondente consolare*, the equivalent of honorary consul. In addition, he went on, the University of Urbino named their Totò Urbino's academic ambassador to America. He ended the ceremony by presenting me with several mementos, including a laminated copy of my fifth-grade report card, a leather-bound volume of *The History of Delia*, and several other tokens of appreciation. The gift I cherished the most was a framed copy of my birth certificate.

The following day, Nino came to drive me to the airport. It took us a while to get going because of the inevitable goodbyes with the friends and relatives that had come to see me off. Before their final arrivederci, some made it a point to remind me not to wait another thirty years to come back to visit. Others even chided me for not staying long enough.

"You came, saw, and left. You hardly had time to go out for dinner with your buddies," an old classmate complained.

"Next time, plan to stay a little longer," urged Aunt Lucia. "You can stay at my house as long as you want. Remember, this is the house where your father was born," she reminded me.

I promised I would be back and for a longer stay. Why not? I was delighted with the overwhelming reception and the honors the town bestowed on me. I was especially proud of the birth certificate, which I showed Nino on our way to Palermo. Nino failed to see my enthusiasm and thought I was making too much out of the piece of paper.

"Yeah, I know! It's a birth certificate. So what? Everybody has one. I got two or three copies somewhere around the house."

I tried to explain that the certificate had a great significance for me, because it represented a validation of my Sicilian identity.

"Why do you need validation? Everybody knows you're Sicilian. Anyone who hears you speak dialect knows you're a genuine Sicilian," Nino countered without hesitation.

Of course, I was Sicilian. But the difference implied in the label *lamericanu* tended to undercut my sense of belonging. I saw it as a subtle reminder that I was an outsider pretending to be one of the locals. This feeling of alienation was somewhat similar to what I experienced in the States. There my friends referred to me as their Italian friend; here, many call me the American. In a way, I lived the irony of being a citizen of two countries and belonging to neither. Nino understood my sense of estrangement and did his best to assure me that I was, indeed, a true Sicilian like himself. At the airport, we arrived early enough to stop at the bar for a cup of coffee and talk about seeing each other again the following summer. By the time we said our goodbyes, I made Nino promise to come and visit me in the States.

EPILOGUE

I returned the following summer and many summers thereafter. After a while, the locals no longer referred to me as *lamericanu* but simply as *professuri*. I decided to take my children to Delia the year they graduated from high school. I wanted them to see where I grew up and meet the people I talked about in my stories. I even took them around the countryside to show them where I had exploded a grenade and stolen the foodstuffs I usually sold to rent a bike or go to the movies. It seemed that everybody the kids met was eager to relate an anecdote about me.

"Once, your papà and I . . ." one of them would begin his story.

"How can I forget the time when your father and my older brother . . ." another would recall.

Still another, "You should have seen your dad when he was a boy. He was such a little devil. He was the scourge of the neighborhood."

People relished the opportunity to tell stories that spoke of their association with the *professuri* in a past they were proud to recall. Sometimes, different people told the same anecdotes. Their versions often varied, as their selective memories spun them into embellished recollections. The kids enjoyed the tales anyway, mostly because they lent an aura of a legend to their father's storied past. More importantly, perhaps, this living testimony, however burnished, gave them a deeper perspective of their father's rise from abject poverty to the celebration of his success. I had made my people proud, and my children delighted in the town's pride.

But the stories didn't tell the whole story. Beneath the fabled anecdotes, there was the narrative of misery, resigned gloom, and high hopes that forged my character and shaped my ambitions. I wanted my kids to know that my strength to endure hardship and persist in the endeavor to live my dream was rooted in my upbringing. More than that, I hoped that the tale of my past would someday be of inspiration to my children, as they thought about their roots and their future. It was my wish that they see my life, not as a celebration of the man but as an example of success that even the poorest of the poor can achieve given the opportunity. I wanted them to believe that the fulfillment of a cherished dream rested on one's ability and determination to chase it. And what better way to turn my wish into a practical lesson than to bring them to my native Sicily where the seed of my dream was first sown.

The desire to encourage my children to chase their dreams grew into a persistent inner voice that, for months, nagged me to leave some sort of a written account of my life. It was then that I began to reflect on my past and collect my notes. When I told Nino about my project, he pointed out that my biography could serve as an example not just for my children and grandchildren. It could also embolden the poor and the hopeless to dream of a brighter future beyond the confines of their wretched, despairing world. Long after we are gone, he was sure, my story would continue to resonate with the aspirations of the millions who emigrated to America, dreaming of a better life. The last time we met, after asking me how my project was coming along, he made me promise to make it available in Italian translation. My story, he believed, would have a special meaning for the many young Italians struggling to make a living in Italy.

Sadly, Nino will never see the Italian text of this narrative. He passed away before I had time to finish this English version and start working on a translation. But I intend to keep my promise and honor his memory. I will soon begin the translation and hope to live long enough to finish it. It is the least I can do to honor the memory of my dear friend. He will always live in my thoughts and in my story.

Made in the USA
Middletown, DE
29 June 2020